JESUS IS MY OWNER

Life with the Sharanahuas

ENDORSEMENTS

Jesus Is My Owner is full of great true-to-life stories. This people group needed Bible translators who would show Christ's love to them. Scotty and Marie did that. Scotty has a personality full of grace and more grace.

I, as a pilot, visited the Sharanahua villages many times, and I can testify that when they began to "make Jesus their owner" (how they describe conversion), it made all the difference in the world. They truly became "new creatures in Christ" (2 Corinthians 5:17). The Word in their language was key.

I recommend this book to you. The stories will fill you with inspiration and joy.

Butch Barkman, Pilot
Former General Director of SIL in Peru
Former JAARS pilot in Peru

It has been my privilege to know Gene and Marie Scott for many years. My wife, Evie, and I have made many pastoral visits to Peru, and specifically to the missionaries that serve with Wycliffe Bible Translators. In each of our visits, we spent time with Gene and Marie and developed a close relationship with them. Our connection with them grew strong through our many times together.

When Scotty finished his book, he sent a copy to me. I read it quickly and closely. What an amazing story—a true story of their lives, going back to the beginning and continuing to the present. The book includes their call to the ministry, their victories, and even some of the tough times. The book is real. It is authentic. It is stirring. So often as I read it, I said to my wife, "Evie, listen to this. It's so good, isn't it?"

I believe that God will use this book in a variety of ways. I believe some individuals will be called into the ministry as they read it. Some will become prayerful intercessors for world ministry. And all readers will be significantly encouraged, truly blessed.

Lareau Lindquist
Founder, Barnabas International

You will enjoy reading Eugene and Marie Scott's experiences over the decades they worked in Bible translation among the Sharanahuas. They individually committed their lives to God's leadership—from their individual calls to serve God, to meeting, dating, and marriage in a foreign land, as well as during severe testings and joys as God took them to a people group, deep into the eastern Peruvian rainforest, people who needed "God's carving."

They were located "across the Amazon watershed," the other side of a seemingly trackless jungle. As we pilots often remarked, "When you get to the Scotts' place you are coming out on the other side of the jungle." Navigating to their river and location in the area where all the creeks and rivers seem to flow at an east-northeasterly (030 compass) heading to the mighty Amazon in Brazil challenged the pilots' and the aircrafts' "radius of action"!

Through many difficult situations the Scotts persisted, showing God's love, providing medical assistance, spiritual leadership, and finally leaving the Sharanahuas with God's Word for salvation, scriptural guidance, and the opportunity for spiritual growth.

Scotty is a man of integrity, joy, and … tears. Honest, sincere, always ready to praise someone and his Heavenly Father, and tears when someone is hurting.

Read on! Enjoy the book! See God's faithfulness.

Doug Deming
Former JAARS pilot in Peru

Scotty is one of the kindest men that I have ever met and his quiet walk with the Lord has always been an inspiration to the rest of us. I especially remember one afternoon when in a meeting of the SIL executive committee there was a seeming impasse on an agenda matter, and emotions were starting to run high. It was then that Scotty, in his own quiet way, suggested that we adjourn and seek in prayer the Lord's will in the matter. His suggestion prevailed, and the next morning when the matter was brought up again, it was resolved in a wonderful way.

A second experience that comes to mind was one Sunday when Scotty was preaching the Sunday morning message. His theme was on the wonders of heaven and, as he was preaching, he suddenly remarked, "I can hardly wait to get there." But then as what he had said impacted him, he added, "but not right away as I still have some things to get finished before then." You can imagine the chuckles from the congregation as Scotty had second thoughts, but we all loved him for his transparency.

We are sure his book will have a great ministry as people read it and respond to Scotty and Marie having shared their lives with them.

Lambert Anderson
Former General Director of SIL in Peru

Scotty and Marie are a wonderful example of a couple who gave a substantial part of their life to meet the physical and spiritual needs of a group of people living in a remote part of the Amazon River basin. They learned and analyzed a language that had never been written before, produced beginning reading books, and helped the people establish a school for their children. Scotty and several Sharanahuas translated the New Testament into the language of these people.

The Scotts' language analysis, as well as the written Scripture in Sharanahua, have been of special help to other translators working in related languages.

As Scotty's supervisor, I appreciated his earnestness in doing the work he was assigned. He was also willing to help others when his skills were needed.

This book tells how they lived with difficult health problems of their own, as well as those of members of the group whom they served, and how they showed God's love for them.

You will enjoy getting to know Scotty and Marie as he shares how they met challenge after challenge and learned many spiritual lessons.

Don and Lucy Lindholm
Former Director of Tribal Affairs, Peru SIL

Scotty, the Holy Spirit working through you as you wrote resulted in my savoring each and every word and story! I found myself challenged, edified, and encouraged in the Lord from start to finish!

Thank you for your ministry and for sharing with great humility how God used you and Marie and your entire network of supporters, workers, and praying saints to bring God's Word to the Sharanahua people. A must-read for anyone who thinks people without Christ can be carefree and happy.

John Williams
JAARS Chaplain

JESUS IS MY OWNER
Life with the Sharanahuas

By Eugene Scott with Marie Scott

ISBN 9781099223808

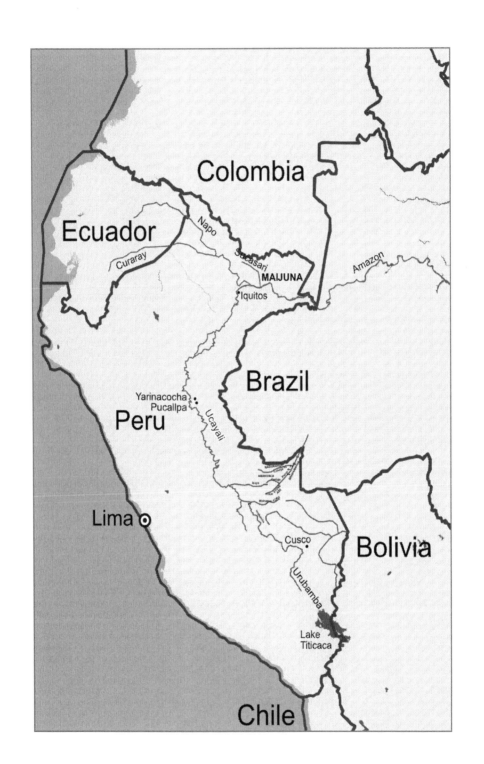

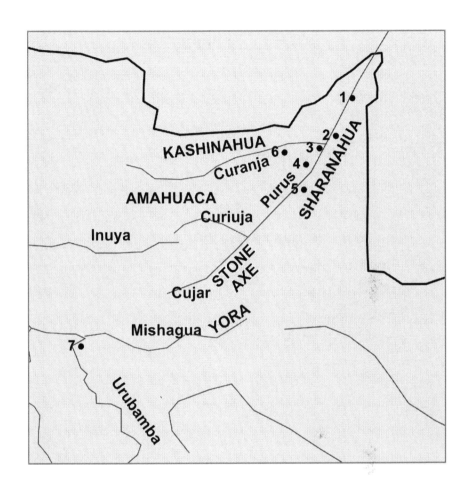

VILLAGES
On Purus River
1. Esperanza (Army post)
2. San Marcos
3. Mouth of the river
4. Santa Margarita
5. Gasta Bala

On Curanja River
6. Conta (Kashinahua)

On Urubamba River
7. Nueva Luz (Matsigenka)

50 km
30 mi

CONTENTS

FOREWORD

When Gene Scott, better known to his friends as Scotty, surrendered his life to the Lord, I'm sure he had no idea of the adventures that lay ahead for him. From a humble home in Washington State he found himself in the middle of the Amazon jungle.

Scotty and Marie lived with a remote tribal group in southeastern Peru for nearly fifty years in order to give the Word of God to people who had never heard the gospel. His days included sitting for hours at the translation desk, traveling by dugout canoe for days on end, or plunging through the jungle looking for unreached people. How does one exist in the most remote jungles in the world with no stores to refill the food supply? He'll tell you how.

What do you do when you make a mistake in a strange cultural setting? You will read how Scotty handled it. Everyday life with the Sharanahuas is an adventure; some circumstances very difficult to see, others a joy and a pleasure.

Aviation was essential to Scotty's translation work with the Sharanahuas. In their remote part of the Amazon near the border of Brazil they were only accessible by air. I was privileged to be one of the JAARS pilots who flew for the Scotts.

In missionary work, a good sense of humor is essential. Scotty tells of a time that I was his pilot and was requested by the chief of the tribe to take a turtle to the army base downstream. I'll let him finish the story.

Scotty's book recounts his experiences from the beginning to the end of his missionary career. As you read this book you will see that his real purpose and desire in writing it is to show the power of God to change lives. Maybe as you read the story of his life you will be moved to join with those who are taking the Scriptures to every written language on the earth.

It has been my honor to work with some of the great pioneer missionaries of our time—men and women who risked their lives to take the gospel to the most difficult areas of the world. None do I admire more than Gene and Marie Scott.

Bernie May
Former JAARS pilot
Former president of JAARS, Inc.
Former president of Wycliffe USA
Founder of The Seed Company

PREFACE

"How can a man 84 years old connect with second graders?"

"Children love stories, and you have lots of them to tell."

My husband and I had been asked to tell children about Peru, not once, but four times during the upcoming year in a public school in North Carolina. Yes, my husband is a storyteller. It is not that he had any more experiences than the average missionary-translator, but he has a way of making everyday happenings come alive. And he loves to tell stories to amuse or amaze.

But he is never happier in his storytelling than when he can tell of the providential hand of the Lord in his life and in his family or in the lives of the Sharanahuas in Peru, with whom we lived and worked for nearly fifty years. For him it is the frosting on the cake if, through his telling of the Lord's work among the Sharanahuas, someone is challenged to join in the task of giving the precious Word of God to the remaining language groups in the world that do not have it.

Marie Scott

ACKNOWLEDGEMENTS

Without the help of my dear wife this book would still not be done. Marie's diaries have been an invaluable help and reminder of some experiences long forgotten. The diaries also helped to insure accuracy where time had blurred some of my memories. As always, her encouragement helped me to keep at it.

The first to prompt me to write a book were two of Wycliffe Bible Translators' former presidents. Bernie May, who flew us out to the Sharanahua communities on several occasions, said, "Scotty, when are you going to write your book?" David Cummings blessed all of us missionaries with his ministry in Peru. Later, on his visit to Waxhaw, North Carolina, we all lined up to shake his hand. I was surprised when he said, "When are you going to write your book?" Then I felt the Lord nudging me to do it.

Our good friend Scott Anderson of Living Church in Englewood, Colorado, spent hours on the phone with us, proof-reading and making suggestions and corrections. He said, "No comma" so many times to us that we presented him with a mug with his picture and "No comma" written on it.

Our daughter Becky Mottola spent many hours going over the book with Marie to proofread and offer suggestions. Besides Becky, our other kids—David, Steven, and Priscilla—and their spouses and Marie's sister Kathy Herzog always encouraged me in this project.

I want to thank Louise Derr for not only proofreading the early manuscript but encouraging me to have it published. Agnes Weaver, an accomplished editor, also encouraged me to write and publish my story.

The final editing was done by Carol Brinneman. We owe Carol a big debt of gratitude for the many hours she spent to make this book more readable and accurate. There were times I wanted to say, "Just leave it like it is." But if I had said that, this book would be lacking the much-needed touch of an accomplished editor. Thanks, Carol.

Thanks are due also to Joyce Hyde for formatting the book for print and for designing the cover. Thanks to Daniel Brinneman for the digital map drawings. We'd like to thank also Frank Doejaaren for his help in scanning the photos.

Other friends who gave me the green light, encouraging words, and prayed for me to finish the book are too many to list. Thanks to all of you.

And, of course, without the strength and counsel from our Lord Jesus this book would not have been finished. To him is all the glory for any good that results from reading this story of my life and those who have taken the journey with me.

Eugene Scott

INTRODUCTION

Writing a book seemed far beyond me. But through the years, at various times, people have urged me to recount the many experiences that my family and I have had as we lived in the jungle of southeastern Peru among the Sharanahua tribespeople.

As my "Stories for a Book" file became larger and larger, I could see how God's hand has been in my life from the very beginning. For that reason I'm including stories from my youth and how God led me over my 90 years of life.

What do I hope to accomplish by writing this book? I'm going to give four reasons.

First of all, I want to bring glory to the Lord who has given me life in Christ—a forgiven life, everlasting life, abundant life. Anything that has been accomplished in my life has been because of his Spirit, his enabling, and his strength and not my own. Christ "began a good work in me" when I was 13 and accepted Jesus Christ as my Savior, and I want him to continue that work until he calls me into his presence.

Secondly, I want anyone who reads this book and wants his or her life to be used of Christ in his service to realize that if the Lord could use me, he can use anyone whose life is dedicated to him.

Thirdly, I hope that some who read this book would be challenged to join us in the global task of bringing the Word of God, the Bible, to the some 1,700 language groups still without any of God's Word in their own language. The vision of the founder of Wycliffe Bible Translators, William Cameron Townsend, was that every language group in the world would have the precious Word of God in their own language. Our Lord Jesus said to ask the Lord of the harvest to send out workers (translators, teachers, pilots, mechanics, computer experts, administrators, all who will help to complete the task) into his harvest field. Those 1,700 language groups are part of the harvest that need workers to go to them to give them the life-giving Word of God.

Fourthly, I want to leave a record of the Lord's faithfulness for my children, grandchildren, family, and friends who have been with Marie and me throughout our ministry to the Sharanahuas and beyond. To them belongs much of the credit for what the Lord has been able to accomplish in our ministry. They have stood with us in prayer and encouraged us throughout our time in Peru and later in our ministry here in the States. Many also have come alongside us with their gifts to make it possible for us to do the work of Bible translation for the Sharanahuas.

If these four goals can be accomplished, then I will feel that writing this book has been worth it. Jesus said, "Apart from me you can do nothing." For any good that Marie and I have done, to God be all the glory! It has been by his grace alone.

Eugene Scott

—1—

FROM DARKNESS TO LIGHT

"Hurry! Come quickly! My Uncle Nairaso is dying!"

I ran with Choro to the house where Nairaso lay in his hammock. One look and hearing the raspy sound in his chest and the labored breathing, I knew that he didn't have long for this world. I hadn't yet had much time among the Sharanahuas and didn't know their language well. An epidemic of flu had broken out in their community. There were no doctors or nurses. I was the only one there who could help them medically or spiritually. Despite giving them antibiotics, some of them succumbed to complications and pneumonia, and several died. I knew Nairaso was going out into eternity, and I felt that I didn't know the language well enough to give him the good news. I thought, *How sad that I can't tell him that there is hope beyond the grave, that Jesus loves him and is ready to welcome him.*

Nairaso's lifestyle was even simpler than that of most of the Sharanahuas. He had arrived from another village just a few weeks before. As I was lamenting my shortage of vocabulary in Sharanahua, it seemed that the Lord was saying to me, "Use what you have."

I got down on my knees beside his hammock with my head close to his and said, "Nairaso, can you hear me?"

He replied, "Yes."

Then I said, "Nairaso, you're dying," which is what the Sharanahuas do in their culture, but we would seldom do in ours. "Wouldn't you like to go to be with Jesus?" Wrong approach. He had never heard of Jesus. He didn't know whether Jesus was good or bad.

"No," he said emphatically.

I got to my feet feeling defeated. Then Choro began to fold his uncle up in his hammock, the way they do when they bury someone. I took hold of Nairaso's wrist. He still had a pulse. I said, "Wait! He's not dead yet." Choro let his uncle back down in his hammock and it seemed the Lord was saying, "Try again."

So I got down on my knees again and said, "Nairaso, can you still hear me?"

Again he replied, "Yes."

This time I said, "Nairaso, let me tell you about Jesus. Where Jesus is, you will never be sick again; you will never be hungry again. Where Jesus is, nothing bad can ever get in there. Where Jesus is, everything is good. Your little boy died just the other day. This Jesus loves the little children, and he took your boy to live with him. He's taking good care of your little boy. Jesus loves you, too. He wants you to come so he can take care of you, too. He's waiting for you. Don't you want to go to be with Jesus?"

This time he said, "Yes."

"Then you pray after me and tell Jesus this." I led him in a prayer to receive Christ. I don't remember exactly what I prompted him to pray. I know for sure it wasn't a deeply theological prayer, but Nairaso called on Jesus, and Romans 10:13 (KJV) says, "For whosoever shall call upon the name of the Lord shall be saved."

After Nairaso had prayed, I got back on my feet. It was quiet for a few minutes, and suddenly he yelled, "I see him!" and he died almost immediately. I was thrilled and shocked all at the same time.

Choro folded his uncle up in his hammock and lowered him into the hole they had already dug for him. As is their custom, they put all his earthly possessions into the hole with him—his few ragged clothes, an old pot, his machete, and that was about it.

After they had covered him up with the dirt, Conshico, a Sharanahua man standing by watching, turned to me and asked, "It's all dark down there where he is, isn't it?"

I replied, "Where his flesh and bones are, it's dark. But his spirit went to be with Jesus, and where Jesus is, it's never dark, always light."

Conshico asked incredulously, "Never dark? Always light?" The Sharanahuas feared the dark because they thought evil spirits were more prevalent in the dark.

"Never dark. Where Jesus is, it's always light."

After pondering this, he asked, and I can still hear it as though it were yesterday, "Never dark—always light where Jesus is? How long have you known about this Jesus?"

"As long as I can remember."

"Did your father know?"

"Yes."

"And your grandfather?"

"Yes"

"And did your ancestors know about Jesus?"

"Most of them."

Conshico stood reflecting for a minute, and then he said, "Oh, what a pity! I'm just now hearing about Jesus. My father never heard, my grandfather never heard, and my ancestors never heard, and they all went out where it's dark."

I thought, *Lord, I can't do anything about his father and grandfather or his ancestors, but thank you for sending me here now so that I can translate your life-giving Word for the Sharanahuas, and they can hear your words, "I am the light of the world.*

Whoever follows me will never walk in darkness, but will have the light of life" (John 8:12).

Later as I pondered the job ahead of me of translating the Bible into a language that had never been written down, I realized that the task was way beyond me without the enabling of God's Holy Spirit. Yes, I had four years of intense Bible study and two summers of linguistic training by the Summer Institute of Linguistics at the University of Oklahoma. I had a deep desire to translate God's Word and introduce Jesus Christ to those who had never heard, but I still felt inadequate to take on this task.

As I reflected on my past life, I thought, *What an unlikely candidate to be a translator of God's Word and introduce Jesus Christ to those who had never heard!*

—2—

THE EARLY YEARS

In 1927 Charles Lindbergh crossed the ocean in an airplane. That was a first. Babe Ruth hit sixty homeruns. That also was a first. And Mrs. Frances E. Scott gave birth to a son. That was not a first. It was her seventh child. That's when I entered this world.

Leonard Scott, my grandfather, uprooted his family from Pinnacle, a beautiful spot north of Winston Salem, North Carolina, and headed west. He stopped in Arizona for a while, and then it was on to the state of Washington. His son, my father, Sidney G. Scott, had met and married Frances Ezell in Ajo, Arizona, and they were married there September 2, 1914. Later my father became a lumberjack in the woods of western Washington.

After the birth of my brother Bob, two years after me, we were eight children. The Depression was about to hit our great country. Mom tried to make ours a happy home, and so we didn't realize that we weren't supposed to be happy if we didn't have much of this world's goods. Sitting around the table was a time for eating garden-grown vegetables, and fruit from our apple, cherry, pear, and plum trees. No one could beat Mom's apple pies and other desserts. Laughter was a staple at our meals. Each of us had our place at the table. Mine was between two of my older sisters. Being low on the pecking order, I didn't get away with much.

Though my brother Bob and I were just two years apart and had the normal amount of skirmishes for that age, Mom taught us to love one another. I can still hear her, if there was a loud disagreement, saying, "There's going to be peace in this family!" And she had a switch from the apple tree to enforce it. My siblings all agreed that I got more spankings than the rest of them, but they also agreed that I deserved them. I knew my Mom loved me, and I knew I had it coming for the things I had done, plus some things she didn't know about, so I didn't resent the discipline she gave me.

My mother was a wonderful woman. Though life was very hard for her, I don't remember her ever complaining. As I grew up, most of my friends came from well-to-do homes, where their fathers were doctors, lawyers, or businessmen. But my friends all liked coming to my house because Mom always treated them like her own; and besides that, she always had fresh homemade bread, buns, or cinnamon rolls to give us. I don't ever remember coming home from school and not finding Mom there. Though my father worked hard in the woods, he was a compulsive gambler and would often gamble away the money that should have helped Mom and the family. As I look back I have wondered how she kept going. But I do know her secret. She was almost constantly singing hymns, such as this one by Frank E. Graeff:

Does Jesus care when my heart is pained
Too deeply for mirth or song;
As the burdens press, and the cares distress,
And the way grows weary and long?

Does Jesus care when my way is dark
With a nameless dread and fear?

As the daylight fades into deep night shades,
Does he care enough to be near?

Refrain
O yes, he cares, I know he cares,
His heart is touched with my grief;
When the days are weary, the long nights dreary,
I know my Savior cares.

She was a quiet woman who walked and talked with her Lord.
I can still hear her singing the songs that ministered Christ's love to
her heart … and later to mine.

When I was probably about 10 years old, my friends and I were
playing ball in one of the many open fields in my hometown. A
young man came along and called, "Come here a minute, boys.
I want to show you something." I immediately felt attracted to
the young man. Something about him suggested friendliness and
kindness. He said, "Sit here on the curb. I want to show you this
little book. It's called *The Wordless Book*."

He showed us a little book with no words, and each page was a
different color. The first page was black. The young man explained,
"That's what our hearts look like without Christ, black with sin."
Next the red page represented the blood of Christ, shed to save
us from our sins. Then a white page represented our hearts made
clean by confessing our sins and accepting Jesus as our Savior. And
last, the gold page represented the streets of gold in heaven where
we will spend eternity with Christ.

He didn't press us at that time to accept Christ, but the seed was
sown in our lives. Sometimes I've wondered if that young man went
on his way wondering if he had accomplished anything by talking to
us. But he did. It was the first time I had heard the gospel explained
that way. Though he didn't ask us to accept the Lord as our Savior
right then, I think all of us boys thought something should change in

our lives. As I remember it, we said, "Alright. The next one that says a bad word gets socked ten times on the arm." That wasn't enough to knock the sin out of our lives, but it was a start.

The church my family attended didn't preach the gospel. When my Mom was a girl and later as a young woman, this denomination did preach salvation through Christ. But by the time I was a boy in that church, they had lost their compass, and weren't accepting the Bible as the only infallible Word of God, and weren't preaching that Jesus Christ was the way, the truth, and the life, and that no one was accepted into heaven except through faith in him.

When I was 13 years old, a quartet of young Mennonite fellows from the Bible Institute of Los Angeles were permitted by our pastor (though he himself didn't attend) to hold a Wednesday evening meeting in our church. The quartet sang hymns beautifully. Then one of them brought a simple gospel message explaining the way of salvation in Christ.

When he gave an invitation to anyone who wanted to receive Christ as Savior, my oldest sister, Beth, who had already given her life to Christ, was sitting next to me and whispered, "Gene, are you sure of your salvation?" I not only was not sure of it, I hardly knew what it meant. When I said that I wasn't, she asked me if I wanted to go forward to receive Christ. I went forward and there in the choir room of that church the young Mennonite fellow explained the way of salvation to me again. On my knees I confessed my sin and asked Jesus to come into my heart and save me. Almost immediately, I experienced the joy of salvation. Jesus became real to me, and I began to read his Word.

There was no follow-up, and I didn't have discernment enough to know that I should leave our church and find one that preached the gospel. For quite a while I tried to live for the Lord on my own, avoiding "worldly pleasures." I didn't enter into a lot of things that my friends were into.

Finally, between my junior and senior years in high school, I decided that I was missing out on too many things with my friends. It was almost as though I said, "Goodbye, God! I can't follow you anymore. It's too hard. I want to be accepted by my friends and do what they do." Of course, I didn't say it, but I acted like it. I became very popular with my classmates. I was invited to all the parties and joined them when they drank, and I began to smoke. Of course, I didn't want my Mom to know what I was doing, though you can't hide it when you smoke. It saturates your clothes. You can't leave the smoke smell behind you. But I don't think Mom knew I was drinking. I drank only with my friends to be one with them. I never drank alone. I kept going to church with the family, but it didn't mean anything to me, and there was nothing there to bring conviction to my heart. Despite this, the Holy Spirit, though grieved, was still in my life, and sometimes I would feel convicted and want to leave the life I was living, but not enough to do it. My life continued far from the Lord on a spiritual downward spiral.

—3—

JOIN THE NAVY AND SEE THE WORLD?

I was a 17-year-old senior in high school in 1945. Many of my friends were 18 and facing the draft as World War II was still raging. Some of my closest friends were planning to go to Seattle; two of them to join the US Air Force, and one to join the US Navy. I decided to go along with them, not to enlist yet, but just to accompany them. I went with the one joining the navy, as he was alone and needed some company. He was ushered into a large room to take the written test, while I waited for him outside the half wall that separated enlistees from those waiting. A non-commissioned officer told me to step right inside to take the test. I replied that I hadn't come to join the navy, only to keep company with my friend who was joining. He said, "Well, it won't hurt you to find out how much you know. Why don't you just step inside and take the test anyway?" That sounded harmless to me; besides, I intended to join the navy after I graduated from high school, so I obliged him.

After we had finished the tests, another non-commissioned officer stepped up and said with a very authoritative voice, "All right, all of you right into this room." I thought of objecting, but I guess I thought, *How can this hurt?* The next thing I knew I was there along with all of the other teenagers being told to strip down, and as I remember, they painted a big number eight on my chest. I passed the physical with flying colors, and then a document was put in front of me to sign to become a part of the United States Navy. I thought, *Oh well. I'll have to join someday anyway, so I might as well sign it.*

My friend who had come to join the navy flunked the physical. He was out, and I was in. This did not sit well with my mother when I got back home to Centralia (Washington) and told her that I had joined the US Navy. I hadn't finished high school yet, and she didn't want to see me joining the navy before I had graduated. Fortunately, they didn't call me until I had finished my senior year.

With a high school classmate, I went to California to visit my brother and family living in Los Angeles. We had been there just a few days when I got word that I was to report for duty in Seattle. So it was back to Washington and Seattle, and then back on the train to go from Seattle to San Diego for boot camp with a lot of other teenagers. One from Everett, Washington, became my best friend.

What a shock it was to us who had just been the mighty seniors of our high school to become low man on the totem pole. Suddenly, I went from being a person to being a number. To this day I remember my navy serial number: 387-50-08. I recall our company commander, a former football player from Oklahoma State. I would have hated to play on the other side of the line from him. No one, but no one, ever talked back to him. In his first talk to us recruits I recall one thing he said, and that was, "You're going to think the devil is an angel compared to me by the time I get through with you." However, his bark was worse than his bite. We didn't see him nearly as much as we saw the platoon commanders, and he wasn't nearly as rough as they were. They were just out of boot camp themselves and wanted to show how rough and authoritative they could be.

The only time the company commander ever did anything to make my life a bit more difficult was on the parade ground as we were drilling. I had already learned quite a bit of parade drill having served for a short time with some of my high school friends in the National Guard in my hometown. One time the company commander said, "Company, short interval, dress right, dress!" The fellow next to me didn't do it right, and so I whispered to him to help him. The company commander said, "You back there talking in ranks!" I was desperately hoping someone besides me had said something, but no. He said, "You know who I mean. Take off your hat. Now put it in your mouth!"

Much to the delight of the rest of the company, but to the incredulity of the company commander, I replied, "It won't fit, sir."

He answered, "Oh! Wise guy, are you?" And he stepped back through the ranks where I was, folded that nice white hat in two and shoved it into my mouth. For about an hour I marched on the parade ground with the rest of the company with my hat hanging out of my mouth. At the end of that time I felt like I had swallowed all of the dust from the parade ground. As we came to a halt in front of the barracks, he said, "Now you can take the hat out of your mouth. If any of the rest of you ever feel like talking while in ranks, ask this sailor how it feels."

I had only two other episodes in the navy that had me wondering if I was going to get something bad, like a court martial, on my record. I was not one to fool around while in the service. I took it seriously and tried to be the best sailor I could be. A couple of times bad things just seemed to come my way unbidden.

While still in boot camp it was our company's turn to serve on the chow line. One of the things we had for that noon meal was ice cream. As we were finished serving and ready to leave, one of the sailors in my company tried to get away with a quart of ice cream. He thought he could sneak it out the door unnoticed and eat it outside, probably with some of his buddies. At the last minute he saw there was a guard at the door checking those going out to make sure nothing was taken out that shouldn't be. The sailor was desperate and shoved the ice cream into my arms and continued on his way. There I was, almost to the door with this illegal ice cream. We all still had our aprons with us, and the only thing I knew to do was put the ice cream in the apron and hope the guard didn't notice. It was a bad decision. He did notice, and said, "All right, Mac, I'm taking you to the officer of the day."

I was one terrified 17-year-old. The officer said, "Sailor, don't you know that it's a serious offense to steal in the navy?"

I replied, "Yes sir." I'm sure my excuse of saying that someone slipped it to me on the way out sounded very lame. The officer could probably see that my knees were almost knocking together.

He said, "Sailor, do you know what I'm going to do to you?"

Thinking the worst, I replied, "No sir."

He said, "I want you to take that ice cream outside, and if you don't eat every bit of it, you're in trouble. You can go now."

Wow! Talk about one relieved and happy sailor; I was it. The fellows in my company were waiting outside to find out what was going to happen to me. Without a word I sat down on the curb there in the heat of San Diego and, much to the amazement of my buddies, began to eat the ice cream. I didn't say a word, just continued to eat the ice cream until it was all gone. No one else got a bite, and I didn't get sick either.

I can still picture it. It was either my sixth or seventh week of boot camp. Our company was standing in formation on the parade ground. Suddenly, the announcement came over the public address system, "The war is over! The war with Japan is over!" A shout of jubilation resounded over the parade grounds. With all of San Diego, the Naval Training Center was beside itself with the thrill of victory and looking forward to peace and all it would entail.

Our company commander gave us liberty to go into the city of San Diego as soon as we returned to the barracks.

There it was pandemonium. Strangers were hugging strangers; smiles were on every face. Happiness on a scale I'd never seen before enveloped the city. I was with two or three of my navy buddies. We were getting hungry, and the restaurants were all full. My friends and I noticed at a drive-in restaurant one man sitting alone in his car. We went over to his window and said, "Sir, would you mind if we got into your car in order to get something to eat? We can't find a restaurant that isn't full."

He said, "You sailors get right in." This was a day to celebrate together. No one knew a stranger.

After boot camp I got the duty I asked for and was assigned to a destroyer, DD 781, the USS *Robert K. Huntington*. It had a complement of just over two hundred men. My best friend from Everett, Washington, Roger Ringstadt, was also assigned to the same ship.

I was made a signalman and thus got to be on the bridge from where the ship was piloted and where the captain spent much of his time. Having just arrived, I was low man, and my first assignment was to make coffee for all the rest of the signalmen.

Soon I learned to send Morse code signals by flashing light. One day the first class signalman told me to send a message to a ship not too far from ours. Wanting to show my ability to send, I operated the light sending the message as fast as I could. The signal came back just as fast, too fast for me to read it. The first class signalman was standing behind me. I feel sure he had anticipated this, and he took the message down for me. Then he said, "You just learned your first lesson. Never send the signal any faster than you can receive it. The person receiving your signal will send it back to you at the same rate you send it to him."

Though I enjoyed the time on the destroyer we never traveled to any other countries, only a short distance off the coast of California. We were on what they called "plane guard." We were on maneuvers with two aircraft carriers, the USS *Hancock* and the USS *Lexington*. Our main purpose for being there was to pick up any pilot whose plane didn't make it after taking off from the flight deck of the aircraft carrier. An aircraft carrier requires a long distance to get turned around, and by the time it did, the pilot may have been lost. The destroyer, on the other hand, can turn around in a much shorter distance to pick up the downed pilot.

Finally, it happened. A plane took off from the deck but didn't gain any altitude and just went right into the ocean. The plane didn't go down nose-first, and the pilot was able to get out unharmed before the plane sunk. We got to him very shortly after and got him onto our deck, much to his delight. Later we rigged up a line with a chair on it and sent him back to his ship. An aircraft carrier had a complement of over 2,000 sailors—almost a floating city. It had a lot of conveniences on it that a destroyer doesn't have. When we sent the pilot back to the aircraft carrier, the carrier sent back on the line a huge supply of ice cream.

After only about four months on the destroyer, my friend and I were transferred to another assignment. I, who wanted to see something of the world, was sent to Pier 91 in Seattle, just 90 miles from home. My friend, Roger, was sent to the island of Kwajalein. Then, as if Seattle wasn't close enough to home, they sent me to Tacoma, just 60 miles from home, to a small aircraft carrier, called a CVE, to help put it "in mothballs," something the navy was doing a lot of since the war was over. My job was to make sure that the compartments that had anything to do with communications were all shipshape, that is, completely in order and clean.

The lieutenant who was over me was a very congenial person. He and I got along very well. One weekend he said, "Scott, I think it's time you were given a promotion in rank. Monday you will no longer be a first class seaman. I'm making you a third class petty officer." I thanked him, and he told me I could go on liberty. I had promised my friend Roger from Everett that I would look up his folks, as Everett wasn't too far away.

While on liberty I decided to stop at one of the many navy tailor shops and have my new third class petty officer chevron sewn onto my uniform, since the officer had said I would be given that rank "the day after tomorrow." After visiting my friend's parents, and as it was summertime and quite warm, I did what most sailors did on liberty: I put my hat on the back of my head and rolled my cuffs up one turn. As I was merrily walking down the residential district in Everett, suddenly there appeared a shore patrol wagon. I never dreamed of seeing one in the residential district of Everett. I quickly "squared up" my hat and put my cuffs down again. The wagon pulled up next to me, and one of the men in it said, "OK, sailor, put your hat back like it was and your cuffs rolled up a notch too, and get in the wagon. We're taking you in to the shore patrol office."

I said, "You wouldn't take me in for something so minor would you?"

They said, "If you don't get in this wagon and keep quiet, we'll book you for insubordination as well." When they got me to the office, the one in charge looked at my liberty card, which said "Seaman First Class," and then at my uniform that had a third class petty officer chevron sewn on it.

"Put that hat back on straight, sailor boy."

17

The officer said, "What are you, Mac, a first class seaman or a third class petty officer? Your liberty card says first class seaman, so that's what you are. It's a serious offense to be impersonating a rank that you're not. I'm writing you up and you will be facing a court martial on your ship." I tried to explain to him that I had sewed the chevron on because I was getting the promotion on Monday. He didn't want to hear any of that and said, "You are to go immediately to your ship and await the "captain's mast." That's what they called the trial of a minor nature. I was dreading having to face the officer on Monday.

When the officer saw me, he said, "Well, Scott, I see you ran into some difficulties on the weekend in Everett. I want you to know that I put that order for a captain's mast into file 13 (the wastebasket), and you will never see it or hear about it again." Talk about one happy and relieved sailor; that was me. And I thanked the officer and was so glad that I had one like him over me instead of a go-by-the-book, officious one. I also believe that although I wasn't walking with the Lord at that time, he made sure that I wasn't going to leave the navy with a bad mark on my record.

Since the war was over, many servicemen were being encouraged to leave the service unless they wanted to make it a career. I was offered a place in a navy band as a baritone player if I would re-enlist, but the thought of not being under orders anymore, and being able to return to my hometown, overrode any desire to pursue a career playing my baritone horn in a navy band. So in August 1946 after just a year and a month in the navy I was given an honorable discharge in Bremerton, Washington. I'm thankful for the time I spent in the navy. It taught me discipline, and it gave me the opportunity to serve my country.

—4—

A PROMISE MADE

After being discharged from the navy, I came back to my parents' home in Centralia, Washington. I enrolled in Centralia Junior College, which had the distinction of being the very first junior college in the state of Washington. Later they dropped "Junior," and today it is called Centralia College. It was just beginning to outgrow its place on the third floor of the Centralia High School building. There were many of my high school friends in the college, and being in the same building with some of the same teachers, it was almost like being back in high school. I was even asked to play in the high school band again. I wasn't living for Christ and was indulging in things that a Christian shouldn't be involved in. As the book of Hebrews tells us, we can enjoy the fleeting pleasures of sin, but it's only for a short time (11:25).

I was not only enrolled in junior college, but I was also making friends with former high school classmates that I hadn't known well earlier. Some of them were from other cities close to Centralia. The camaraderie was great.

One young fellow in particular became a very close friend of mine, Lloyd Bevington. One time he and I began to discuss which one of us could run the fastest in the 100 yard dash. Somehow this became a big topic in the college until it was decided to hold the race on the high school and junior college track. I'll never know how it happened, but it just gathered steam until everyone was excited about it. My friends good-naturedly told me, "Scotty, either you win that race or you are in big trouble. We've placed our bets on you." Others were saying the same thing to Lloyd. The date for the race was announced. Lloyd and I took our stance like any professional track star, the dean fired the gun, and we were off. The student body was cheering for their choice. I've probably never in my life run any faster, and I barely nosed out Lloyd. There were shouts of jubilation from my cheering section, and then we *all* dissolved into laughter so hard that it was difficult to tell who won. Probably the college had never had such enthusiasm over a race that didn't count for anything. Lloyd and I continued to be close friends and together we had other experiences that had a lasting effect on our lives.

When I was 20 I had to make a decision whether to continue in junior college or accept a permanent appointment as a clerk in the Centralia Post Office. That kind of an appointment didn't come often to one as young as I was. Another thing that made the appointment to the post office attractive was that I knew Uncle Sam wasn't going to go broke any time soon. This gave me confidence that I wouldn't have to be concerned about financial security, and starting at such a young age could give possibilities for advancement. Though I had to drop out of junior college to work full time in the post office, I continued to hang out with my friends.

At that time Youth for Christ was just getting started in my hometown. My older brother Ezell asked me to come and play my baritone horn in the orchestra in YFC. I never could turn my brother down, so I went. No one there knew that I wasn't following the Lord. The Youth for Christ director, Victor Hovda, a real man of God, but not knowing my double life, asked me to lead the orchestra and to be the assistant Youth for Christ director. Again I couldn't seem to say no. I would go to Youth for Christ meetings and feel convicted when the message was given, but I continued to go from Youth for Christ to a Saturday night dance with my friends, which usually included drinking. This double life was becoming very painful for me. I remember at one point thinking, *I can't keep this up. I either have to go all out for Christ or turn my back on him completely.*

One evening Lloyd and I were heading for a party. We picked up a case of beer, and as we were driving along we saw a couple of soldiers hitchhiking. It was the night before Thanksgiving. It was cold out and, having been in the service ourselves, we wanted to help these two soldiers. We decided we would take them to the edge of the Chehalis city limit where they would have a better chance of getting a ride south on the main highway. We opened a bottle of beer and offered the soldiers a bottle. We were driving through Chehalis and made the mistake of drinking as we drove along. The police saw us and pulled us over. Fortunately, they let the soldiers go, but they made Lloyd give them the keys to his dad's car, and made us both get into the police car and took us to the Chehalis city jail. Without a word the jailer took us to a cell, ordered us in, and locked the cell door.

There we were, in this dark, dank, cold cell in November, with not even a place to lie down even if we had felt like it, which we didn't. Lloyd and I were to have helped the sportscaster for KELA, the local radio station, to be his spotters for the broadcast of the Thanksgiving Day football game between the Centralia High Tigers and the Chehalis High Bearcats, and here we were in the Chehalis jail.

After we had been there for an hour or more with no word from anyone, we rattled the cell door to get some attention.

When the old jailer came to the cell door, I asked him, "Why are you keeping us here? We haven't done anything bad."

He answered, "You're here for being drunk, and it will cost you ten dollars to get out. Your friend is in here for drunken driving, and it will cost him one hundred dollars to get out." I wasn't drunk, nor had Lloyd been driving drunk. You don't get drunk on just part of one bottle of beer. We didn't have ten dollars between us.

Then our thoughts turned to our parents and the humiliation they were going to feel when this came out in the paper. The *Centralia Chronicle* had a section called "The Locals" where any misdemeanor, jail sentence, or anything similar was published, and everyone read that almost as much as the headlines. I knew that if my mother read that about her son, it would just about kill her. Lloyd and I were despondent and didn't know what to do. They weren't going to let us out.

In the middle of the night Lloyd said, "Gene, do you know how to pray?"

I said, "I don't know if God listens to guys like us, but I'll try." I prayed saying, "Lord, if you will get us out of here without getting our names in the paper, I'll never do this again, and I'll serve you forever."

We were in the cell all night and didn't sleep a wink. Early in the morning they let Lloyd call his dad to tell him where we were. Mr. Bevington came and by that time the chief of police had arrived. He said to Lloyd's dad, "I have boys of my own, and I know how it is. If you'll just pay the fine, we'll let the boys go. It won't go on their record, and no one will even know it happened." Lloyd and I heaved a sigh of relief. I was so thankful that the Lord had answered the prayer for us, but I'm not sure that Mr. Bevington thought shelling out 110 dollars was an answer to prayer. Lloyd and I barely made it to the football field in time to be the spotters. After the game I returned home to Thanksgiving dinner. Mom thought I had spent the night at Lloyd's house, and I didn't tell her differently. She didn't know how thankful I was that Thanksgiving Day.

—5—

THE PROMISE KEPT

The Youth for Christ director, Victor Hovda, urged the youth to go to some meetings over in Yakima, Washington. I had no desire to go to more meetings, but I did have a desire to drive my older brother Thurman's new Dodge car. He offered to let me drive it to take the young people to Yakima. So in order to drive the new car I took the other young people and went.

I had no idea what I was getting into in Yakima. As soon as I stepped into the auditorium I could sense there was something different than I had ever felt before. I didn't know that for at least a year a group of men and women had been praying fervently that God would do something new, something deep, something lasting, a genuine movement of the Holy Spirit in conviction and renewal.

As the meetings got started, a strong spirit of conviction swept over the five hundred or so people in attendance. Men, women, pastors, and missionaries began to confess their sins and get right with the Lord. The people began to give cheerfully, lavishly, even hilariously for missions. A dishpan was placed in front of the podium for an offering plate. Some were even offering to the Lord the keys to their cars. At one point the leader of the meetings stood in the dishpan as a symbol, quoting 2 Corinthians 8:5: "They gave themselves first of all to the Lord." As the Holy Spirit continued his work, I was getting more and more uncomfortable. I thought, *If these godly people have to confess their sins and get right with the Lord, where do I stand? I must have one foot in hell.* The Holy Spirit was working so profoundly that revival was taking place. People continued to confess their sins, get right with the Lord, and experience afresh the joy of salvation.

Dr. Armin Gesswein, a Lutheran pastor working under the auspices of the Charles E. Fuller Evangelistic Association, was the scheduled speaker, but the Holy Spirit was working so powerfully that he was not yet able to give his messages. Finally, one of the people in the congregation stood up and said, "Dr. Gesswein, we have come a long ways to hear you, and we're not getting to hear you."

Dr. Gesswein, who was very instrumental in the beginning of Billy Graham's ministry, and was greatly used of the Lord in stirring people to pray and experience revival, replied, "Dear brother, we have come here to hear from the Lord, and we are hearing loud and clear."

As the Holy Spirit continued to move deeply among us, I could stand it no longer, and I finally went forward. The leader, Pastor Bill Cady, looked at me and said, "Young man, did you have something to say?"

I said, "I have been the biggest hypocrite." Then, as the tears began to flow, I could say no more. I was not aware of the 500 or so people there; I was only aware of the Lord. Though I had accepted Christ at age 13, this was the first time that it struck me that if I had been the only person in the world Jesus would have died for me. My sins put him on the cross. I thought, *Oh what have I done to you?* I said to him, and no one else heard me, "Lord, please forgive me. Here's my life if you can use me."

Afterwards an elderly woman whom I didn't know came to me and said, "Young man, I have been observing you, and you have confessed your sins, and your desire is to be emptied of them, isn't it?"

I answered, "Yes."

She said, "That's wonderful, and we have to do that in order for the Lord to be what he wants to be in our lives. You have emptied yourself of sin, but God doesn't want you to remain empty. He wants to fill you with his presence. Have you ever received the Holy Spirit? By that I mean, have you ever welcomed him into your life? When you accepted Jesus as your Savior the Holy Spirit took up residence in your life. He is resident, but he wants to be president. He wants to control your thoughts and actions to glorify Christ in you. Just as by faith you accepted Jesus as your Savior, now would you like to welcome the Holy Spirit to be in charge of your life?"

When I said that I wanted to do whatever the Lord wanted me to do, she said, "Then right now you can pray and ask the Holy Spirit to be in control of your life." I then prayed a simple prayer asking the Holy Spirit to control my life from then on. I didn't have any ethereal experience, but I experienced a deep, settled peace.

As I walked out of that meeting, I ran into a friend of mine from my junior college days. He said, "Let's go have a drink together." Always before when asked to do something I knew I shouldn't, I didn't seem to have the willpower or the strength to say no for fear I would offend my friend. This time it came so easy to say "No, thank you" because I didn't want to offend my Friend Jesus, and the Holy Spirit gave me the strength to say no.

When I returned to my hometown, at the next YFC meeting I stood before the people, and though I didn't find it easy to do, I confessed to them the double life I had been leading and that from now on I wanted the Holy Spirit to be in charge of my life to glorify Christ. Again a great burden was lifted, and I felt clean. I had nothing more to hide. I had been transparent before all the people gathered there. I spent time in the Lord's Word and in prayer, and continued my work as a clerk in the post office.

Soon after the meeting in Yakima, I looked up my friend Lloyd, and said, "Do you remember what we told the Lord while we were in jail? I'm finally keeping my promise. I have given my life to Jesus, and I want to serve him from now on."

Lloyd said, "I'm glad for you, but I'm just not ready to do that yet."

Many years later when Marie and I came back from Peru on furlough, I saw Lloyd's wife, Shirley. She told me that Lloyd had died of cancer. She said that before he died he told her, "Tell Gene that I asked Jesus to be my Savior." I look forward to seeing Lloyd in heaven.

While working in the post office in Centralia, I had the night shift for a while and would go right home after work to avoid any temptation to return to the life I had been leading. One evening as I was leaving the post office one of my junior college friends bumped into me and said, "Come on, Scotty, let's go up to the Legion Club for a while." I knew what we would find there, but in a moment of weakness I agreed and went with him. I remember feeling so uncomfortable sitting there with the fellows on all sides drinking and smoking. I didn't join in their drinking and smoking, but I did join them in playing cards to gamble. I felt so convicted and after a short time excused myself to leave.

They said, "Come on, Scotty, the night is young. Stay awhile longer." But I replied that I had to work the next day, so I needed to get home in order not to be sleepy on the job.

When I got home I picked up my Bible. I didn't know the Scriptures well. I opened it without looking for any particular verse. I opened right up to Hebrews 6 and read the chapter and was horror-stricken to read verses 4 through 6. I don't think I had ever read those verses before. "It is impossible for those who have once been enlightened, who have tasted the heavenly gift, who have shared in the Holy Spirit, who have tasted the goodness of the word of God and the powers of the coming age and who have fallen away, to be brought back to repentance. To their loss they are crucifying the Son of God all over again and subjecting him to public disgrace."

When I read that, my heart sunk because I thought those verses applied to me. Had I not stepped back from my commitment and gone back into sin? I remember praying something like, "O Lord, I don't want to go back into the world I once lived in, back to my former way of life, but it looks like you're through with me." I think I must have gotten down on my knees several times that night, pleading with the Lord.

The next morning I went to Victor Hovda, who was also a pastor. He had been a spiritual mentor to me. I told him that I had blown it. He asked what I had done. When I told him, he said, "Where do you think conviction comes from?" I said that I thought it came from the Holy Spirit.

He said, "Well, if conviction comes from the Holy Spirit, do you think he would bother convicting you if he was through with you?" I said I guessed not. "Then get down on your knees, confess your sin to the Lord, and you are forgiven. The slate will be clean. He not only forgives, he forgets."

I can't describe to you the peace and joy it brought to me to hear his welcome words, and then to sense that the sin was taken care of and I was again free in Christ.

One of the things I learned through this experience in 1948 is that, apart from our salvation, there is no such thing as a once-and-for-all experience that will take care of us for the rest of our lives, as wonderful as that experience may be. We must daily look to the Lord for victory over sin and the control of his Spirit over our lives. The apostle Paul said, "I die daily." I believe he meant that he died daily to sin. The Lord allowed me to fail that time in the Legion Club so that I would learn that the Christian life is a day-by-day, moment-by-moment experience of relying on him for victory. Yesterday's experience may be wonderful, but I realized I must come daily, hourly to him. "Thou wilt keep him in perfect peace, whose mind is *stayed* on thee" (Isa. 26:3a KJV, emphasis mine). This verse is the secret: constantly having the Lord in mind, having him control the thoughts, desires, and motives. I wish I could say that I have constantly done that, but it is my goal.

—6—

THE MERCY OF GOD

My wife, Marie, has said that someday she is going to write a book entitled *My Husband and His Nine Lives*. I doubt she will ever really do it, so I'll just share a few incidents that show the Lord was at work to keep this man alive in order to be able to do the Bible translation for the Sharanahuas.

When I was a child, our house was just a half block from the Milwaukee railroad. I must have been 8 or 9 years old when one of my friends, who lived close to the railroad tracks, couldn't resist the temptation to take a "railroad torpedo" off the track. In that era, the railroad used to clip torpedoes to the rails to give a signal to the engineer. The torpedo was about three inches square, bright red, and in big, bold, black letters was written DANGER. The torpedo was filled with powder and powerful enough when set off to be heard over the roar of the railroad engine.

My friends and I decided that we wanted to hear the big bang. So we built a bonfire and stood back and threw the railroad torpedo into it. When nothing happened we got a long pole and raked it out of the fire. Then we tore a little piece off of the corner so that the powder was exposed and threw it back into the fire. Still nothing happened. We raked it out again, and I said, "It can't be dangerous or it would have gone off. They just don't want kids like us taking it off the rail to hear the bang."

I put it on the curb, got a big rock and came down on it with all my might. We got to hear the big bang alright but it was more of a roar than we had anticipated. The rock was blown all to pieces, and some of it hit my friends and younger brother Bob, who were standing close by. The powder and rock came up into my face. I must have closed my eyes when I brought the rock down or I would have been blinded. My ears rang so loud that I couldn't hear anything else.

My mother and older brother had just stepped outside and said, "Oh my! It sounds like a bomb has been dropped on us."

I started to run down the street, even though I couldn't see where I was going, yelling, "My head's blown off!" A neighbor came out and picked me up. My face looked like I had smallpox. I think my ears rang for about two weeks after that.

Later a man that worked for the railroad told me, "Those railroad torpedoes are very powerful. You should have lost your arm, if not your life."

Ever since then I've had a healthy regard for any sign that says DANGER. I thank the Lord for sparing one foolish boy whose curiosity overcame good sense. Later, we never heard of any railroad accident resulting from my friend having removed the torpedo from the rail.

***

One crisp winter day, when I was about 12 a couple of my friends and I went down the railroad tracks to a small pond. Though the sun was shining brightly, it was bitterly cold. I had on my older brother's hip boots. We didn't think the pond was more than about knee-deep, and we wanted to walk across it.

My friends said, "You have on boots and we don't, so you go out and test the ice to see if it will hold us."

As I was walking across, we began to hear a "crack, crack." We were laughing, wondering how long it would be before the ice gave way. Suddenly, it did give way. We were still laughing until I continued going down, and the water was in above the hip boots and almost up to my neck. It was no longer a laughing matter. About one foot deeper and I would have been just about as frozen as the ice I had been walking on. The ice was too thick to break off to get back to the shore, but not thick enough for me to get myself back onto it and, besides, the hip boots were filled with water making any movement difficult. My two friends got a long pole and put it out to me dragging me across the ice to shore. Somehow I survived that near disaster also. (Could God have had a hand in it?)

***

One beautiful spring day when I was a senior in high school, the sponsor of the Hi-Y Club (High School YMCA) took some of us up to Mt. Rainier. Even though I lived only about 60 miles from Mt. Rainier, and on a sunny day I could see it clearly from my back yard, I had never set foot on the mountain. My folks never owned a car to make the trip. This trip with my high school friends and the sponsor was a dream come true for me.

When we came down from the mountain and the sponsor let me off at our home, my Mom met me with the news, "Four of our boys have been killed."

At first I thought she meant all four of my brothers, but I then I reasoned, *How could that be, when they are all so far apart geographically?*

Then Mom told me that seven of the high school boys had been coming back from a dance at 3 a.m. The driver went to sleep and went head-on into a fir tree at the side of the highway. I wasn't living for the Lord in those days and so easily could have been with them if I hadn't gone to Mt. Rainier. Four of them died immediately, and one more died the next day. Only the driver and one of my best friends, Waldo King, survived. Waldo was unconscious for about a month but finally returned to full health. What a sobering time this was in our high school. I had never attended a funeral before and now there were funerals for five of the young fellows. I thought about the life I was living but again put off giving my life over to Christ to be used of him.

***

After high school I entered the navy at the age of 17. World War II ended while I was in boot camp in San Diego, California. After a few months on a destroyer off the coast of California, I was sent to Seattle, Washington, just 90 miles from home. So much for the slogan, "Join the navy and see the world."

Hitchhiking home one weekend, I got dropped off at Fort Lewis. From there a soldier and I got a ride. We hadn't noticed anything out of the ordinary when the driver and his companion picked us up, but we hadn't gone far when we saw that they had both been drinking and the driver was all over the road.

We asked him to let us out, but he replied, "I wouldn't think of it. Nothing is too good for our servicemen." Then he handed back to us what little was left of the quart of whiskey and said, "Have a drink, boys."

The soldier whispered to me, "I escaped death serving overseas for three years. Now I'm going to get killed by a drunk driver."

Then the driver said, "I'm going much too slowly. I have to get you servicemen to your home quicker." He sped up, went off onto the shoulder of the highway, tried to correct, and turned the car over. As we were rolling over across Highway 99, which used to be the main highway between Seattle and Los Angeles, the soldier, probably reacting automatically from his army training, dove across my legs, partially pinning me to the seat as we rolled. Thankfully, there were no cars coming from the other direction. Miraculously, none of the four of us were hurt except that the passenger next to the driver had a pretty bad cut from going through the windshield. Almost unbelievably the car, though its top was smashed down, would still run.

The driver said, "Come on, boys. The car still runs. We'll get you there yet."

We replied, "Not on your life!" By this time we were only about 15 miles from my home in Centralia. I went to a nearby gas station and called my brother-in-law Curtis Ellis who came and picked us up.

The soldier and I were pretty shook up, and I offered him our home to stay in for the night before he continued his trip. He was very happy to take me up on the offer. He wasn't hurt, and all I had was a slightly skinned-up head. I'm sure it would have been worse if the soldier hadn't dove across my legs. Again our wonderful, compassionate God was looking out for me. He had plans for my life and wasn't through with me yet.

***

While Marie and I were in Peru in 2001, trying to finish the translation of the New Testament into the Sharanahua language, I needed to see a urologist in Lima. He did a biopsy and then sent me later to the pathologist to bring the results to him. Our son David being in Lima at that time took me to the pathologist.

When I received the written report from the pathologist, the envelope was not sealed. I said to David, "This is about me. I think

I'll look and see what it says." When I saw the word *carcinoma*, I said, "Oh, that doesn't sound so good."

David, who didn't know any more about cancer than I did but wanting to encourage his dad said, "I think that's the easy kind, Dad."

When the urologist looked at the report I could tell by the look on his face that it wasn't the easy kind. He said, "You have cancer. On a scale of one to ten you are ten and it's probably into your lymph nodes and bones." I felt like I had just been given a death sentence. The doctor added, "I've never known my pathologist to make a mistake."

I must admit that at that moment I didn't have that promised "peace that passes all understanding." It came later. Marie was out in the jungle at Yarinacocha. I called her and told her the news. It was prayer meeting night there, and all the folks went to the Lord in prayer for me.

The head of our clinic, Joy Congdon, said, "Scotty, you need to go to the States and have another opinion."

Marie and I flew to Dallas, arriving on a Sunday, and the very next day one of our nurses, Jean Lindholm, got me into the Methodist Hospital to one of the leading urologists in the States. It seemed like a miracle to get me in that quickly. He did a preliminary exam and told me that he pretty much agreed with the pathologist's report from Lima that I had a massive cancer.

I asked him if he could operate and he replied, "A man of your age, almost 70, we don't usually do that."

I responded, "Well, I'm still playing basketball." I thought that might help to hear that I wasn't too old.

The urologist smiled and put his big arm around my shoulders and answered, "I'm not giving up on you, but this is going to take a lot of prayer." Wow! Was that ever music to my ears! Not only was he a noted urologist, but he was also trusting in the Lord.

Blood work, a biopsy, CAT scan, and bone scan were done, and I was told to come back in a week for the results. As Marie and I waited in his office, the doctor finally arrived after having had to answer an emergency call. He said, "Forget all those ugly things I told you. You don't have any cancer." What a shocking but wonderful announcement!

All I could answer was, "Praise the Lord!"

To which the doctor replied, "Yes!"

That evening at our mission's center in Dallas, those who were there from Peru were having a prayer meeting. Don Burns was praying and said, "Lord, we don't know what you did in Scotty's body, but we believe you did a miracle and want to say, 'Thank you!'" Those were my sentiments exactly. Again, the Lord had spared my life, and Marie's declaration that I couldn't bow out until the translation for the Sharanahuas was completed became a reality.

In a Peruvian store, if you're given something extra for your money, it's called a *yapa*. After all these close calls, the Lord has given me a yapa: many more years to my life.

***

During our last years in Peru, the Peruvian government asked to assume ownership of our mission's *lakefront* property. Since Marie and I were among the fortunate ones to have a house on the lakefront, we had to move farther back on our center. So we were moving our things into our new home for our last few years in Peru. I decided I would take the 2 x 4-foot frosted sheet of glass that our son David had fixed for me to put over the desk to relieve the glare while I was working on the translation. It made it easier on the eyes. I decided to put it up in the loft of our new house until I made up my mind where it would best fit. There was no staircase up to the loft so I got a ladder. I had gotten the glass up there but decided to move it just a trifle. I was standing with one foot in the loft and one foot on the top rung of the ladder. I didn't realize that the floor had just been waxed, and when I leaned to straighten up the sheet of glass, the ladder slid out from under me. In a case like that with everything happening in split seconds you don't think, you just react. I grabbed the sheet of glass and somewhere in my rapid descent I let go of the glass, which shattered. A piece of the glass hit Aurora, our house helper standing there, and cut her hand, fortunately not too severely. I didn't land on the many shards of glass on the floor but on my back on a narrow stairway and right where I had had a spinal fusion done years before. I literally bounced across the floor and somehow ended up with my head almost under the dining room table.

I can still see the look of horror on Marie's face as she witnessed the whole thing. I couldn't speak at first. Marie called the only medical person on the center at the time, Nurse Carol Sagert. When Marie called, Carol got there almost immediately. She thought for sure that I would be paralyzed and began to stick me gently with a needle to see if I had any feelings in the legs. Then she asked me if I had any feelings. I replied, "Carol, I have lots of feelings. None of them good right now." Then some of the men came and strapped me down to a stretcher and drove me to the hospital some 6 miles away in Pucallpa. Dr. Muñoz took x-rays and found no broken bones. He said, "For a man 70 years old to fall that far and not break any bones, that was a miracle." As to Marie's statement "You can't bow out until the translation is all done," the Lord was making sure it was a reality. All praise to him!

Our granddaughter Giordana, after hearing of yet another close call, remarked, "Grampa, when you get to heaven, the angels are going to say (with a swift wipe across her brow), '*Whew!*'"

—7—

"WHERE DO YOU WANT ME, LORD?"

I was busy sorting mail in the post office in Centralia, Washington. While I had to concentrate on making sure the mail went to the right places, my mind was also on what I was going to do with the rest of my life. I was a young man of 20 and had recently given myself to the Lord unreservedly. I wanted nothing more to do with a life of dissipation. After a year in the US Navy, I knew something about discipline. Now I wanted some *Christian* discipline in my life. I voiced that to the Youth for Christ director in my hometown. He said, "If what you want is training in the Scriptures, learning Christian discipline with a heavy emphasis on missions, Prairie Bible Institute in Three Hills, Alberta, Canada, will give you all of that." I put that in the back of my mind and took it to the Lord in prayer. I felt the Lord had used the YFC director to steer me in the way I should go.

So as I continued to put the letters in the right pigeonholes, I determined to go into the assistant postmaster's office and tell him that I would be leaving my position as a clerk to go to a Bible institute to prepare for ministry for the Lord. He responded that I was throwing away a permanent appointment as a clerk in the post office, a position not many got at my young age. He said I just had a yearning to travel, that there wasn't much money in the ministry. He told me to fill out a leave of absence and get this out of my system and come back to the post office. In order to please him, I filled out the leave of absence, but I knew that I would never return. Having "put my hand to the plow," I was determined not to look back.

When I dedicated my life to the Lord, I was so glad that I would no longer be causing grief to my dear mother by my lifestyle. But she was disappointed when I said I felt the Lord was leading me to Prairie Bible Institute in Canada. She knew nothing about Prairie but had heard it was a radical school, which it wasn't, unless you call training men and women in the Scriptures and preparing them for service for Christ radical. My oldest brother, Sid, and my oldest sister, Beth, had both gone to the Bible Institute of Los Angeles, known as Biola, a fine institution that turned out many wonderful pastors, missionaries, and Christian workers. Though in many ways I would have liked to follow in my brother and sister's footsteps, I felt the Lord was calling me to go to Prairie, but I didn't want to disappoint my mother again. At that time I attended a Bible study and prayer meeting. They highlighted the verse in Matthew 10:37 "Anyone who loves their father or mother more than me is not worthy of me." That seemed to seal it for me that I should go where I felt the Lord was leading me. Still it pained me to think of hurting my mother again. God had a solution for that.

Mom said, "Gene, let's go talk this over with Mrs. Milem. She has a lot of wisdom and might have some good counsel for you." Mrs. Milem was an excellent Bible teacher and a graduate of Biola. I readily agreed to go with Mom to talk it over. She listened to what Mom said and to what I said about the way I felt the Lord was leading me.

With godly wisdom she said to Mom, "Frances, if Gene feels God wants him to go to Prairie, let's give him our blessing. He's still very young, and if after a year at Prairie he feels he wants to continue his training someplace else there is plenty of time for him to do that." Mom accepted Mrs. Milem's counsel, and I was able to go to Prairie knowing that Mom would not grieve over my decision.

After each year of study at Prairie Bible Institute, I worked in the summer with Victor Hovda, who besides being the Youth for Christ director was also a missionary with the American Sunday School Union in southwest Washington. The slogan of the ASSU was "Reach the otherwise unreached of rural America." This slogan fit so very well with the mission I was to go with later, Wycliffe Bible Translators. Wycliffe's goal was to translate the Bible for every people group in the world that didn't have God's Word in their own heart language. Another thing that helped to prepare me for work with Wycliffe was that the ASSU was a nondenominational organization, as is Wycliffe. I learned that all evangelical groups have the same main goal, leading people to Christ, and helping them to become grounded in the Scriptures. One should learn to work with any group that was sound in the fundamentals of the faith and not allow periphery issues to keep one from loving, fellowshipping, and cooperating with other denominations or groups. Vic Hovda was one who emphasized knowing God's Word. His young people camps produced several who went on to be missionaries on foreign fields. I learned so much from him. He had me teaching daily vacation Bible school and sometimes bringing messages, when needed, in one of the rural churches.

I'll never forget the first message I ever brought, even though no one else remembers. I was in a church in East Olympia teaching daily vacation Bible school there. That Sunday morning we were waiting for Vic to arrive to bring the morning message. It came time for the message, and Vic still wasn't there. The elderly Norwegian superintendent of the Sunday school stood up and said in his Norwegian brogue, "Vell, someting has happened so Brother Hovda couldn't make it, so Yene (Norwegian for Gene) is going to bring the message." That's the first that "Yene" knew he was going to preach. Between the pew and the pulpit I was saying, "Help, Lord!" I had nothing prepared. The Lord brought to mind Revelation 21, and I brought a message on heaven. I don't know how heavenly it sounded, but the Lord helped me to get through it.

After four wonderful years of immersing myself in the Scriptures at Prairie Bible Institute, and three summers working with the American Sunday School Union, mostly in young people's work, I was seeking the Lord for direction in my life, what he wanted me to do with this preparation. It was time to make another decision. Where and in what capacity did the Lord want me to serve him?

At the close of my senior year, several mission organizations were represented at Prairie. They set up their booths with literature about their mission, and a missionary attended each booth to answer questions and attract students to their particular mission. As I was walking past the Wycliffe Bible Translators booth, the young missionary-translator asked me, "Have you considered Wycliffe?"

Prairie Bible Institute at that time didn't offer Greek or Hebrew, so I responded, "Oh, I would never fit in that organization. I don't know Greek or Hebrew, so I would never make a translator."

The translator replied, "Who said you had to know Greek or Hebrew in order to be a translator? We have translation consultants who know Greek and Hebrew who will make sure your translation is accurate. Why don't you take our Summer Institute of Linguistics course to find out if you have an aptitude for linguistics and translation? Then even if you don't join Wycliffe, the course will help you in learning a foreign language."

That rang a bell with me. One of my classmates had told me, "I took the Summer Institute of Linguistics (SIL) course, and I liked what I was being taught as well as the Wycliffe people teaching it. If I was not already committed to going with another mission board, I would gladly go with Wycliffe Bible Translators."

I took these two suggestions to be the Lord's way of guiding me, and I applied and was accepted to go to the SIL course held at the University of Oklahoma, in Norman, Oklahoma.

—8—

TRAINING TO BE A TRANSLATOR

Leaving Prairie Bible Institute, I returned to Centralia to be with my parents and other relatives in my hometown. My brother-in-law Howard Collard was there with my sister Beth and family on furlough from their work as translators to the Mayo people in Mexico with Wycliffe Bible Translators. (Even though I knew they were serving with Wycliffe, I did not feel this affected my choice of missions.) Howard was going to the Summer Institute of Linguistics at the University of Oklahoma to take some special courses. I was going to the same place to take my first summer of linguistics. It worked out perfectly for me to travel with him to Oklahoma. We traveled in his Plymouth station wagon on this long trip from Washington. I hadn't known Howard well, but the trip gave us plenty of time to get to know one another. I found him to be one of the most Christ-like men I have ever known. What a blessing it was for me to have him for my roommate that summer.

Talk about shifting gears; I had to go from the prairie of Alberta, Canada, with its sub-zero weather, to the heat and humidity of Oklahoma. In those days many of the buildings at the university weren't air conditioned. A fan in the dormitories had to suffice. I remember more than once working on a paper and having it stick to my arm from sweat. I had never been in such thunderstorms as they had in Oklahoma. Once in a while we were given warnings of an approaching tornado. Fortunately, they never hit us.

Not only was the Oklahoma weather new to me, but linguistics was something I had never tackled before. The linguistic terminology left my head spinning: phonology, morphology, phonemics, phonetics, semantics, and syntax. What did I know of these? Nothing! But I was about to find out. We ate, slept, and lived linguistics. I never found the classes easy, but often they were fascinating.

At the close of the day the students would often pile into a car and go to OD's, a popular restaurant, to have a coke. One evening the guys came into my room and said, "Come on, Scott, time to close the books and take a break."

I said, "Sorry, guys, but I'm not ready yet for classes tomorrow, so I'll have to take a raincheck."

Someone said, "Come on! All work and no play…, you know."

Much to my delight my roommate Howard came to my rescue, "Leave him alone. He wants to be ready for tomorrow."

No one was going to dispute the seasoned missionary-translator. So I was off the hook. It wasn't that I was more studious than the others, but maybe it took me longer to be ready for classes than it did for some of them.

Being with people who were from many different schools and backgrounds showed me that Prairie Bible Institute didn't have a corner on turning out missionaries. I was deeply impressed with the godly lives of the staff of SIL. Besides those serving with Wycliffe, recruits from other missions were there to learn linguistics. I had a good time of fellowship with many of them.

I found the teachers of SIL very congenial and patient with those of us who had never studied linguistics before. Because of the heat and lack of air conditioning, it was sometimes hard to stay alert even though the teacher was good. One class that I thoroughly enjoyed was Field Problems. It came right after lunch, and sometimes the heat was almost unbearable. The teacher, Harold Key, kept our attention and also had a great sense of humor.

One especially hot afternoon Hal said to the class, "I want all of the single women to stand." After they all stood he said, "OK, now I have everyone awake. The single women are awake because they're standing. The single fellows are awake because they're looking to see who is eligible. The married women are awake because they're looking to make sure their husbands are not looking. I don't remember what he said would make the married guys be awake, but I'm sure it was something that had us all in stitches.

SIL wasn't all studies. Every afternoon after classes, we could participate in volleyball, tennis, swimming, and once in a while softball. Every Friday evening there was a get-together in the auditorium where we would be treated to music and sometimes a hilarious skit or other program. I was asked to join a brass quartet, which I thoroughly enjoyed. We comprised two trumpets, a trombone, and my baritone. We played for the group once in a while on Friday evenings and also were asked to play in churches, and once even on the radio in Dallas, Texas.

As the summer was winding down and we were coming close to the end of the linguistics course, the mission began interviewing those of us applying for membership in Wycliffe. I found the interviews polite and to the point. But one interview almost cost me acceptance. The interviewer, Otis Leal, Wycliffe's candidate secretary, was famous for using examples.

Otis gave me this example: "There was an island of 50,000 people, all starving, but a relief agency was set up to come to their aid. Then there was another island with only 5,000 people and they, too, were starving with no relief in sight. If you had a food supply to distribute, to which island would you go?"

After pondering the question for a few moments, I answered, "Well, I guess I'd go to the island of 50,000 people and start giving out the food as fast as I could until it was all gone."

Otis replied, "That's fine. A lot of people feel that way, but they're not Wycliffe people."

I was taken aback and said, "Otis, I've read Wycliffe's policies and thought I was in agreement. Would you mind running over that example again?"

This time I realized that I hadn't caught the point that there was a relief agency set up to come to the aid of the big island, while there was nothing on the horizon for the smaller island. Maybe I'd had a mental lapse when Otis gave the illustration. Anyway, with the illustration restated I came down on the side of the smaller island, not just because otherwise Otis would have disqualified me, but that was really the way I felt.

There were two or three other interviews, which I felt went well, and also, though we hadn't realized it, we were being observed by the staff all summer. They gave their observations to the board making the decision about who would be accepted as members. One other deciding factor was a Bible test. After four years in a Bible institute, I didn't find that test too difficult.

Finally, the big day arrived. In August 1952 I was accepted as a member of Wycliffe Bible Translators and the Summer Institute of Linguistics. Having prayed much that the Lord would lead as to whether or not I was to join Wycliffe, my heart was filled with praise and thanks, and I felt it a great privilege to be a member of this mission.

—9—

JUNGLE CAMP

I then returned again to my parents' home in Centralia and enjoyed being with all my family there, knowing that I would soon have to leave them again for a longer period of time. At the time, before being assigned to work in a foreign country, you were required to take a training course in Mexico in the southern state of Chiapas. This training was called "Jungle Camp." There were five of us going, four from Washington and one from Oregon. So, as 1952 was winding down, we all piled into Don Johnson's Pontiac for the long trip south. (Don was a shirttail relative of mine, my older brother Ezell having married his cousin Susie Kjesbu.) Don was from Mossyrock, Washington, as was Furne Rich. Her husband, Rol Rich, was from Beaverton, Oregon. Jeanne Grover was from Pateras, Washington, on the other side of the mountains in eastern Washington. I completed the five. I was the only one who was not a graduate of the Bible Institute of Los Angeles. They forgave me for being from Prairie Bible Institute. We had a wonderful time. I don't remember any bad vibes in the car all the way from Washington to Mexico.

Crossing the border from Texas into Mexico was much different from crossing the border into Canada on my trips

to Alberta. Canada didn't even require a passport or even register-
ing our names. Going into Mexico was a whole new ball game. A
passport was essential. Our car was inspected to make sure nothing
illegal was being taken into Mexico. We all had to register at the
border. This was my first introduction to hearing a predominant
language other than English. The Mexican officials understood
English, but they were pleased if we could speak Spanish, which
the five of us could not. After a cordial experience we were on our
way to southern Mexico. I remember seeing landscapes covered
with cactus. I said, "This would be a bad place to have to parachute
out." All along the way we found the Mexican people very friendly
and helpful if we needed to ask directions. Though the food was
new to us, it was delicious.

Arriving in Mexico City we were warmly welcomed by
Wycliffe colleagues. The headquarters lodged in a hotel named
after a famous Aztec Indian named Quetzalcoatl. They had short-
ened the name to Quetzal and then gave it a gringo flavor by
calling it The Kettle, perhaps because it was always "steaming" with
activity. We were treated to a trip to the famous Aztec pyramids in
Mexico City and to other historical and interesting places in this
metropolis.

After a week or so in Mexico City, the five of us once again
loaded into Don's Pontiac and were on the last lap to Jungle Camp.
On the way we stopped in the delightful city of Oaxaca. I soon
learned that despite the way it was spelled, it was pronounced
Wah-ha-ka. While there, we were treated to a band concert in the
plaza. I was all set to hear some good Mexican music when much
to my surprise the band struck up "On Wisconsin."

In going through the city of Tuxtla I remember having the
most delicious and perhaps the first filet mignon I had ever had.
The last stop before Jungle Camp was a small Mexican village,
Ixtapa. From there we were flown into the camp on the Jatate River

by a Missionary Aviation pilot, Jim Lomheim, a wonderful friend whom I had met at Prairie Bible Institute.

At last we were really into the jungle of southern Mexico. There were perhaps fifty of us trainees. Don and I joined Elmer Wolfenden and Bob Saxton in a hut for single fellows. It was made of thatch and mud, with no flooring. The staff at Jungle Camp, like the staff at SIL, were all congenial people. We learned how to live and survive in the jungle and had courses in carpentry, cooking, canoeing, medicine, and more, including butchering.

In the medicine course we were taught how to give injections. I didn't realize at the time how much I was going to need this training later in our work with the Sharanahuas. We practiced first by giving injections to an orange. Then we practiced on each other giving a placebo injection. We were taught that after you put the needle in, you were to aspirate a little to make sure there was no blood, for if there were blood in the syringe, you were to pull the needle out so as not to inject into the bloodstream. My partner for shot giving was Will Kindberg. When I aspirated, the needle accidentally came clear out, so I had to give another injection. Fortunately, Will didn't pay me back when it was his turn to give me the injection.

All this training was at what we called "main base." After several weeks at main base we were ready for the second phase of Jungle Camp: "advance base." To get to advance base we had to take a long hike through the jungle. As I remember it, the hike took more than one day, so we had to string our hammocks for an overnight on the trail. Those who wanted to could take turns riding on one of two mules or a horse. Most of us had not had experience in riding either. I never asked to take a turn, as both of my previous experiences with a horse as a child had bordered on disaster.

That evening on the trail, we were assigned a small group with whom to cook and share our food. The one in my group who was to cook the beans literally spilled the beans. We had nothing else allotted to us for food that evening. We had been taught that sometimes you have to improvise and use your imagination when nothing else is available. We were camped by a small stream and someone (not me) noticed that there were lots of little snails in the stream. So my group went snail gathering. It took quite a while to get the snails out of their shells, but after being boiled, they were quite tasty (I won't say what kind of taste) and, after all, they were better than nothing.

The next day we arrived at our destination, close to the Lacandon people. Phil and Mary Baer were the translators working among them. Our advance base camp was far enough away from the Lacandons so as not to bother them. All of us were to make our shelters called *champas*. I was assigned a champa with a couple of other single fellows and one of our staff. To build our champa we looked for trees that would make good, straight poles. I found one that looked very straight. I was feeling lucky at my good fortune at finding such a sturdy, straight, small tree and began to hack away with my machete to bring it down. When I chopped it clear through, much to my chagrin, the tree didn't fall, but the end buried itself right next to the stump of the tree. I hadn't realized that the top of the tree was tightly wound around by a lot of vines, not allowing the tree to fall. Later I was going by that same place and another fellow was chopping on the same tree not realizing that he was about to get the same surprise I got.

Each of us had to do a project while at advance base. I chose to identify trees by their leaves, and that included doing drawings (I'm the world's worst artist). Fortunately for me, we weren't graded on our project; we were just supposed to do it.

I thoroughly enjoyed both main base and advance base at Jungle Camp. Being single I didn't have the added responsibilities of those with a family. At advance base sometimes in the evening we would sit around a bonfire while someone gave his testimony.

Jungle Camp was a time of bonding, learning the life stories of some of our fellow "jungle campers," and to appreciate them. By the time we finished Jungle Camp there was a lot of love flowing among us. Also we learned to appreciate and love those on the staff who were dedicating their time to serve us.

I think we traveled a little faster on the way back to main base than we did going out to advance base, as we made it back in one day. A couple of fellows who were a bit more adventurous than the rest of us went at a little faster clip. As the rest of us stuck together with the staff, we heard a shout from a trail quite a ways above us. It was our two adventurous friends shouting, "Hey! You guys, you have the wrong trail!" They soon realized that they were the ones who had taken the wrong trail.

One of the things we all looked forward to when we arrived back at main base was the tradition of treating the incoming hikers to a delicious hamburger. After having had snails, we were going to savor those hamburgers. But I got heat exhaustion on the way back from advance base, the only time that it has ever happened to me. I had spent some time losing what I had eaten at lunch. Much to my chagrin I was not able to join the others feasting on the hamburgers. By the next day I was fine again.

After our Jungle Camp experience, four of us—Eugene Loos, Ken Jacobs, Elmer Wolfenden, and I—were assigned to stay on and start building a new dining room at main base. We took turns, with two of us going out to bring in poles while the other two stayed behind at the base, sawing up the poles and getting them ready to build. Ken and I took an old white horse named Jiatano (pronounced He-a-ta-no), got some poles hooked up behind her, and with the harness connected to her load in place, made our way slowly back to the base. One of the four guys, who was from the city, wondered what took us so long. But he didn't know Jiatano. So the next time, *all four* of us went out to get the poles. The one from the city was going to show us how to get Jiatano moving. After we got the poles in place, he said to Jiatano, "Giddyup!" Jiatano had other things in mind, namely a rest, and she laid right down in the harness. We guys were laughing so hard that we almost needed a rest too. Ken, who was raised on a farm, got Jiatano up and gave her a swat on the rear, and she slowly started her march back to camp. Never again did we hear anything about how long it took to get the poles.

Besides Jiatano, there was a mule called Negrita, who was blind in one eye. I was leading Negrita back to camp as she pulled a pole. We had dug holes in which to put the posts for the dining room. I forgot that she wouldn't see the hole if she was coming up the hill with her blind side approaching it. She stepped into a hole, and I was feeling very bad thinking that she might have broken her leg. When I told Eugene about it, he said, "I wish you had killed her because she just about killed me. I was behind her crouched down and she kicked. Fortunately, I had my hand up and her hoof caught my hand instead of my face." So there was no love lost between Eugene and Negrita.

At Jungle Camp I learned about the jungle in which I had never lived, how to live closely with fellow jungle campers in a day-to-day situation, how to live on less than I was accustomed to, how to appreciate the gifts that others had that I didn't have, and how to listen to and follow the instructions of the staff. For me Jungle Camp was an experience I cherished.

—10—

ORIENTATION AND ASSIGNMENT

Upon finishing our time at Jungle Camp, we had one more summer of linguistics study at the University of Oklahoma in Norman. This time Don Johnson and I roomed together. What a prince of a guy Don was. I never heard a cross word out of him, and it was absolutely a delight to be his roommate. Later Don was to become the director of the work in Ecuador.

One of our main teachers that summer was Elliot Canonge, who did the translation for the Comanche in the United States. His wife, Viola, wasn't there that summer, so Elliot, when he wasn't teaching, hung out with us single fellows. He was an excellent teacher and also had his own sense of humor. I remember him putting a test on the board, and as he was writing, he said, "Oh, this is a doozie! I hate myself when I do things like this." That gave us *so* much confidence, but we loved him anyway.

From Norman, Oklahoma, we traveled to Sulphur Springs, Arkansas, for orientation before traveling to the country where we felt the Lord wanted us to serve. We all enjoyed our time at Sulphur Springs, a beautiful, small community. It was the place where the first Summer Institute of Linguistics was held in an abandoned farm house in June 1934. The few students sat on nail kegs as they didn't have chairs yet.

A lot of changes had taken place by the time we arrived in Sulphur Springs. There were several nice, sturdy buildings plus a gymnasium. Again, orientation was a pleasurable experience as we listened to those who had blazed the trail for us who were soon to walk on it. Everyone who taught us brought treasures and insights from their own experiences. Hal Key, later to become director of the work in Bolivia, was our main teacher, and we had others who gave us one-time talks. Al Townsend (no relation to Cameron Townsend) told us about the beginning of the work in Peru. One speaker I especially remember to this day was Dick Pittman, associate director of Wycliffe Bible Translators. Besides stories on his vast experience, he brought us a devotional. He told us, "In your quiet time with the Lord each morning, you should latch on to at least one verse that you can use to encourage others, besides encouraging yourself."

Just 2 or 3 miles from Sulphur Springs lies Noel, Missouri. Some of us decided to go to Noel on a Sunday to take in one of the morning services. We chose to go to a Methodist church. It was a good choice, as the pastor, Rev. Pitchford, brought an excellent message. Afterwards a very friendly woman in the congregation, Mrs. Scott, no relative of mine, invited all of us to her home for Sunday dinner. And oh, could she cook—fried chicken, mashed potatoes and gravy, and delicious pie. Fortunately, I was thin in those days and could put away quite a bit without it showing. A real bond of fellowship developed out of that meeting, and we were often invited to come back.

After orientation, Wycliffe held their biennial conference there at Sulphur Springs. We single fellows were assigned the basement of one of the buildings. We affectionately called it "the dungeon." I hadn't realized it, but at Jungle Camp I had contracted malaria and now at Sulphur Springs it hit me full force—high fever, chills, and vomiting so hard I broke a blood vessel in my eye. I was "confined to the barracks," to use an old navy term. One of my favorite teachers at SIL was Howard Law, a PhD who was a translator in Mexico. Howard had been crippled by polio, but it didn't stop him from doing what he had to do. Howard heard about my sickness. I could hardly believe it when I saw him coming down the steep steps with a tray of food for me. That title of PhD didn't negatively affect Howard's loving, servant heart. One of the favorite verses of the founder of Wycliffe Bible Translators, William Cameron Townsend, affectionately known as "Uncle Cam," was Mark 10:45: "For even the Son of Man did not come to be served, but to serve, and to give his life as a ransom for many." I saw this verse lived out time and time again by Uncle Cam and many others in Wycliffe.

Those of us in orientation classes were allowed to stay for the biennial conference. Many of Wycliffe's leaders were there: Uncle Cam, Dr. Kenneth Pike, Dr. Bob Longacre, Dr. Ben Elson, and many others plus delegates. We could sit in on the sessions even though we didn't have a vote. I remember one session when the item on the agenda got rather emotional. Uncle Cam in his loving way stood up and said, "Beloved, I suggest we take a couple of hours away from the session right now and just seek the Lord and his guidance." Later, I was standing near some men, and I heard one of them say, "What is Uncle Cam thinking of? We have so much on the agenda, and he's asking us to take two hours off to pray." Being the new kid on the block, of course, I didn't say anything, but I thought, *I'm glad God put such a godly man, Uncle Cam, as the director of Wycliffe.*

Now it was time to accept an assignment to the field where the Lord wanted me to serve. I was asked to join the advance to Peru, South America. Even while I had been studying the Scriptures at Prairie Bible Institute, I had felt a tug in my heart for the people of South America and had often joined a group praying for that continent. I took it as the Lord's leading when the opportunity came to go to Peru. One of the verses the Lord used in my calling was Romans 15:20 where Paul said, "It has always been my ambition to preach the gospel where Christ was not known." I said, "Lord, if you could use me to take the gospel to a tribe that had never heard of Christ, I would consider it one of the highest privileges I could ever have." Thus the Lord prepared the way, and it was on to Peru for my life's service for Christ. And that was another decision that changed my life forever.

—11—

DAVID FARAH, ONE OF A KIND

I first met him in Sulphur Springs, Arkansas, in the basement of one of the buildings at the Wycliffe complex. He was wearing a loud sport coat and singing a popular song, and I wondered, *What kind of a fellow am I going to be sharing this basement with?* It didn't take long to discover that David Farah was a very congenial fellow with a refreshing sense of humor and a deep commitment to Christ. We were together during all that time of orientation for new members of Wycliffe. And by the time the session was over, we had formed a close friendship. David went to a different session of Jungle Camp than I did, but we met again for the following summer of linguistics study at the University of Oklahoma.

After talking and praying about it, David and I decided we would ask to be partners to go out as translators to one of the tribes in Peru. We met in Miami to fly together to Lima, the capital of Peru. It was then that David told me of meeting one sweet woman named Gloria Corsello and that they were engaged. That was the end of our short-lived partnership. On February 18, 1954, David and I embarked from Miami to fly to Lima. This, of course, was before the days of jets. As I remember, counting stops, one in Panama and the other in Guayaquil, Ecuador, it was a 12-hour flight on a DC-6. On the layover in Guayaquil, we were allowed to get off the plane. That was our first introduction to the hot, steamy weather of South America. Stifling to me, I was glad to get back into the plane and on our way to Lima.

Now at the age of 26 I remember the thrill of landing in the country that was to be home to me for I didn't know how long. I thought, *Here I am finally in the country to which the Lord has called me.* I had no idea that this was to be a journey in Peru of almost fifty years. Neither Dave (that's what his friends called him) nor I knew Spanish to any extent, and we certainly didn't know our way around Lima. We had expected one of our Wycliffe colleagues would meet us at the airport to take us to the Lima "group house." But we didn't see anyone that would be classified as a North American. So for an hour Dave and I cooled our heels waiting for someone to show up who could help us. I was glad that I wasn't alone. You don't panic when Dave is around. What a welcome sight Harold Goodall was. He had been given some misinformation and thought our flight was due an hour after we had landed. We couldn't have had a friendlier person to be the first to welcome us to Peru. Later Harold was to be elected the director of the Peru branch eight years in succession. That gives you an idea of how much Harold was esteemed by us all.

Harold hailed a taxi, and we were on our way to the group house. It was located in a residential district of Lima. The street it was on was named Llupaque Llupanqui, named for a Quechua chief. Dave and I were warmly welcomed by the several colleagues who were staying there at the time.

Mrs. Cudney had come to Lima a short time before we arrived to serve as the "house mother." A gracious hostess, she immediately made Dave and me feel right at home. The atmosphere at the group house was one of a loving, cordial family. We ate our meals together, and helpful advice was given to Dave and me from the first.

Don Burns served in Lima in public relations. He spoke Spanish so well that it was said that if he were in another room where no one could see his blond hair and North American appearance and could hear only his speech, a Peruvian would take him for a fellow Peruvian. Don took us down to the immigration office to get our visas and any other official papers we might need. It was obvious that he was well known there, and the Peruvians working in the immigration office responded to him in a cordial way. What a blessing it was to Dave and me to have Don with us to show us the ropes and make sure that we were officially inscribed into the country as linguists under the Ministry of Education.

Our first assignment in Lima was to take a Spanish course. All of us were beginners, and we had a very friendly, helpful young Peruvian woman as our teacher. As I remember, we had about only two months of intensified Spanish study, including lessons on Peruvian culture.

I was struck by the friendliness of the Peruvian people. The only time I heard any tone of disapproval was when I was coming back to the group house in a *collectivo*. A collectivo was like a taxi, but it always took the same route. The passengers knew which route it would take and wait by the curb and flag it down. The driver would keep on picking up passengers until his collectivo was full. There was one set rate. When you got to the corner where you wanted off you would say *"Esquina por favor"* ("At the corner, please."). And the collectivo driver would know to stop. Many of the taxis and collectivos had painted on the window *"Cierre despacio por favor"* ("Close it slowly, please."). I hadn't been in Lima long and didn't understand Spanish as well as I wanted to. I was alone and coming back to the group house in a collectivo. When we were nearing my corner I said in my best Spanish, "Esquina por favor" ("At the corner, please"). The chauffer obligingly stopped, and I got out, closing the door behind me.

The chauffer said, *"Mas fuerte por favor!"* ("Shut it harder, please!")

I supposed I had closed it hard enough, but thought, *If he wants me to shut it harder I will oblige him.* So I shut it harder. All the other passengers in the collectivo laughed uproariously except the driver.

He said, *"Que tal hombre!"* meaning, "What's the matter with you, man!"

I didn't know that when he said "Mas fuerte por favor," he was saying it ironically.

When I told a Peruvian professor friend about it, he laughed heartily and said, "That will teach the driver not to say anything he doesn't really mean to a North American."

While Dave and I were in Lima, we continued to learn about Peruvian culture. We were there during *Carnival.* Carnival is much like Mardi Gras in New Orleans. During that time pranks are played on innocent people, and everyone is expected to take it good-naturedly. The favorite trick is to throw water on the passerby. Usually it was a balloon filled with water. Dave and I needed to go to downtown Lima, and we were trying to escape the water treatment. We had almost arrived back at our group house and were congratulating each other in having escaped without getting wet. We were so close, and all we saw was an elderly woman out watering her lawn. She looked so innocent that we never dreamed what would happen next. Suddenly she turned the hose on us. We looked at one another, dripping wet. Then we both burst out laughing as the elderly woman looked at us with a mischievous smile.

After a few months in Lima, Dave and I were assigned to go out to Yarinacocha, the mission's center. Our destination was Pucallpa, a city in the jungle. The flight was in a twin engine DC-3. Flights were made only in the daytime and when the weather was clear. From Lima to Pucallpa the flight had to cross the Andes Mountains where one of the peaks towered at 22,000 feet. The DC-3 flew at only about 17,000 feet. It had to be a clear day so the pilot could see to go between the peaks. The cabins were not pressurized. Each passenger had an oxygen hose to use whenever needed. It was a 2-hour flight. We landed on a dirt airstrip in Pucallpa, which at that time was a city of about 10,000. Pucallpa had no paved roads. We were met by an old but very serviceable Burma Jeep. Besides the driver, Uncle Cam was there to meet us. Uncle Cam exuded friendliness and made us feel very welcome. The 6-mile trip from the airport to Yarinacocha was one dusty, bumpy ride.

What a welcome sight Yarinacocha was. Many of the homes and buildings at that time had thatched roofs made from the many palm trees surrounding the center. It was located beside a 9-mile lake named Yarinacocha. *Yarina* was the name of a certain class of palm tree in the area, and *cocha* was the word for "lake."

Dave and I were taken to the single men's dorm. It was owned by two men: George Insley and Phil Cheesman. George was one of the Jungle Aviation and Radio Service (JAARS; now known as JAARS, Inc.) pilots. He had flown on many missions over Germany in a B-24 during World War II. George had received many medals for his service, including the Distinguished Flying Cross. Phil Cheesman was the only Englishman there; he worked in the finance office. Phil had been an officer in the Royal Navy. To give a name to the men's dorm, George and Phil decided to combine their last names and call it Chinsley House. Dave and I joined the other four fellows in Chinsley House and were each assigned a bunk and a row of drawers. Dave was assigned to work in the finance office, while I was assigned to be the shipper. This entailed ordering supplies for those serving out in the tribes and seeing that those supplies were packed and taken down to the hangar to be loaded into the plane on the day of a flight. Each plane had a weight limit, so it was my job to weigh each box to be sure to not exceed it.

Dave and I both were enjoying our assignments at Yarinacocha. The fellowship with the translators and support personnel couldn't be beat.

Tribesmen or women traveled to Yarinacocha to take the bilingual school course, called the Teacher Training Course. These courses were taught by professors from Lima or Pucallpa with some of our colleagues assisting. One of the young professors from Lima was a single fellow, Elias Flores, so he stayed

Dave Farah and Scotty as new arrivals in Yarinacocha.

with us in Chinsley House. Dave and Elias had many a friendly chat. Dave shared the gospel with Elias, and though Dave's grasp of Spanish was limited, he led Elias to Christ.

After Dave and I had been a couple of years in Peru, that lovely woman that I had heard about arrived in Peru, and one very happy Dave Farah was there to meet her. Dave and Gloria had a beautiful wedding on the front lawn of Uncle Cam and his wife Elaine's home at Yarinacocha. I deeply regretted that I was unable to attend. Dave had asked me to be best man at his wedding, but I was away, having been assigned to be Bob Sandberg's temporary partner to the Maijuna people.

After Dave and Gloria were married, they were assigned to go to Bolivia to take part in a new advance. Though I missed Dave very much, I was happy for him and Gloria that they had the joy and privilege of helping to reach the tribes in Bolivia to give them the Word in their own languages.

Dave served in various capacities in Bolivia and was elected director for several years. As always, Dave made friends wherever he went. He had many friends among the people in the capital of

Bolivia, La Paz. One of his friends, a Colonel Banzer, had a difference of opinion with the party in power in Bolivia and was put in prison. Dave went to visit him and gave him a New Testament. After Colonel Banzer was released from prison, he became the president of Bolivia. When Dave went to congratulate him, he told Dave how much he appreciated that visit. He said, "You were the only one who visited me when I was in jail." The president asked that all the schools in Bolivia be given the Spanish version of the New Testament. Dave and Gloria are still two of our best friends, and we are blessed every time we have the joy of being with them.

—12—

YARINACOCHA:
UNCLE CAM'S VISION A REALITY

The Peruvian government invited the Summer Institute of Linguistics to send linguists to all of the more than forty minority language groups in the Peruvian jungle. Uncle Cam knew that in order to fulfill this task he would need a center of operations in the jungle, a place from which both floatplanes and wheel planes could operate. And he needed a plot of land big enough to allow for expansion, looking forward to the day when there would be translators working in every language.

A Brethren missionary in the area of Yarinacocha, Joe Hocking, was an American loved not only by fellow missionaries, but by all the Peruvians who knew him. In fact, the Peruvians of the area loved and trusted him so much that they voted him in as mayor of Pucallpa, the nearby city. Joe met and admired Uncle Cam. It was inevitable that a friendship would blossom between these two pioneers, both with a passion to see the otherwise unreached have the gospel of Jesus Christ in their own language. Knowing of Uncle Cam's vision to see a center in the jungle that would serve missionary-linguists and be used to reach the tribes, Joe said, "Cam, I know just the place for you. Come and let me introduce you to Yarinacocha." When Uncle Cam saw the beautiful lake, he immediately knew that this was the place God had chosen.

From a small beginning, Yarinacocha became a center for housing the linguists and support personnel, which included pilots, aviation mchanics, teachers, doctors, nurses, printers, radio technicians, radio operators, administrators, literacy experts, buyers, government relations personnel, farmanagers, mechanics (to keep the generator and vehicles operating), community development personnel, house parents (to care for translators' children during school sessions while their parents were out in villages at work), a commissary manager, financial managers, plus other necessary personnel God used to accomplish the task of providing the Scriptures for every tribe in its own language.

Yarinacocha in its peak years, around 1970.

How fortunate we were to have Uncle Cam and his lovely wife, Elaine, with us in Peru for nine years. Uncle Cam exuded friendship. He had a way of making everyone feel they were important to him. He always gave his full attention to anyone with whom he was conversing. His laugh and his whole demeanor was infectious. Peruvians loved him. He was a friend to presidents and government officials, but also to tribespeople who some might think of as not very important. To Uncle Cam everyone was important.

Marie and I were amazed when on the Peruvian Independence Day Uncle Cam and Elaine invited us to join them for a picnic at a favorite spot a few miles from Lima. On such an important day one might expect they would invite someone who was more noted in our group, but Uncle Cam wanted new arrivals to immediately feel accepted. It was a thrill to Marie and me to have this time alone with Uncle Cam and Elaine.

Uncle Cam tried to take part as much as possible in all the activities on our center. At 5 p.m. when the sun was going down and the heat of the jungle was abating, you would find him joining the rest of us for a game of volleyball. What a serve he had!

He and Elaine often invited government officials to their home at Yarinacocha. After enjoying one of Elaine's delicious meals and fellowship around the table, Uncle Cam would invariably ask the Peruvian friend to read a portion of Scripture from a Spanish Bible.

Uncle Cam was so admired by Peruvian government officials that Peru's President Fernando Belaunde Terry gave the highest Peruvian award for foreigners, the Order of the Sun (*El Orden del Sol*), to Cameron Townsend in honor of his and the Summer Institute of Linguistics' service on behalf of Peru's minority language groups.

Shortly after receiving this honor, at one of our Sunday evening meetings, Uncle Cam showed us this medal and said that it was awarded to him, but it was because of the work of all of us in Peru. Then he said, and I'll never forget it, "Beloved, what are we going to do with medals like this someday? We're going to cast them at the feet of Jesus where they belong."

I don't expect to find a more loving and godly man than Uncle Cam. What a privilege to have known him and to try to follow his example.

Yarinacocha became a small, self-sustaining community. We had our own commissary. We were a nonsectarian organization. Workers came from almost every evangelical denomination. Uncle Cam didn't want us as foreigners to take the place of responsibility in Peruvian churches but leave that to the national Christians. Also he wanted us to be focused on our task and goal of Scripture translation. He didn't want us to be sidetracked by getting involved in the work of any church but to leave that important work up to our brothers and sisters from other missions. These missions included the South America Mission, the Christian and Missionary Alliance, the Brethren, the Mennonites, the Swiss Indian Mission, and other wonderful, Christ-centered evangelical missions. We enjoyed good relations with those missions, and they often attended our Sunday services at Yarinacocha and the Sunday evening services in Lima.

We didn't have a pastor as such at Yarinacocha, but we took turns bringing a message from the Scriptures that the Lord had laid on our hearts. Often Uncle Cam himself would bring the morning message. His exhortations were always fresh and encouraging. I can still hear him saying, "Beloved, God has called us to love everyone. We must tell the truth, but even that must be done in love. Why, God has called us to even love our enemies."

In the evening the service was more informal; we often heard reports of what God was doing in a particular tribe. There was time for personal testimonies and prayer requests and prayer. Uncle Cam made prayer a high priority. When I initially became part of the Yarinacocha community, we met twice a week at 6:30 a.m. for prayer. It was not compulsory, but it was well attended. There were Sunday school classes for our children as well as for adults. Once a week we got together in small groups for prayer in the evening, and once a month there was a day of prayer.

Every year a Peru branch conference was held. At that time we started off the sessions with the first morning dedicated to praising the Lord for who he is and what he had done for us. Then after prayer, we elected our director and our executive committee for the year. After that we discussed items on the agenda. Motions were made and items voted on to become part of our policy. During the day and then again at night we would hear reports from the language groups. Of course, one of the thrills of conference time was singing praise to our Lord. We didn't lack for musical talent as there were several gifted pianists. Other musical instruments were played to the glory of God and to the delight of the listeners. Not a few could sing solos that blessed us all. After conference sessions about five o'clock in the afternoon we could play volleyball, basketball, or tennis.

At the first conference I attended in 1954, we didn't have a conference speaker from outside our organization. We brought daily devotionals ourselves. When I got a note asking me to bring one of the devotionals, as did other new members, I have to admit that it scared me. I thought, *There's Uncle Cam, Ken Watters, Harold Goodall, and other leaders whose walk with the Lord I admire, and then there's me.* But the Lord reminded me that when I asked him for a message, I had the same access to his Holy Spirit as these men of God did. After that year, we had outstanding Christian leaders come to be our speaker at each annual conference. They usually spoke once in the morning and once in the evening. It was a time of encouragement, sometimes of correction, a time of binding us together in love, a time of spiritual refreshment.

At one of our conferences, the first meeting started off in an unusual manner. As we were singing a hymn, I was standing next to the screened wall, and I saw a small snake heading toward me. I didn't know if it was poisonous or not, but I didn't have time to ask him. I had nothing else with which to attack him but the hymnal. So I threw it with all my might onto the floor. That got the attention of everyone around me. I missed the snake, who continued on his way. As others saw him coming, John Bush, one of our airplane mechanics, who looked like he might make a good football linebacker, seeing the problem, picked up the end of the bench and used it to pulverize the snake. End of problem; end of snake; back to singing our hymn. When the speaker got up to speak he said, "My, you people do have a different way of starting your services."

At the height of our work at Yarinacocha we numbered some three hundred people. That was counting translators, support personnel, and children. We were one big happy family. Our children called the adults "uncle" and "aunt." To this day when I meet some of the people who grew up in Yarinacocha, now grown and with their own families, they still call me "Uncle Scotty," and I like it. One speaker said of Yarinacocha, "I've seen more love per square inch here than I've ever seen before." No, we weren't perfect by a long shot, but people knew how to ask for forgiveness, and many times there were tears and reconciliation.

To this day every July 28, the Peruvian Independence Day, children who grew up at Yarinacocha gather together, if they can, in Dallas, Texas, at the Wycliffe campus and celebrate. A Peruvian flag is displayed. They sing the Peruvian national anthem, eat

Our home for nearly fifty years had a lakefront view.

Peruvian dishes, and drink *chicha morada* or Inca Kola. Reminiscences fly thick and fast. It's a time to reconnect and enjoy being together again. The parents of these former children also often participate in the festivities.

Once a year there was a *clausura* (graduation exercises) for the Teacher Training Course. Teacher candidates were chosen for their aptitude to learn. If they didn't know Spanish yet, the linguist would help them through the courses. Professors would come from Lima, Pucallpa, and other places in Peru to teach the native people in Spanish. Then the newly taught indigenous people would go back to their community to teach in their own native language what they had learned. At the graduation exercise, dignitaries from Lima, some of them government officials, came to observe for the first time the education of tribal people. On at least one occasion, Peru's minister of education attended. It was a thrill to the graduates to be presented their diplomas by such a high official. The graduation exercises were always on Saturday, and many guests from Lima stayed overnight. Uncle Cam invited them to come to our Sunday evening service in our auditorium, and most of them did.

The Peruvian press always came, too. Marie and I met one of them and invited him to our house. In the course of the conversation he said, "There's something different about this place. I feel a peace here like I've never felt in any other place." I don't remember what we said to him at that point, but we knew that the peace he sensed was the peace of God that permeated Yarinacocha. That reporter then went from our house to our neighbor's next door, Ted and Lillice Long. Ted never lost an opportunity to witness for Christ. He led many a Peruvian into a relationship with Christ as Savior. That's what happened with this reporter. After a time of friendly conversation, Ted, who had grown up in a Latin American country, led the reporter to Christ as the reporter, in prayer, asked Jesus into his heart to be his Savior.

Those in the Peruvian press who interviewed Uncle Cam found him to be the congenial person we all knew him to be. Uncle Cam exhorted all of us to make any Peruvian who came to Yarinacocha to feel welcome. He would say, "Beloved, be gracious to anyone who comes here. Let all feel welcome. We have nothing to hide, so show them around the center if they want to know more about us." That was Uncle Cam, a friend to everyone.

—13—

THREE MONTHS WITH
THE AMAHUACAS

I had looked forward to this day in 1955 with keen anticipation. I was actually going to be flying out to serve in a tribe in the Amazon jungle of Peru. The sky was clear except for an occasional white, fluffy cloud. In the air one could see for miles. I remember that in the navy on board the destroyer, in any direction I looked, all I could see was the ocean. Here, flying over the jungle, instead of the blue of the ocean, you could see nothing but one big green blanket of countless trees. The pattern of green was broken on occasion by a stream or river or by a tree that had blossomed yellow.

JAARS' first pilot, Larry Montgomery, was at the controls of the Piper Super Cub. As I sat next to him, I heard him singing at the top of his voice, "Fear thou not for I am with thee. I will still thy pilot be." Then he said, "Scotty, I bet you think I'm just up here flying along without a thing to think about. Actually, as I fly I'm constantly thinking 'If we should have engine failure, can I see a place up ahead where I could put it down, or that place we just passed, could I glide back to it?'" I was glad we didn't have to find out where to make an emergency landing. JAARS airplane mechanics made sure of that.

About two and a half hours after leaving Yarinacocha, an airstrip cut out of the jungle loomed ahead of us. Called Varadero, it lay between the headwaters of the Inuya and Curiuja Rivers. Larry skillfully lined up the Super Cub to touch down on the 250-meter strip. From the air it looked awfully small to me. But Larry put the plane onto it smoothly. I was glad not only that the Lord was watching over us, but for Larry's professionalism as a pilot. He had spent years as an army pilot. I got out of the plane to be greeted by the translator for the Amahuaca people, Bob Russell. He had already had six months living among these people and had begun to learn the language.

This place was like Paradise to me. There were no gnats, and all was quiet except for the occasional call of a macaw, other birds, or howler monkeys. When we said goodbye to Larry, and the Super Cub droned off, leaving us alone, we would not see another English-speaking person until the plane returned.

When I arrived among the Amahuacas, I knew it was a temporary assignment that would end when Bob married Delores in about four months. The location at the headwaters of the two rivers was extremely isolated—no way to get there except to land on the very small airstrip or to take a dangerous walk up the Inuya River.

As long as my assignment kept me there, I wanted to be an asset and help to Bob. Bob's time spent with the Amahuacas had given him a proficiency in jungle living that I had not yet attained. Sometimes his skills at getting things done so speedily and my lack of it grated on my nerves. I found myself envying his quick and efficient ways of doing things and resenting the suggestions he would give me to help me where I lacked.

Since the Amahuacas weren't coming to us as anticipated, Bob left with one of the four soldiers who were stationed not far from us to go to the Amahuaca community. I was left all alone to answer the radio when it was our time to check in. No one was there within hearing distance. I talked out loud to the Lord and said, "Lord, my first assignment, and I can't get along with my first partner. Forgive me, Lord. Take away the resentment and replace it with Calvary love, a love that doesn't keep score of supposed slights or hurts, a love that is not so easily offended."

Our thatched-roof house was built without a floor. With Bob being gone, I went into the house to find something to fix for lunch. As I was on my knees on the dirt floor looking at what we had for food, I got a feeling I was being observed. I looked cautiously behind me, and there stood three young, husky Amahuaca men staring at me, leaning on their tall bows. They were completely naked except for a monkey tooth belt. I confess that my hair stood on end, seeing them standing there silently. I had not heard a sound as they entered the house. I managed to give an Amahuaca greeting, which Bob had taught me. Much to my relief all three responded with grins and an answer to my greeting.

When Bob got back, I said, "Bob, I want to ask your forgiveness for a bad attitude I've been having toward you."

He replied, "Scotty, the Lord has been talking to me also, and I ask your forgiveness for not being more sensitive," or words to that effect. We had prayer together; the atmosphere was changed. God answered prayer, and love flowed between us.

Bob said, "When there are only two people together for a long time in an isolated place, the lines of communication have to be kept open. You have to be able to pray together. I was with one partner who just clammed up and wouldn't say anything. We didn't have prayer together over our needs. And that is excruciatingly painful." I was so glad that it wasn't like that anymore between Bob and me.

It was then my turn to go to the Amahuaca village. I was 26 at the time and in very good health. One of the Peruvian soldiers in the small post close to Bob's house went with me. The trail was not very well marked, and a lot of it went up and down hills. Sometimes I had to get down on all fours to pass under a tree fallen across the trail. We crossed small streams along the way and were able to get a refreshing drink. It was an all-day hike.

The Amahuaca houses were built up on top of a ridge. That way, they could see any enemies who might come to kill them. Their dogs would always give a warning if someone was approaching. The ridge was so high that parrots would fly by almost horizontal to the houses.

After a couple of nights with the Amahuacas, it was time to return home. Some of the Amahuacas went with us, taking with them food for their time at Varadero. I saw one elderly Amahuaca woman taking a huge basket of corn. She carried it on her back, with a wide vine across her forehead attached to the basket to hold it in place. Seeing her, I was ashamed to go without carrying something. I knew that I wasn't able to take as big a basket as she was carrying, but I got it across to them to let me take a smaller one. They obliged, fixing it up for me with the vine across my forehead just like they were carrying theirs. Again it was up and down hills, crawling under fallen trees, and wading through streams, and I was having a hard time keeping up. At one point the sole came off of my tennis shoe, and I had to tie it on with the shoestring.

Late that afternoon I staggered into our location, one exhausted young man, perhaps as worn out as I had ever been. Bob took one look at me and exclaimed, "What in the world were you thinking, carrying that basket of corn on your back on such a hike as that?"

I said, "Well, look at the load that elderly Amahuaca woman was carrying. Shouldn't I have at least carried some?"

Bob replied, "That elderly Amahuaca woman has been carrying things on her back since she was a little girl. Her body is used to it, yours isn't. I never take any more than a blanket and an extra pair of clothes on a hike like that." Welcome to the jungle and living with the Amahuacas. I was learning what I could and could not do.

Bob Russell was one of the most dedicated, efficient, and capable missionary-translators that has ever been my pleasure to know and work with. I couldn't have been more pleased when he asked me to be best man at his wedding in Lima.

—14—

A MONTH WITH THE MAIJUNAS

Translator Bob Sandberg needed a partner for a river trip he was planning in the area where the Maijuna[1] people lived. Being single it was easy for me to move from one assignment to another. When the director, Harold Goodall, asked me to go, I was glad to accompany Bob. Since it was going to be a month of nearly constant travel on the rivers, it would be easier for me to make the trip than it would have been for his wife, Ruth.

Bob and Ruth had a home among the Maijunas on the Sucasari River. The Sucasari is a small tributary near the confluence of the Amazon and Napo Rivers. It's about five hours by outboard motor downstream on the Amazon River from the city of Iquitos. Iquitos is the capital of the state of Loreto, and the largest city in the jungle.

One of our pilots took us from Yarinacocha to Iquitos where Bob had a canoe waiting to be readied for our trip to the Sucasari. He had to tar the bottom of the canoe to make it "seaworthy." All of this was new territory for me. I had never been to Iquitos. After being with Bob Russell at the headwaters of the small

---

1 For those who worked in Yarinacocha when we were there, this people group were known as Orejon. However, in recent years the people rejected that name, which was disparaging, and chose to be known as Maijuna (People).

Inuya and Curiuja Rivers, even the great Urubamba (a tributary of the Amazon) seemed small compared to the mighty Amazon at Iquitos.

Our canoe was powered by an outboard motor, a 2 horsepower Penta. I thought, *This is faster and easier than paddling or poling the canoe, but just barely.* When we arrived at the mouth of the Sucasari, I was amazed at how narrow a river it was. It was starting to get dark at one point in our trip, and on occasion Bob was having a hard time seeing the bends in the river. One time we didn't navigate the bend quick enough, and the bow struck the trunk of a tree at the river's edge. It jarred the tree enough that fire ants cascaded down on top of us. If it hadn't been that the river was also inhabited by alligators, I think we would have jumped in to get the ants off.

On the way we came across some Maijuna men. One, who was the chief, offered me a drink from the gourd he had in his hand. We had been taught in orientation to not turn down something offered unless there was a good reason; otherwise, we ran the risk of offending those we had come to serve. I could see no good reason for turning down the offer of a drink and did not want to offend the chief. After Bob had some friendly conversation with the Maijunas, we continued our river trip. Bob said to me, "Well, you just made a good impression on the chief. Do you know what the drink consisted of that he offered you?" I admitted that I didn't, but that it tasted good. Bob said that it was a masticated drink: fruit chewed up and spit into a gourd and served. I was glad that he waited until after I had drunk it to tell me.

In Peru at that time, a *patron* was someone who had indigenous people working under him. Often these workers were exploited and treated almost as slaves. There were exceptions, of course. A certain *patrona* lived right across the river from Bob and Ruth's home among the Maijunas. She treated the Maijunas under her as her personal property. Bob had been told that she was holding a young Maijuna woman as her personal slave, and against her will.

When Bob and I had arrived in Iquitos, the patrona also happened to be there with this Maijuna woman. Bob, wanting to see the Maijuna woman freed to return to her family, went to the Iquitos police department to inform them that the woman was being held against her will. The police captain called in the patrona and told her to bring the Maijuna woman with her. He also invited Bob to come, and I accompanied Bob. The captain asked the patrona what her relationship with the Maijuna woman was. She answered that she was her property and she was to do what she was asked to do. The captain interrupted her when she said that the young woman belonged to her, saying, "Señora, your property? Here in Peru we don't own people. Slavery is not allowed." Then he asked the Maijuna woman if she wanted to stay with the patrona or return to her own people. She replied that she wanted to return to her own people. So the captain told the patrona that she could no longer keep the woman and asked Bob if he would take her back to her people, which Bob readily agreed to do.

When we got back to Bob and Ruth's house on the Sucasari River, the young woman returned happily to her people, but Bob had not endeared himself to the patrona. One evening after dark we heard the sound of an outboard motor. It sounded as if it were leaving the patrona's house across the river. Bob thought it was probably her taking another Maijuna away with her on another trip.

He said, "Let's go out and intercept the boat to make sure the patrona is not taking another Maijuna away against his or her will." So off we went with a motor with more horsepower than the 2 horsepower Penta. Bob was steering the canoe while I held a powerful flashlight at the bow as we skimmed over the water in hot pursuit. Then I remembered that Bob had told me that a Peruvian man who worked for the patrona had told him that if he interfered anymore in the affairs of the patrona, he would kill him. Suddenly, I didn't feel so safe holding that powerful flashlight. I felt like a sitting duck, a perfect target for anyone who wanted to shoot.

I went back to Bob and said, "Would you like to trade positions? You hold the flashlight, and I'll steer the canoe." I was only kidding, of course. (Well, halfway kidding.) It turned out that the canoe was not the patrona's. Bob had a friendly conversation with the owner of the canoe, and we returned home.

On one of our trips up the Napo River we spotted a large boa constrictor wrapped around an alligator that was about 6 feet long. The boa seemed to be at least 20 feet long. There was no doubt which was going to win the battle. That alligator would soon make a good meal for the boa. After crushing it, the boa would swallow it whole and then lay contented on the shore until it was digested. Knowing that the boa wasn't going to let go of that alligator and couldn't hurriedly unwrap himself from it, I decided to get close and take a picture. Just as I was set to take the picture, the alligator gave one last effort to free itself and let out a loud "Oomph!" It so startled me that I almost fell backward into the river. The old Bolsey camera didn't have a light meter on it and, unfortunately, I didn't choose the right setting. Looking closely, you can make out the boa and alligator, but I would have never shown the picture at a slide presentation at church!

Sometime after that, we stopped on the bank of the river. Bob and I had just gotten back into the canoe. He stepped too heavily on the side of it, which threw us both into the river. It was unexpected, and I was holding the Bolsey camera that Mrs. Cudney had loaned me to take pictures on our trip. When that camera went flying and sunk into the river, I felt terrible that I had perhaps lost it. The river was muddy, and you couldn't see underneath the surface. Bob and I stripped down to our shorts and dove in to find it.

After quite a number of dives without success, I said, "Bob, the Lord knows where that camera is."

"That's right, Scotty. You dive and I'll pray."

This time when I dove I felt the strap floating above the camera and was able to bring the camera up with great rejoicing. Thanks to the Lord, the lost was found. We opened the camera to dry it out in the tropical sun, and amazingly it worked again. All praise to the Lord!

We spent almost as much time, if not more, on the river than we did at Bob's house. I jokingly told him that when we got back to Yarinacocha I was going to put in for sea pay. We would often stop on the bank of the river, make a small fire and cook up some soup to go with a roll. And our evening meal was about the same. I think I lost over 10 pounds during the time I was with the Maijunas.

Bob was a congenial person, and I enjoyed his great companionship and learned a lot from him. He even gave me some marital advice should I ever get married. After the month with Bob, it was back to Yarinacocha and my assignment there.

—15—

INITIAL CONTACT WITH
THE KASHINAWAS

After ending my assignment with Bob Sandberg and the Maijuna people, Harold Goodall called another single fellow, Ken Kensinger, and me into his office. "We have reliable reports of an unreached people group on the Curanja River, which flows into the Purus River. We would like for you fellows to go there to make an initial contact with the Kashinawas. Would you be willing to go?" Both Ken and I said we would.

Sharanahua thatched homes dot the riverbank.

The Aeronca floatplane took Ken and me out to the Purus River at the mouth of the Curanja where there was a Sharanahua community, a 4-hour flight.

The translator to the Sharanahuas, Cecil Hawkins, introduced us to the chief of the Sharanahuas and explained to him that we would like to have someone take us upstream on the Curanja River to the Kashinawa village. The chief, Alfonso, said that he and some other Sharanahuas would take us.

We waited for a few days while the Sharanahuas decided who was going to go and got together enough food for the trip. While we waited, Ken and I dispensed medicine for the Sharanahuas as it was needed. They brought one man to us that had a huge boil on the side of his abdomen.

We got on the radio and described the boil to Dr. Altig, the doctor back at Yarinacocha. He said, "You're going to have to lance that to get the poison out. You probably don't have anything else to lance it with, so boil up a razor blade. Do it with deliberation, not slowly."

We did as the doctor told us. When it came time to lance it, Ken said, "Scotty, you have to do this. I don't think I can." I would gladly have turned the assignment over to him, but since he said I had to do it I decided I would.

Remembering that the doctor said to do it with deliberation, I plunged the razor blade into the middle of the boil. We had a turtle shell there to catch the pus that would come out. We knew the boil was swollen badly, but we didn't know that much pus could come out.

Ken said to me, "Scotty, you're looking really pasty."

I replied, "Ken, you don't exactly look like a rosebud yourself." Mission was accomplished, and the Sharanahua man healed nicely.

When it was time to start the trip, three or four canoes loaded with Sharanahuas, Ken, me, and our supplies began the trip up the

Curanja. At that time, on the Purus and Curanja Rivers, there were no motors, so it was five days of paddling and poling to get us to Conta, the Kashinawa community. When you think of the jungle, you have visions of a hot, steamy part of the world, which, most of the time, it is. But we made our trip upstream during the dry season in July. At that time of the year, a cold wind sometimes blows over the Argentine pampas, across Bolivia, and over the Peruvian jungle. The temperatures have been known to get down even into the forties, which in the jungle, when accompanied by a wind, make it extremely cold. This cold snap is called a *frio* or *sur* (because the cold wind comes out of the *south*). It hit as we began our trip. Ken and I put on two pair of pants, a couple of shirts, and jackets, and still we were cold. The Sharanahuas seemed to be enjoying the trip even if it was cold.

On the way upstream one man stood in the bow of the canoe with a sharp eye out for big fish. They could tell when one was just below the surface of the water, and they stood poised to harpoon it. Also, Ken and I might never see it, but the Sharanahuas, through years of practice, could always spot a game bird or monkey in the trees as we made our way upstream. Then they would pull the canoe over to the edge of the river while one of them would scramble into the jungle to shoot the game. The men still had bows and arrows, but they also had 16 gauge shotguns that they now used more often than the bow and arrow if they had the shells. At other times they would spot a wild boar or a tapir and that brought meat for everyone.

At one point one of the Sharanahuas was shooting at a monkey high up in a tree. I hadn't seen the man shoot the arrow. Then they began to shout at me. Not knowing the language, I had no idea what they were yelling about until an arrow landed a few yards from me. They had been warning me to get away as the arrow shot straight up at the monkey and had missed and was bound to come down close.

The first night, when we pulled off onto a sandbar, the Sharanahuas quickly made temporary shelters of bamboo poles, tying palm leaves on with vines. Then they hung their hammocks and mosquito nets. Ken and I put down our sleeping bags on the sand and crawled under our mosquito nets. Before we bedded down for the night, I got out my baritone horn that I had brought along and was going to entertain with a little music. A Sharanahua man, Conshico, said, "Don't play it now." Then I realized that it hadn't been too long ago that they had to be careful of an enemy group coming to attack, and to hear my horn from far away in the jungle could let the enemy know where we were. Later when we arrived at the Kashinawas, Conshico asked me to play my horn. I think he wanted to make sure I wasn't offended by his asking me not to play before.

A couple of days before we arrived at the Kashinawa community, one of the traders, who would go up and down the rivers selling to and exploiting people, passed us in his canoe. He went ahead of us to tell the Kashinawas that we were dangerous and to not trust us. The Kashinawas later told us what he had to say about us. These traders wanted to keep the tribespeople in ignorance, so that they could continue to cheat and exploit them, and they knew that we had come not only to give them God's Word, but to teach them to read and write and to count and add. The Sharanahuas, who had already had a translator family living with them, told the Kashinawas not to believe the lie of the trader concerning us, that we would not harm them but help them. The Lord prevented us from starting our time with the Kashinawas under a cloud of suspicion.

Soon the Sharanahuas left to return to their community, and Ken and I were left alone with the Kashinawas. They were a very friendly people and generous, sharing their food with us. It was watermelon season, and they brought us more watermelons than we could possibly eat. After we had eaten part of a watermelon, Ken and I felt we couldn't eat another bite. So when it was dark with no one around, we threw it as far as we could out into the jungle. A few minutes later one of the Kashinawas called us with the watermelon in hand and said, much to our embarrassment, "You dropped this." We quickly learned nothing goes unnoticed by the Kashinawas.

Soon they were busy making us a house. It was bigger than we needed, but they seemed to enjoy working on it. It was a community project. They brought in corner posts of an ironwood. They were so hard it was almost impossible to drive a nail into them. We were amazed at the strength of the Kashinawas as they carried these heavy posts. They would fold up a shirt and put it on their shoulder so that the wood wouldn't dig into their flesh. Then two or three of them would hoist the heavy post onto their shoulders. They brought in about 1,500 palm leaves

Friendly Kashinahuas brought food to Scotty.

for the roof and left them on the ground a few days to dry. Then, using vines, they tied them to the poles on the roof. A well done thatched roof would last about seven years.

We learned to eat and enjoy their food, of which there was an abundance. There were many types of fish, pheasant and grouse types of birds, wild boar, tapir, turtles, and monkeys. Some food I enjoyed more than others, but we ate whatever they brought to us. Besides the meat there was plenty of yuca, corn, papaya, peanuts, and bananas of all types, including big plantains for cooking. I was fortunate, too, that Ken was a good cook and enjoyed cooking. I was glad to let him do it whenever he wanted to.

Our initial trip to the Kashinawas couldn't have been more cordial.Ken and I enjoyed fellowship together, and we had a congenial time with the Kashinawas. They seemed to enjoy having us around. As we began learning their language, we gave the Kashinawas medicine when it was needed and, of course, they were happy with that.

Though we had also enjoyed the Sharanahuas, both of us said that we were glad we had been assigned to the Kashinawas instead of to the Sharanahuas because the Sharanahuas seemed like a much prouder people. They considered themselves superior to the Kashinawas. Later we found that the Kashinawas considered themselves superior to the Sharanahuas.

—16—

GOODBYE KASHINAWAS, HELLO SHARANAHUAS

After we returned from the Kashinawas, Cecil Hawkins, the man who, with his family, had begun work with the Sharanahuas, was asked to take an administrative post at Yarinacocha. In order for him to do that, someone needed to take his place among the Sharanahuas. Director Harold Goodall asked me if I would be willing to do that, and they would send someone else out with Ken. The Lord sometimes has a way of making us eat our words. Ken and I had said that we were glad that we were called to the Kashinawas and not the Sharanahuas. After praying about it, I felt that the director asking me to go to the Sharanahuas was the Lord's way of getting me to go. The Word says in Hebrews 13:17, "Obey your leaders and submit to their authority."

Shortly after I had agreed to go to the Sharanahuas, the son of the high school principal at Yarinacocha said that he would like to assist a linguist-translator where he could. I was happy to take Terry Smith, a tall, strapping teenager with me. Many times the teenagers at Yarinacocha went out to one of the tribes to assist a linguist in need of a short-term partner. Among other things, Terry wanted to do some of the cooking. He asked me one day if it would be all right if he called his mother on the radio to ask her how to cook a certain dish. He wanted to do it just right. At one point Terry even dug the hole for the burial of one of the Sharanahua men.

The Sharanahuas had never seen anyone that tall and that blond. They were delighted that Terry had come out with me. He was a big help to me and was glad to help the Sharanahuas any way he could. His being there freed me to spend more time with the Sharanahuas and learn their language. Later, upon graduation from college and linguistic training, Terry went as a translator-linguist along with his wife, Carla, to the Panao Quechuas in the highlands of Peru.

—17—

GOD BRINGS MARIE INTO MY LIFE

In 1955, shortly after Terry and I had returned to Yarinacocha, I was leaving a Sunday morning service when Dr. Altig stopped me. "Scotty, let me look at you. Your eyes are turning yellow. I'm sure you're coming down with hepatitis. I think you better go home and rest." It's harder to rest in the jungle with its beehive of activity and hot, humid climate than to go to Lima and stay in one of the apartments at our Lima Cudney Center (the former group house now so named in honor of our beloved Mrs. Cudney who for many years was the guiding hand there). So into Lima I went to get out of the jungle heat and to enjoy the cooler, more relaxed atmosphere to see if I couldn't quickly get over the hepatitis.

While there recuperating, a beautiful young woman arrived en route to Bolivia to serve as a translator. She had an eleven-day layover. When I heard her name was Marie Herzog, I thought I better go over and introduce myself. I told her that I had played in a brass quartet at SIL at the University of Oklahoma with her sister, Dottie Herzog. We struck up a pleasant conversation and found that we had quite a few mutual acquaintances besides her sister. She played the piano, and I had brought my baritone horn into

Lima, so we decided to make some music together. One thing led to another, and we ended up spending a few enjoyable hours together.

It seemed that all of the jokers in our mission happened to be in Lima then. I had barely met Marie when "helpful comments" were made while we were seated at the same table for a meal. One comment I have always remembered: "Come on, Scott. You have to make your move. The lady's not going to be here forever, you know." Who needs enemies when you have friends like that?

Despite those kinds of comments, we continued to spend quite a bit of time together. We even went to the basketball court to shoot some baskets. By this time I was feeling better, and I felt up to playing a basketball game of "freeze out" with Marie. I thought she might be quite athletic like her sister Dottie. We played just one game, and she beat me, but she never beat me again. She wasn't quite as athletic as Dottie.

All too quickly her eleven days were up, and she was on her way to Bolivia. I never knew whether I would see her again or not. The Lord had directed her to Bolivia, and I was anxious to get back to the Sharanahuas. But hepatitis had been for me a blessing in disguise. If I hadn't had hepatitis, I wouldn't have come into Lima, and the chances are that Marie and I never would have met. Did God have anything to do with that or what? As we played our instruments together, I think the thought went through my head that I would enjoy making music with this woman for the rest of my life. More about our relationship later.

—18—

MY FRIEND RON HILL

After saying goodbye to Marie, I was soon over hepatitis enough to return to Yarinacocha and prepare to go back out to the Sharanahuas.

Ron Hill, who had just completed his training at Princeton Theological Seminary, came from Oklahoma City. He had visited SIL in Norman. Ron liked what he saw and wanted to be more involved. He was a very likable young man, and I felt a bond with him almost from the first. His desire was to please God, and he wanted above all to serve him. I needed a partner, and he wanted to get some experience in a village situation. We met at Yarinacocha and agreed to go out together. Ron wanted to help in any way he could, and we had a great time of fellowship during the short time we were at the mouth of the Curanja River. It was a time of ministering to the medical needs of the Sharanahuas. Of course, I was anxious to learn the language and show the love of Christ to the Sharanahuas and to Ron. In 2 Corinthians 5:14 the apostle Paul said the love of Christ compels us to go. A missionary or translator should not go for any other reason. Any other reason will be a failure in the sight of the Lord.

While we were living with and ministering to the physical needs of the Sharanahuas and trying to learn more and more of their language and culture, I began to feel nauseated at times. I noticed I was having more of the hepatitis symptoms I had had before, only more pronounced this time. It was definitely a relapse.

Ron said, "Scotty, you have to get on the radio and call the doctor. You're looking really yellow." I was afraid that if we called the doctor the administration was going to think I was a poor medical risk and send me back to the States.

I said, "No, Ron. The plane will be coming for us in a couple of weeks, and I will be alright until then."

He replied, "Come on, man. You need to call the doctor. I don't want to have to take you out of here in a box."

Being the senior partner, I had the last word. It wasn't the smartest thing I ever did, but in spite of that the Lord was answering prayer that I wouldn't get too sick.

The day finally came for us to go downstream by canoe to Esperanza, the military base on the Purus River. Our PBY Catalina was to meet us there to take us back to Yarinacocha. It was coming to deliver supplies en route to one or two of the other tribes in the area. The Cat, as we called it, was an amphibious plane used much by the US Navy during World War II. It had been a gift from the Mexican government to the Peruvian government for helping the indigenous peoples of Peru. The Peruvian ministry of education had turned it over to our mission to be used in the work of literacy and translation. It could take up to nearly thirty passengers. Its wings held enough fuel to deliver several 50-gallon drums of gas for JAARS planes to utilize at different strategic locations.

When Ron and I arrived in Esperanza, we were graciously invited to stay at the Peruvian Army base to await the Catalina's arrival. The military personnel treated us royally. The Cat had scheduled a stop on the way to leave off supplies for another translation team. But upon landing there, the nose wheel was damaged, and they could not come on to Esperanza. They had to return to Yarinacocha, land on the lake, and get the nose wheel repaired before they could make a landing on the airstrip to get us. That meant a delay of eight days.

There I was with hepatitis, living at the army base where the food was mainly fried plantains (cooking bananas), fried fish, and yuca, a diet someone with hepatitis should avoid. Ron and I prayed, and I believe the Lord did one of his miracles. While everything indicated that subjecting my liver to that diet should make me sicker, amazingly enough, I kept getting better. By the time the Catalina came to get us, all of the symptoms of hepatitis, or nearly so, were gone. Praise the Lord! I didn't even have to mention it to the doctor.

Ron Hill left Peru thoroughly sold on the work of Wycliffe to reach all the language groups in the world with God's Word. He became an ordained Presbyterian pastor, but his love of Wycliffe and his concern for Bibleless people stayed fresh.

A few years later he invited Marie and me to stay at his home in Oklahoma City while we were on furlough, and we got to go to his church and enjoy fellowship with him and his family. Sad to say, when Ron was still in his early thirties he had a heart attack and died. Apparently, he was born with a heart defect. I look forward to seeing Ron again in heaven where we will worship together with Sharanahua believers forever.

—19—

SHIPPER AND RADIOMAN

After Ron and I came back from the Sharanahuas, I was asked to be the shipper at Yarinacocha, buying and sending supplies to the translation teams.

I was also asked to be one of the radio operators at Yarinacocha. The radio operator's job was to maintain contact with the planes flying over the jungle, noting in a log their position, their heading and altitude, and the estimated time of arrival at their destination. The pilots would call in every 15 minutes. Also the radio operator kept the pilot informed of the weather—ahead of him and back at Yarinacocha. Another of my duties was to check in every morning with the teams out in the tribal locations and later with those working in the Quechua dialects in the Andean Mountains.

The linguists would ask for a set time to talk with the doctor or perhaps with one of the linguistic consultants or with the director. The translator-linguists could also call in anytime that they needed to, and the operator would put them in touch with whomever they needed to talk. Sometimes there would be calls from Lima. Perhaps a Peruvian government official in Lima wanted to talk to our director. On Saturdays the radio operator set up times when the translators could talk with their children who were in school at Yarinacocha. The radio operator's job was a busy one that called for being alert and taking down and giving out all the necessary information. Having served as a signalman in the navy may have helped me to enjoy the assignment, though I knew that if I was to follow the calling to be a translator to the Sharanahuas, it had to be a temporary assignment.

Being the radio operator was not without its humorous experiences. One person, whose first language probably was not English, was spelling something for me and the word had a "u" in it. He said, "U as in Yugoslavia." Well, he had the phonetics right if not the spelling. Another person ordered twelve dozen candles. When the plane arrived the translator was handed a box with not just twelve dozen candles, but with twelve dozen packages of candles.

Sometimes people from our sister missionary organization South America Mission used our frequency to talk to their children who were enrolled in our school at Yarinacocha. Children have no qualms about repeating what they hear, or saying whatever is on their minds. One child, in talking to his parents, telling what all had been going on the past week said, "The other day did the teacher ever blow her stack!" The "whole world" listening in on the radio enjoyed that tidbit of information, much to the chagrin of the teacher if ever she found out about it.

One of the things I enjoyed as radioman was listening in whenever Uncle Cam talked to someone over the radio. We had a radio code of subjects we could or could not talk about on the radio. "Never bring up political or negative topics. Don't talk about finances." I think Uncle Cam had a lot to do with the radio code.

The radio wasn't always used for business; sometimes it was used for encouraging. I remember early one Christmas morning when unexpectedly Uncle Cam walked into the radio room and asked, "Scotty, are all the folks out in the tribes listening right now?"

"Yes, Uncle Cam." Being Christmas morning he no doubt figured that no one would be monitoring our radio frequency.

Sitting down before the mike, he said, "Good morning, beloved. Merry Christmas to all of you! This morning I'd like to share a few verses with you from the precious Word of God." And he proceeded to give a heartwarming Christmas message to all.

I was so glad I got to hear that. It must have thrilled the workers that our beloved founder was taking part of his Christmas morning to greet them and share the Word with them.

—20—

A BOLIVIAN JUNGLE WEDDING

During the time I served as shipper and radioman, Marie and I corresponded by mail whenever the PBY Catalina took supplies from Peru to Bolivia, which was three or four times a year.

After a year or more of serving in this job, I decided that it was time to know more about Marie other than through an occasional letter. I didn't want anyone else to know what I had in mind, so I kept this to myself and the Lord. The grapevine at Yarinacocha was well and active. I drummed up courage and went to Harold Goodall's office which, at that time, was in his house. I asked him if it would be alright if I took my vacation by going with the Catalina on its next trip to Bolivia. Rumors had a way of getting around at Yarinacocha, and the word had gotten out, from our pilots no doubt, that Marie and I were corresponding. So when the director's wife, Juanita, heard me say I would like to take a vacation in Bolivia she said, "This sounds interesting!" So much for secrets.

Harold gave his OK, and so I planned to go to Bolivia. But when it was time for the scheduled flight, I became sick. I prayed, "Lord, if you want me to go to Bolivia, if you have in mind for Marie and me to join our lives in service for you, please put your healing hand on me so I can go." Previously, I had prayed, telling the Lord that if Marie was sent to a tribe in Bolivia I would take it as from him that it was not in his plan for us to marry, as I didn't want to take her away from a tribal assignment. In Bolivia, being shorthanded, they made Marie the shipper.

The scheduled flight for Bolivia was canceled on the day it was to go. The next day I was feeling fine, and I took that as an indication from the Lord that I should go. Unknown to me, Marie had prayed, asking the Lord not to let me get on the flight if it wasn't his will for us to be married. So when I arrived on the flight in January 1957, she had a pretty good idea why I had come.

In Bolivia, the Tumichuqua Center resembled Yarinacocha's. There was a beautiful lake, but it was much smaller, as was the center itself. And no place to get away from the center! We were surrounded by jungle on all sides. It was much too far to walk to the nearest small town, and there was no road anyway. So in the evening we went down to the airstrip to have some privacy. We sat down on a log and in the course of conversation I asked Marie if she would consider marrying me. I told her that I didn't want her to feel rushed, so I asked her to pray about it (she had already been doing that) and then to let me know. The next night when we went down to the airstrip, again it was not long before mosquitoes came out in full force. In order to escape them we got into the Helio Courier airplane. Then Marie gave me her answer, "Yes," she would marry me. Perhaps Marie had the distinction of being the first one ever to be in a Helio to give her answer to a proposal of marriage.

I was scheduled to go back to my assignment in Peru, and we planned to be married in Yarinacocha, probably in June. It was planned that another fellow, Gil Prost, and I would go on the flight scheduled to take me back to Peru. En route we would land on the border of Bolivia and Peru to do a survey to find out if there were other tribes in the area needing to have linguist-translators learn their language to give them the Scriptures.

The day of the flight in February the air was hot and muggy, hardly a cloud in the sky and no breeze. All the Wycliffe workers came to the airstrip to see us off. Marie and I took one last walk around the airstrip to say our goodbyes. When we arrived back to the Helio Courier, Gil was already in the plane in the back seat with a 15-gallon drum of gas tied down on each side of him. Gil was about 6 feet 4 inches tall, and so I said, "Gil, you need some room for your long legs. Let me sit back there, and you sit up by the pilot." But he wouldn't hear of it, so after director Hal Key led in prayer for the flight, I got in the front seat next to the pilot, Willis Baughman.

The Helio Courier has a short takeoff and landing capability. Empty, it will get airborne in 100 meters. Fully loaded it will get off in 300 meters. As we taxied to the end of the airstrip for takeoff, I had utmost confidence in our pilot and in the airplane. We were not overloaded. As Willis gave it full power, and we were going down the airstrip, I looked out the window and waved to those standing on the edge of the airstrip. Any moment I expected the Helio Courier to do its thing and get us up in the air like a home-sick angel. We got about a meter off the ground, and that's all. It all happened so fast I didn't even have a chance to be nervous. First, the roar of the engine on takeoff, then WHAM! as we hit the stump at the end of the airstrip. The plane flipped over. And then there was a deafening silence. It was a strange sensation to be hanging upside down and backwards, held in by the harness straps.

I believe I was the first one to say anything: "Is everyone OK?"

Willis said, "I'm OK." "How about you, Gil?" His head had come forward and struck something, leaving a small gash on his forehead.

Gil didn't answer, and Willis said, "We have to get out of this fast before it catches on fire!"

Gil, who must have been stunned, did hear the word "fire," and was out the back door before Willis and I could get out.

Willis surveyed the smashed Helio and said, "Maybe I can get over this, but if I had killed one of you, I don't know that I could have ever gotten over that."

Meanwhile all the people watching the takeoff were horrified to see the plane flip over. All they could see were the wheels sticking up in the jungle. The director, not wanting Marie to see me smashed, if that were the case, told her to run to the radio and have the operator call Yarinacocha and tell them that there had been an accident.

Everyone rushed to the airplane. Hal Key, seeing the three of us standing there unhurt except for the gash on Gil's forehead said, "Alright, now we're going to sing the doxology." I don't think I was able to join in very heartily, but after we had sung "Praise God from whom all blessings flow...," Hal turned to the Bolivian workers who had also run down to see what had happened and said, "You may wonder how we can sing praises to the Lord when this new airplane lies here smashed. Well, God can give us another airplane, but if we had lost these three lives, we couldn't have brought them back again. So we can with enthusiasm sing praises to our wonderful Lord."

Not only did the Lord spare our lives, but the mechanics were able to repair the damaged Helio later and put it back in service.

The accident didn't make me lose any confidence in the pilot whatsoever. The director told Gil and me, "If you want to show Willis that you haven't lost any confidence in him, volunteer to go up with him in the Aeronca to take pictures of the accident." This Gil and I did without hesitation or qualms.

I will never believe that the accident was Willis' fault. The Helio Courier has a tall rudder. It was found some distance from the airplane, leading to the conjecture that the rudder might have had a crack in one of the hinges causing it to shake loose, which would cause a drag, not allowing us to get airborne. After this accident the Helio Courier Corporation built the Helio with three hinges on the rudder. Perhaps as a result of our accident and the corporation adding the third hinge, other accidents may have been prevented.

The Lord shut the door to me going back to Peru at that time. In those days it was considered improper for a Christian unmarried couple to travel together. I could have traveled alone via La Paz to Peru. Then later Marie would have had to travel alone the same route, something she wasn't anxious to do.

She suggested, "Why don't we just get married here and go back together?" That sounded like a good plan to me, and after praying about it, that's what we decided to do. We set the date for March 25, the year being 1957. We had a couple of months until that date, and I was able to help in Bolivia in a few capacities. Marie continued her assignment as shipper, while we waited for the wedding date.

As we waited, I realized that Marie hadn't had much opportunity to really get to know me, and it didn't seem fair. I asked her to take a walk with me again out in the jungle. There where no one was around I said, "Marie, there is much that you don't know about me, so I'm going to tell you all the negative things I can think of about me, and I'm sure there are more. If after hearing all these things about me you want to back out, there is still time." After hearing all those things she still wanted to go through with it.

When I told the missionary-pastor Rev. Joe McCullough, who was to marry us, what I had done he said, "Don't do that! She'll find out soon enough."

While we were waiting for the wedding date, Hal Key said, "Scotty, why do you want to go back to Peru? There are tribes right here in Bolivia that need translators."

I answered, "Well, I just haven't felt called to leave my assignment in Peru to take up an assignment here in Bolivia."

That night, and I have a feeling that Hal had something to do with it, someone stood outside my window where my bed was and in a loud voice shouted, "Scotty! Pacahuaras (a tribe in Bolivia) calling!" The next morning I said that somehow it didn't sound like the voice of the Lord to me.

I hadn't come to Bolivia thinking I would get married there, so I didn't have anything that resembled wedding clothes. I borrowed someone else's suit and shoes. In fact the only things I was wearing of my own were my shorts and socks. Marie borrowed a wedding gown from Gloria Farah. One couple even loaned us their wedding rings for the ceremony until we could get to Lima to buy our own. We had to wait for a Bolivian official to arrive by horse before we could start the ceremony. He was to perform the civil part of the marriage to make it official, and he was about an hour late. The jungle was hot. Someone got a large palm leaf and fanned Marie as she sat in the wedding gown waiting.

Marie, God's permanent partner for Scotty.

We cut our wedding cake with a decorated machete. The tricks played on couples who had been married in Yarinacocha had become widely known. Hal told his colleagues there in Tumichuqua, "We're not going to be like those 'savages' in Peru. There are certain things you can't do to Marie and Scotty." He told them they couldn't throw rice on us because the Bolivians watching would think that a horrible waste of good rice. They had me take Marie in a wheelbarrow appropriately decorated with tin cans tied to it from the director's house where we had been married to the airplane. The plane was to take us to a hotel in the little jungle town of Riberalta, a few minutes away by air. That evening, as we looked out the window of our hotel room, we could see clouds of mosquitoes waiting to get in. Not to worry! The bed with its corncob mattress was covered by a mosquito net.

Later, on our way via train to Peru from La Paz, Bolivia, Marie thought, *Here I am going off with this man that I don't really know—for the rest of my life*. But since that time we have had sixty action-packed years to get to know one another, and we can say that our love for each other has only grown over that span, despite all the negative things I told her about myself beforehand.

—21—

A LITTLE DETOUR

When Marie and I arrived back in Peru, one of my friends congratulated me on my new assignment.

I said, "What assignment?"

He replied, "Haven't you heard?" When I said I hadn't, he announced that I was to be the Lima buyer. That meant staying in Lima and doing all the buying for orders from Yarinacocha. Needless to say, I was shocked. So we wouldn't be going right out to the Sharanahuas after all.

Later, I found out that my friend Bob Russell had gone to our director Harold Goodalland told him, "Don't send Scotty and Marie immediately out to the tribe. Adjusting to married life and a new culture and language at the same time is too much. Delores and I did that, and I don't recommend it. To begin their life together, give Scotty another job for a while."

Our life together has just started.

Harold took Bob's advice and thus I was assigned to be the Lima buyer, and Marie was given a job in the finance office as well as taking some Spanish classes. In hindsight Bob's advice was well given and we could see the wisdom in it. I'm glad that we didn't go directly to the tribe where Marie would have been exhibit number one. Later, when we went to the Sharanahuas together for the first time, the people were always looking at us through the cracks in the walls or going to the living room where it was open to them to stare at us whenever they wanted to, which was most of the time. It's not for nothing that the Lord laid down the rule to the Israelites in Deuteronomy 24:5, "If a man has recently married, he must not be sent to war [in our case, sent to the tribe] or have any other duty laid on him. For one year he is to be free to stay at home and bring happiness to the wife he has married."

The time in Lima was a good way to start our marriage. We wanted to absorb as much of the Peruvian culture in Lima as possible. Life in the capital, the big city of Lima, is, of course, another world away from life in the jungle. At first Marie and I had to begin our life in Lima as "house parents" to the single women who lived in an apartment two blocks away from the Lima group house. While we enjoyed the fellowship we had with the women, it really wasn't conducive to being alone to start married life.

We were told about an elderly Peruvian couple who were looking for boarders to share their ample house. Marie and I were happy to share the home with Señor and Señora Galdoz. We shared breakfast and supper with them, and the conversation was delightful.

One thing we had to get used to was having supper close to ten in the evening. Supper was not just a snack, but a full course meal. After I got home from my buyer job around seven in the evening, Marie and I would sometimes have an apple to hold us over until the ten o'clock supper.

We enjoyed Señor Galdoz's sense of humor, and they treated Marie and me like their children. In fact, we called them Papa and Mama Galdoz. Thanks to this loving couple, our Spanish vocabulary picked up as did our grasp of Peruvian culture in the big city.

—22—

FINALLY, OUT WITH MY PERMANENT PARTNER

In January 1958 Marie and I were finally going to begin our work together among the Sharanahuas.[2] Because of bad weather we didn't leave Yarinacocha until 10:30 that morning, and after stopping halfway to gas up the plane, we arrived at 3:30 that afternoon. As the floatplane taxied to the bank, it seemed the whole village was out to greet us.

This was a new experience for Marie, so here she gives her first impressions:

> "As we climbed the bank to the village the people all crowded around us excitedly chattering in words that meant absolutely nothing to me.[3] The people were short with straight

_____

2 The Sharanahuas live in three main villages along the Purus River: Gasta Bala, the farthest upstream of the three; next, Santa Margarita; and then San Marcos. Quite a few Sharanahuas have moved downstream to Esperanza, the seat of government and a military post. A few family-sized settlements are sprinkled in between these larger villages. They cover the distance of about 100 miles as the crow flies, or from about six to sixteen hours between Gasta Bala and San Marcos by water, depending on the swiftness of the river, whether they are traveling with a motor or with paddles and poles, and whether they are traveling with the current or against it. The population when we were living there was approximately 500. Today, according to the Ministerio de Cultura of Peru, it is about 669.

3 The Sharanahua language can be heard on http://www.scriptureearth.org. Look for "Sharanahua" on the alphabetical list to hear Scripture read.

black hair and dark skin and eyes. They were a hardy people from working to survive all their lives. Some were painted with the red paint made from the seeds of the *achiote* plant, others with black from the *huito* plant, or a combination of the two. Their clothing came from the stores in Pucallpa, available to them through the traders in the area. They seemed to be as curious about us as we were about them. They were friendly and jovial, eager to learn what they could from us. This would be our new family.

"The village had about nine houses set upon stilts three feet off the ground with no walls and roofs thatched with palm leaves. There was no furniture, except possibly a crude bench to sit on. Clothing was draped from the rafters, along with hammocks, which were easily dropped to hang. These were their chairs by day and beds by night. Beside each home was a small cookhouse with a mud floor, no walls, and a thatched roof. Small fires were burning in some of them, with well-used cooking pots blackened by the flames, as the evening meals were being prepared.

"Standing in sharp contrast to the simple homes stood one larger building, made of the same materials. That was

Romu makes a paddle while his wife spins cotton.

A hardy people; work is not easy.

to be our home. It was built by the first man to contact the Sharanahuas, Cecil Hawkins, who, after three years of living with these people, was transferred to administrative work at Yarinacocha. After seeing the simple homes without walls around me, I was relieved to walk into a house that was divided into four rooms with a crude table, benches, and beds. Shelves were built for dishes and supplies. The walls, windows, and ceiling were covered with *tocuyo*, a kind of heavy muslin cloth that kept out the pesky gnats. Soon the supplies in the plane were unloaded and moved into the house, and I was able to arrange our things, making the house our home."

One of the things I, Scotty, remember about our arrival was the dehydration I felt, just as I had experienced there before. It seemed I was constantly thirsty the first day. As soon as we arrived, a couple of Sharanahua men went out into the jungle and came back with two long poles to serve for putting up our radio antenna. George Insley, our pilot, helped us get the kerosene lantern going and stayed all night. He left the next day but ran into bad weather and had to come back to stay another night. When George left the following day he was able to go all the way back to Yarinacocha.

Marie soon has the kitchen set up and ready to go.

We had to boil water that children brought to us.

Now we were really alone with each other and the Sharanahuas in one of the most isolated parts of the Amazon jungle of Peru. To this day there is no road to get there. It's only accessible by air. One of our pilots on arriving at the Sharanahua village for the first time said, "Well, if this isn't the end of the world, you can see it from here."

Marie knew it wasn't going to be easy learning a new language[4] and learning to deal with the heat and gnats. But at the same time she had the inner peace that this was where the Lord wanted us and that he would provide the strength, the wisdom, and the joy to do his will. Over our years among the Sharanahuas, I was always amazed that in spite of the heat and the clouds of gnats, Marie would quickly straighten up the house and get our things in order upon our arrival.

No doubt every missionary and translator who goes to the people they hope to reach for Christ wants to announce to them as soon as they set foot on their territory: "God loves you. Jesus died for you to save you from your sins and give you eternal life." But you can't do it until you learn their language and culture.

When we first went to the Sharanahuas there was no medical help, no doctor or nurse in the area. We were it. We had a little training in giving shots and recognizing sicknesses while we were in training in southern Mexico. Ministering to their physical needs, as we learned the language, was one way of demonstrating to the Sharanahuas the love of Christ.

Every morning they arrived at our house for treatments for one thing or another. We prayed and gave out medicines, bound

---

4 Sharanahua is a member of the Panoan language family. The alphabet consists of twelve consonants, four oral vowels, and four nasal vowels. The consonants are c, ch, f, hu, m, n, p, qu, r, s, t and y. The vowels are a, i, o, and u with their nasal counterparts, which are written an, in, on, and un. The language is tonal, with a high and low tone. The word order in sentences is adverb first, followed by subject, object, and then verb.

up wounds, and gave shots as needed. Intestinal parasites were the most common ailment. The people didn't boil their drinking water, and the river where they got their water was used for everything—washing clothes, bathing, and sometimes a latrine. So they were bound sooner or later to have intestinal parasites. They came with other ailments, too, and when we couldn't diagnose a case we would call on the radio to the doctor in Yarinacocha, describe the symptoms, and he would advise us as to what treatment we should give. He would say, "If this doesn't work, call again." Then he would prescribe something else.

When the Sharanahuas saw how quickly they got over their sickness from getting an injection, they would sometimes think we

Dispensing medicines at school.

weren't doing the best for them if we gave them pills instead of a shot.

The Sharanahuas seldom forced their children to do something they didn't want to do. Sometimes, if the child didn't want to take pills, the mother would take the pills in her hand as though she was going to give them to her child. Then, as Marie or I were attending to another patient, the mother would swallow the pills herself.

There were two or three albino Sharanahuas. One they called Yoshi, which meant "spirit." Yoshi, who was about 8 years old, was terrified of shots. One day his mother brought him with a fever. When I was ready to give him the shot in his buttocks, he was so scared that he tensed up. When I plunged the needle in, his buttocks were so hard, much to the hilarity of the Sharanahuas watching, that the needle bent over. Yoshi leaped up and fled into the jungle, and I don't think he ever submitted to a shot again.

One of our patients was our good friend the shaman Bidisario.[5] He was our next-door neighbor, a very robust man who was healthy most of the time. One day he came to us with a cut from his machete that opened the skin almost to the bone on the back of his hand. I knew he needed stitches, but I had never given any stitches in my life. Besides that, we had no suturing needles or suturing thread.

We called the doctor on the radio and he told us, "In the absence of suturing needles and thread, you are going to have to boil up a regular sewing needle and thread and do the stitching with those." We didn't have any anesthesia either, but the doctor said that I needed to do it anyhow as that would help the wound to heal without infection. The doctor tried to take me through the different steps for suturing, but I was not looking forward to putting Bidisario through this ordeal without anesthesia. In fact, I was not looking forward to putting myself through this ordeal without anesthesia for him.

Sometimes you have to do things you aren't trained to do when you're the only one available to do it. I followed the doctor's instructions, and Bidisario stood there stoically while I tried to shove the needle through his tough skin, which was almost like leather. He did grimace from the pain, and I was grimacing inside from the anguish I was putting him through. When I got the stitch in place I was shaking too much to tie the knot so Marie had to do that. I probably should have put in another stitch but I couldn't bring myself to put Bidisario through the ordeal again, and

---

5 No family names are given in this book. The Sharanahuas rarely called a person by his name, let alone a family ("last") name, unless dealing with a mestizo or answering for a government document. When talking to one of their own, they always used a kinship term. We had to write down their names for vaccinations. Often one parent would say to the other regarding their child, "What did we name this one?" If they wanted to distinguish between two siblings then they would use the Spanish name. They made allowance for us using their names until they took us into the kinship system. Then we were supposed to use the kinship term while talking with them or referring to them (see chapter 51, "Zacarias").

I wasn't sure I could do it again anyway. The wound healed without infection, and that made not only Bidisario happy, but it made me happy that "our labor was not in vain."

One of the aggravations in village life was domesticated pigs, which were allowed to run freely throughout the community. I tried to raise a garden near our house, but each time the neighbor's pigs would come and root the plants up and eat them. I even tried to wall off the garden by putting up a bamboo fence around it, but the pigs rooted through it.

One day as Marie and I were outside our house talking to some Sharanahua children, a pig came wandering down the path. Marie, wanting to scare it away, asked one of the boys to give her his bow and arrow, the bow being only about a foot across with a little tiny arrow. The boys used them to shoot little lizards and thus be ready later to learn to shoot the bigger bows and arrows that their fathers used. Marie took the bow, and not dreaming she could hit the pig or that if she did it would do any harm, took aim and shot. Much to her amazement and to the amazement and amusement of the Sharanahua children, the arrow stuck in the rear part of the pig, who was not amused and went squealing down the trail back to the shaman's home where it came from. Pretty soon Bidisario's wife, Fushna, came storming down the trail convinced that one of the boys had done the foul deed. Somehow Marie had disappeared into the house before Fushna got there. Bidisario and Fushna loved their animals and didn't take kindly to anyone mistreating them.

Another time *I* couldn't disappear into the house. Bidisario was upset that one of his animals had been mistreated. I had gone out to the Sharanahuas without Marie to help put a new thatched roof on the house. Floyd Lyon, a pilot, had brought out some supplies to me. As we were sitting on the floor of the house, eating a meal and talking with the Sharanahuas visiting us, Bidisario came stomping down the path to our house with a canoe paddle over his shoulder. There was a Mastanahua (a neighboring tribe to the Sharanahuas) there visiting us, and it seems that someone had told Bidisario that this Mastanahua had kicked his dog, making Bidisario furious.

As he approached the Mastanahua, he said something like, "So you kicked my dog, did you? Well, we'll see about you."

With that he took a stance in front of the Mastanahua with the paddle, posed like Babe Ruth getting ready to take a mighty swing at the ball. I could see that the Mastanahua might well lose his head. Praying, and not knowing what else to do to prevent a catastrophe, I stepped up to Bidisario with a cup of coffee and offered it to him. Knowing that in their culture to refuse something offered you is an insult to the one offering it, Bidisario laid down the paddle and took the cup of coffee.

I wish I could tell you that Bidisario later came to Christ. He had gone hunting, and when he didn't come back late that afternoon, the Sharanahuas went to look for him. They found him just sitting on the edge of the trail with the game that he had shot still strapped to his back with vines—and he was dead. The Sharanahuas were all amazed because they said, "There was no blood. No one had shot him or done him any harm; he just died." He is the only Sharanahua that we know of who died of a heart attack.

Another very small tribe, linguistically very close to the Sharanahua, was the Chandinahuas that lived just upstream from the village where we lived. The Sharanahua chief Alfonso often took me there to minister to their physical needs. One man had a disease where the skin was peeling off over his entire body. He just lay in his hammock suffering. I wanted so much to give him something that would bring healing, but nothing seemed to do any good. Finally, the man died. So another man, a Yaminahua, whose dialect is closely related linguistically to Sharanahua, took the widow for his wife, and they went to his village some distance away. This man did not want Siwa, the widow's little girl, who was about 2 years old, so they left her with an aunt. Marie tells this story from a mother's perspective in chapter 24, "Unfair!"

The Sharanahuas are generous people and brought us all kinds of bananas similar to those sold in the States and a myriad of other kinds of eating bananas, plus the plantain, a large cooking banana. They also had a plentiful supply of papaya, and yuca (manioc or cassava root), which is one of their staples much as potatoes are for us. In addition there were peanuts in abundance and watermelon, both seasonal. Meat also was plentiful. There were all kinds of edible fish, the largest and for some the most delicious—the *paiche*—which could be as much as 12 feet long. Some meats we enjoyed more than others. They often eat monkey meat. We didn't turn it down when brought to us, but it wasn't our favorite dish.

One Sunday Marie and I stepped out of our house to go visiting. Our house, like the others, was right on the edge of the jungle. Often animals would venture close. We looked up in our lemon tree and there sat a monkey. I thought, *This is a chance to repay some of the villagers' generosity.* I asked Marie to keep an eye on it while I dashed into the house to grab my .22 rifle. When I got back outside the monkey was still sitting there in one of the top branches. Taking careful aim I got him right in the head. Walking over to retrieve it, I saw a string around its neck. My heart sunk as I realized I had shot someone's pet monkey. Even though Sharanahuas eat monkey, they would never shoot someone's pet monkey. One of the young boys sauntered up to our house. Hoping that he didn't come from the house where the

We spent many hours getting acquainted.

125

monkey came from, I offered the monkey to him. He took one look at it, saw the string around the neck, and recognized it as their pet monkey. He walked sadly down the trail to his house.

Pretty soon the father came storming down the trail and said, "Why did you shoot our pet monkey? My wife and children are home crying."

I tried to explain to him that I didn't realize it was a pet, that I thought it had come out of the jungle. I didn't see the string tied around the neck. I didn't know their language well enough then to give a real good apology, but I gave him some shotgun shells with which to shoot another mother monkey and take the baby, which rides on her back, for another pet. This mollified the owner, and he went back home with less anger than when he came. I'm sure the Sharanahuas made allowances for this foreigner's lack of knowledge of their culture and that I couldn't see as well as their men could to spot birds in the trees and monkeys with a string on the neck.

Part of what we could do to help the Sharanahuas was to figure their accounts with the traders. They hadn't learned to count in high numbers yet. We could also weigh the rubber they collected to make sure they got what they should for their work. The Sharanahuas were very thankful for our help, but it didn't endear us to the traders who were in the habit of exploiting them. We tried to show Christ to the traders also while at the same time trying to make sure the Sharanahuas were not ripped off in their exchanges.

One day Marie prepared a meal for the visiting commanding officer of the Peruvian army post, a day's journey by canoe downstream. After the meal I talked to him about some of the traders trying to take advantage of the Sharanahuas' inability to figure their own accounts. He was very receptive and said that he would try to put a stop to that practice. Also, on occasion, we would invite one of the traders in for a meal, to be hospitable and to show that we wanted to be their friends.

—23—

THE WOOD CHIP THAT TALKED

The Sharanahuas have a beautiful language, but no one had ever reduced it to writing. No one had made an alphabet for them. They had no schools or any way to learn to read or write. They had never written anything in their lives. Marie and I had to learn their language and their culture, then devise an alphabet for them and teach them to read and write.

Once when I went from our house at the mouth of the Curanja River to a house at the other end of the village, I got there and discovered that I needed a certain kind of medicine. Rather than take the time and energy to go back to my house, I asked a young Sharanahua boy to go for me and bring back the medicine. I didn't have any paper with me, so I picked up a chip of wood and wrote the message to Marie on that. I told him to give the chip to Marie

Baby Dave slept peacefully, unaware of the trauma around him.

and she would give the medicine to him to bring to me. When Marie read my message on the chip, she gave him the medicine, and he brought it to me. It was an amazing thing to that little Sharanahua boy that a piece of wood could talk. Their word for *writing* is the same as their word for *carving*. So to them, God's Word is God's Carving.

—24—

UNFAIR!

Marie tells Siwa's story here from a mother's perspective.

A little orphan girl, burned by fire, starved, and left on the riverbank to die—that was Siwa's condition when brought to us. I will never forget the first time I saw her. I didn't even realize she was in our house. The room was full of Sharanahuas and Chandinahuas, and she lay in filthy rags, a tiny heap in one corner. Scotty saw her first and went over and tenderly picked up the bony frame and sat her on his knee. Her hair was cropped off close to the head, revealing a large, infected lump and many small sores. Her only possession was a dirty, ragged dress. It barely covered her emaciated body, which had only a little more flesh than was needed to hold the bones together. Her tummy was swollen, the skin stretched tight from worms and extreme malnutrition. Her sad, careworn face looked like that of an old woman rather than of a 2½-year-old.

As I looked at this poor, forsaken bit of humanity, I compared her with our own chubby, healthy little son David, born six months before in August 1958. My heart cried out, *How cruel and unfair life is. We must help to give her another chance.*

As I heard her story told by her people, my heart ached even more. Her father had died of a disease less than a year before. When her mother remarried, her stepfather didn't want her and took her mother far away to his community. She was left with her grandmother, who cared little for her. At night Siwa slept next to a fire to keep the mosquitoes away and to keep herself warm. One night she rolled into the fire, badly burning her legs. Rather than give her proper care at this time, her grandmother left her on the riverbank to die. But later her people brought her to us.

Siwa was a Chandinahua, who were looked down upon by the Sharanahuas, so we were soon told by the Sharanahuas that the best thing to do would be to throw the little girl into the river.

Instead, we took her into our home, praying the Lord would put a love for her into the hearts of one of the Sharanahua families so that when she was restored to health there would be a home waiting for her.

Scarcely a whimper passed her lips as Siwa watched her people, glad to be rid of the "burden" they had brought, walk out the door, leaving her behind to live with strangers who barely spoke her language. Her new home was far different from her previous one. This home had walls, windows, and doors. There were tables and chairs, dishes, pots and pans, a stove, books, papers, pencils, and many other things that she had never seen before. She was soon to find out, too, that she was to sleep on a cot rather than on the ground as she had previously done.

Siwa was a little reluctant to let me remove her ragged dress, but when she realized that a pretty shirt was awaiting her, the reluctance was soon gone. A bath in a tub of water was a new experience. She sat there puzzled and passively allowed me to scrub at the crusted dirt, which took several warm baths to remove. After the first few baths, she caught on to the idea, and all I had to do was hand her "her" bar of soap and put her in the tub and she went to work to get herself clean.

Early the next morning we contacted our doctor at Yarinacocha by radio. As we described Siwa's condition, he diagnosed the case. He prescribed a diet for her and sent out some medicines on the floatplane that was coming out that very day. If she were to survive, we knew we would have to rigidly follow the diet the doctor prescribed: one ounce of milk every hour. But what were we to do between feedings with a little girl who could think of nothing but food?

In the days that followed I felt like a prison warden, saying no to every desire and request of a starving child. She would sit quietly and watch me as I worked around the kitchen, and then the minute I turned my back she would be down off the chair eating a forbidden scrap of food that she had her eyes on or perhaps a piece of dirt to ease the gnawing hunger. I watched the clock eagerly and was as happy as she was when the minutes had ticked by and it was time for the next tiny ounce of milk.

And yet the doctor's prescribed milk diet was working. The torturing diarrhea was letting up. How happy we were after a week to wake up and find a clean bed and know that Siwa had not had to suffer so in the night.

By this time she seemed like our own little girl and what a joy she was to us! Her tiny baby voice rang through the house as she gradually opened up and talked to us, usually in short phrases such as "*Dikapo!*" ("Listen to that!"). Then she would say, "Your baby is talking," or "Your baby is crying," or perhaps she would mimic a birdcall outside. The tribal barriers were breaking down between her and the children of the village, and they loved to sit outside the window and chatter with her or, better yet, to come inside to talk to her. We were encouraged by this and began to wonder which home would open up to her when she was completely well.

Even though her condition seemed to improve, and we were able to gradually increase the amount of milk given to her, Siwa still craved dirt and food. We had to watch her constantly. She knew she was being watched. Then one morning she was too sly for us. We woke before five o'clock in the dim light of the early morning to hear dishes rattling in the kitchen. There sat Siwa in the middle of the kitchen table eating corn and leftover stew right out of the pot.

We're not sure if this actually had anything to do with her decline or whether she was too far gone when she was brought to us. From that day on we watched Siwa slowly slipping away from us. The diarrhea returned and became more painful than before. At times she would even refuse the milk we offered her. The last three days she was with us we expected she would go, but the night's rest seemed to help her rally, and we would hope again.

In her last day, she seemed to want nothing but love and affection, so we took turns holding and rocking her most of the day. Scotty was taking his turn in the rocking chair, while I was putting the supper on the table, and very conveniently Chichi, the grandmother of the tribe, walked in and said that she would be willing to hold Siwa while we ate. We were happy to see this act of concern, again feeling that the tribal barrier was being broken down.

But we didn't realize what was going on in Chichi's mind as she held the little girl. Perhaps she thought of us as a couple of young upstarts who didn't know how to take care of the sick. She must have thought we were starving the little girl to death. At any rate she took the case into her own hands and just before she left Siwa she asked her if she was hungry. What a question! But the next question hurt even more. "Do you want some meat and yuca?" Scotty explained to Grandma that our doctor had studied for many years and knew a great deal about this type of sickness, and so we were following his directions.

Grandma was not very happy about having her offer turned down, and her parting remarks to Siwa struck terror into her heart. We didn't hear exactly what she said but the effects were evident. Siwa's eyes filled with fear and for some time after that she would not be left alone with Scotty. She seemed to realize that death was near, and perhaps she was connecting him in some way with death. It just about broke Scotty's heart not to be able to comfort her at this time.

When we put her to bed for the night, she began to call her mother, "*Uwa, uwa, owu!*" (Mama, mama, come!"). Of course, her mother was miles and miles away and couldn't hear the pitiable cry of her little girl. Her calling for her mother tore at our heartstrings, and we couldn't stand it. Scotty got up and picked up Siwa and carried her to our bed and put her between us. Her fearful eyes pleaded for assurance that she wouldn't die. For three days now everyone had been telling her that she was going to die. She now realized it and felt she was alone in it. Our limited knowledge of the language left us helpless to console her and tell her of our love for her, and those who knew her language had no love to show.

We left a flashlight burning to lighten the interior of our mosquito net. Gradually the fear eased from her eyes, and the three of us slept, though fitfully, for about two or three hours. After that, in too much pain to sleep, she lay there between us crying softly and pleading with her eyes for something to take the pain away. We knew that the end was near, but that same determination that had kept her living through so much misery kept her with us hours after we thought she would be gone.

I prayed softly as Scotty spoke simply to her. "Siwa, you are going to God's country. God loves you. In God's country you will not be sick. In God's country you will not have any pain. In God's country there is no crying. In God's country you will not be hungry. There is lots of food in God's country." In the dimming light of the flashlight we couldn't see her face, but we were thrilled to hear a ring in her voice as she responded, "*Shara*" ("That's good.").

That's the last coherent word she spoke. We watched her constantly until the end—watching the suffering increase, watching death take over. She couldn't swallow anymore, but from time to time we would put a wet washcloth to her mouth, hoping it would help the dryness and the thirst.

Our precious little girl, Siwa.

We prayed that she would be gone before dawn. We feared that as soon as the Sharanahuas found out she was dying the women would come and wail over her. But instead of the women, the Lord sent some of the men to come encourage us. They stood talking in low tones until shortly before Siwa left this world. Pablo, the Sharanahua who was helping us learn his language, was the last man to leave. With tear-filled eyes he said, "I won't be coming to study today. I think I'll go hunting." And he left.

After the men had left, the boys who were still there started laughing. So Tacarumba, one of the boys about 8 years old who had stayed in our house during much of the time Siwa was with us, said to his friends, "Don't be laughing. She was like one of their own."

About 15 minutes after Pablo had left, Siwa looked like she was going to cry. But no cry came. Instead the little body relaxed and a look of peace came over her face. She was in the arms of Jesus.

While the men had been with us they had offered their assistance in her burial, so immediately Scotty went to tell them she was gone. Little Tacarumba, who had seemed to care most during her short time with us, had been there for her to the very end. He tenderly bent Siwa's arms and legs into the position they put them for burial according to their custom and helped us wrap her in a sheet.

Scotty picked up the little bundle and we walked quietly to the grave that had been made ready. A number of the Sharanahuas stood around watching as our next-door neighbor, Bidisario, laid the little body to rest. Bidisario explained to us as he did it that he was pointing her feet in the direction of her home and her people.

As we walked back to our house that now seemed so empty, once again my heart cried out, *Unfair!* as I looked at our happy son, David, in my arms. He didn't realize what was going on. He didn't lack for food, clothing, or love. We were so glad that the Lord allowed us to show his love for two weeks to little Siwa before he took her into his arms.

A few hours later the beauty of death for one going to be with the Lord dawned on us as Scotty said softly, "You know, Marie, a few hours ago I was trying to tell Siwa about God, and now she knows far more about him than we do."

Since Siwa's time, many Sharanahuas have come to Christ, so the way they felt about her and others like her has been replaced by the love of God.

—25—

SLOW SPEED AHEAD

On our first furlough from Peru, we were leaving Boonville, Indiana, where Marie's father was a pastor, and heading west to my folks' place in Centralia, Washington. We were pleased with the 1953 Dodge we had purchased from another Wycliffe translator who had returned to Peru. He had just had a new valve job done on the car, which ran smoothly.

One of our stops en route was Oklahoma City where my friend Ron Hill lived, my teammate to the Sharanahuas before I met Marie. Ron was now assistant pastor of a large Presbyterian church. Just before we entered the city, the car started to develop disturbing sounds. After a while it began to shimmy at an alarming rate, and I wondered if we would make it to Ron's home before it conked out. Fortunately, we made it.

The next day Ron took me to his mechanic's garage. After checking over the car, the mechanic said, "I'm afraid I have bad news for you. The rods in your car are completely shot. It will take new ones to repair your car." I knew we were talking about major repairs. I asked him how much it would cost. He said about four hundred dollars, which to us at that time was a huge sum. We had only two hundred with us. I thought that perhaps because the mechanic knew Ron and knew I was staying in his home that he might allow me to put the two hundred down and pay the other two hundred when our next monthly check came from Wycliffe. But he told me he was working on a small margin and just couldn't do it. I didn't blame him one bit for not being willing to repair it without having the full amount. He didn't know me in the slightest and could be out the payment on the repair of the car and his time if I didn't come through with the amount due. I asked him how far he thought we could get with the car in its present condition. He said, "Oh, that's hard to say. If you go just about 25 miles an hour you might get another 1,000 miles out of it. On the other hand, you might not make it out of the city limits."

So there was the diagnosis. That cold winter night in Oklahoma City I questioned the Lord. "Lord, what am I going to do? The mechanic says I might not be able to make it out of the city. Marie is several months along in her pregnancy. I don't dare try to make it over the Rockies to Washington. If the car should quit in one of the mountain passes, we would be out in the cold with Marie in her condition. Lord, what would you have me do? You know I'm not a mechanic. We don't have the funds, and I can't ask for a loan from my friend. Lord, please show me what I'm to do. Do I dare go back to Indiana at 25 miles an hour, keeping off the freeways?" To try it or not to try it, that's the question.

"Lord, it seems the only answer is to trust you to keep the car going until we get back to Marie's folks' place. There we can wait for our check to cover the cost of repairs." The Lord gave that "peace that passes all understanding" that this was his will. Finally, I could sleep.

The next morning, off we went at 25 miles an hour. It would be against the law to travel on a freeway at that slow speed, so we had to take other highways. As we traveled along, every time we came to another small town we would burst into the "Praise the Lord" refrain of "To God Be the Glory." We knew all praise belonged to him for keeping this sick car going. As you can imagine, drivers were often less than happy with us as they were forced to go at such a slow rate of speed. In hindsight I should have had a sign painted to put in the back window saying "Sorry, this is as fast as this car will go until it gets some new rods." Since I didn't, the only thing I could do was smile at the furious faces as their cars passed us. Maybe that made them all the angrier, but it did something for me.

How appropriate that one of our overnights along the way was in Wickliffe, Kentucky. It's spelled a little different than the way our organization spells Wycliffe, but close enough to make us feel the Lord had chosen this very place for us that night.

On we went, mile after mile, with thanksgiving in our hearts for the way the Lord was keeping the car functioning. After about 700 miles of 25 miles an hour we drove up to Marie's parents' house. In order to make the surprise complete, we knocked on the door. We will never forget the look of absolute shock on Marie's dad's face. He thought that by this time we would have been getting close to Washington.

Sometimes my father-in-law's boldness shocked me. It did this time as he said, "We're going to go to my friend who is a Christian and owns a car dealership and garage, and tell him, 'We come to you in the name of the Lord and ask you to fix this car without charging this missionary.'" Of course, I couldn't do that, but we did go to dad's friend, and he ordered a new rebuilt engine from Sears to install in our car for four hundred dollars, and we could pay for it on time.

As soon as the engine was installed we were off for Washington, and we never had a bit of trouble with that car the rest of our furlough. Our friend who sold it to us had no way of knowing that the rods were about shot. At the same time we were to return to Peru in 1960 with our second son, Steven, in tow, a Wycliffe airplane mechanic from Bolivia with nine kids was just arriving in the States and needed a car. It worked out perfectly for him to take ours, as we were leaving from Florida, and he was just arriving there for their furlough. The car ran well for him the whole time he was in the States. So, Lord, thank you for the way you take care of your own.

—26—

TRIAL THROUGH FIRE

Friday, July 16, 1965, started out like any other day with the Sharanahuas. It was dry season and thatched-roofed homes were like boxes of tinder just waiting to be lit. I had planned to go downstream that day, but something came up that kept me from going.

We were having a new latrine made and decided to burn down the old one that wasn't too far from our house. Our house, like the Sharanahuas', had a thatched roof made of palm leaves tied to the poles by vines. Like theirs, our roof, too, was as dry as it had ever been. I asked the Sharanahua men if there was any danger burning something that close to our house, though they had made other fires closer than that, which always concerned me. They assured me there was no danger because the wind was blowing away from the house. So a couple of the Sharanahua men set the old outhouse on fire. After the fire had been set, the wind shifted directions and was blowing toward our house, but it still seemed far enough away that it wouldn't present a problem.

Marie was standing outside our house talking with Custoti as she hung clothes on the line. Chichi, the oldest Sharanahua woman in the community, who was standing beside them, calmly said, "Why is your house on fire?"

Marie called me, and we looked up to see a hole about the size of a basketball burning the crown of our house. I knew that in a matter of 2 or 3 minutes it was going to be a roaring inferno. I rushed into the house and grabbed the two-way radio. Marie dashed in to pick up a few diapers. By the time we got back outside my worst fears were realized. I knew that as soon as the fire burned through the dry vines holding the crisp, withered leaves to the roof poles, all the leaves on the roof would collapse to the floor together. The Sharanahua men wanted to run back into the house to get more things, but I said, "No! I can stand to lose my things, but I couldn't stand it if I lost one of you in the fire." I had hardly gotten the words out of my mouth when the roof came down with a roar.

A local Spanish priest and I ran around the house to the gas shed, which contained the 50-gallon drums of aviation gas. The fire was so hot that we had to circle at a distance to get to the shed. We rolled the drums down the bank to the river. If they had caught on fire, I dread thinking of what might have happened to the whole community. Later we discovered that the shed, too, had burned to the ground. Praise the Lord that the drums had been rolled away before the shed burned.

As Marie and I stood with our two boys, David, 7 years old, and Steven, 5, surveying what used to be our house, now burnt completely to the ground, we said, "Well, we just lost all our things, but we didn't lose our children or any of the Sharanahuas, so we can praise the Lord." One of the Sharanahua women seeing the house burning feared for our lives, thinking the whole village might burn. So she took our 14-month-old daughter, Becky, and ran out into the jungle with her. As we stood there, the priest came to us and said, "You've just lost your house and have no place to stay. I have two houses. Come and stay in one of those."

As we were going down the trail to his house, we remarked again on the goodness of the Lord in keeping anyone from getting burnt, and Marie managed a smile. One of the Sharanahua women seeing her smile said, "Don't smile! Cry! You just lost all your things." But Marie told her that we could smile because the Lord had kept everyone from being burned.

When our family got to the priest's house and we were alone, I said, "Let's think of some verses to encourage each other." Our little 5-year-old Steve quoted one verse he knew: "Rejoice in the Lord always: and again I say, Rejoice" (Phil. 4:4 KJV). As the Word says, "Out of the mouths of babes..." (Matt. 21:16 KJV).

Not only did all our things burn—a small kerosene refrigerator, an outboard motor, a .22 rifle, and more—but also all our language analysis, word lists, and preliminary translations, which we had written in notebooks and on 3 x 5-inch cards. For Marie personally, what hurt the worst was losing her diary. That represented four and a half years of recording what had gone on in our lives. In the days before the computer, there was no backup to our linguistic and translation work.

We later got a letter of encouragement from one of our professors of linguistics, Elliot Canonge. Among other things he said, "It's my opinion that all first translations should be burned up anyway."

The bottles for our little 14-month-old Becky had all burned, but during the night she cried real hard only twice. The next day when pilot Jack McGukin came to get us in a floatplane, he stepped out onto the float with a baby bottle of milk in hand. What a welcome sight for both mother and daughter!

—27—

THE FIRST SHARANAHUA SCHOOL

By 1966 Marie had prepared primers, checking carefully with the Sharanahuas to make sure everything was accurate before the books were printed. Most of the Sharanahuas had never held a pencil before, never saw writing in their language, never tried to read or write. We prayed the Lord would cause this first experience at learning to read and write to be a good one. We wanted the Sharanahuas to think of school in their language a valuable thing to do.

These were the early days of our time among the Sharanahuas, and at that point they didn't consider women to be as valuable as men. Of course, we knew that women were just as valuable as men, not only to us, but also to God. But we felt it best, at the outset, to invite only men to the classes.

We were very pleased when nearly all the men turned out. At this time we didn't have any desks or chairs, so the men sat on the floor and used our benches as tables. We started by teaching them Sharanahua syllables, for example, *po, pa, mo, ma*, etc. Some of the men caught on quickly, while it was very difficult for some of the older ones. Progressing with the syllables, the primers then introduced them to simple words of one or two syllables. Soon the men were making good progress. After a short time of teaching only the men, we brought in women and children—both boys and girls.

Also we taught them basic arithmetic. They had a counting system, but it went only to 20. Beyond 20, they just said *ichapa*, which meant "lots." Their numbering system went like this:

fusti = 1
rafu = 2
rafu non fusti = 3 (literally 2 + 1)
rafu non rafuri = 4 (2 + 2 also)
mucu fustiti = 5 (1 hand)
mucu foshca fusti = 6 (1 hand and 1 thumb)
mucu naman cayanoati = 7, 8, or 9 (1 hand and the middle finger)
mucu rafu = 10 (2 hands)
mucu rafu non tau fusti = 15 (2 hands + 1 foot)
tau rafu = 20 (2 feet)
ichapa = any amount over 20

It didn't take us long to realize that what they were actually doing was counting on their fingers and toes. They didn't know the Spanish numbers at all, so we had to teach them which numbers were larger than the others. We were very pleased at how quickly they learned.

After they had been in school for several months, we were able to observe which ones were doing the best. We chose two of the most promising Sharanahua men to take the Teacher Training Course at Yarinacocha. While there, whenever the students didn't understand, they would get extra help from the linguist-translator working in their language. After the bilingual course was completed, the students would go back to their own communities and teach their people in their own language. Thus Marie and I no longer had to spend our time doing the teaching and could concentrate on the translation of the Scriptures. In the early days we checked regularly on the schools and the Sharanahua bilingual teachers. Later on, only an occasional check was needed. We were very pleased to see how well they were teaching and how well the students were learning.

—28—

NEW BEGINNINGS FOR
THE SHARANAHUAS

In Isaiah 43:19, God wanted his people to join in his excitement and joy. He says, "See, I am doing a new thing! Now it springs up; do you not perceive it? I am making a way in the wilderness and streams in the wasteland." We were in for some excitement too.

We had encouraged the men of the village to think about building a real school, like the mestizo (person of mixed European and Native American ancestry) town downstream had, with desks and chairs, instead of sitting on the floor, as they had been doing in our home.

So in 1968 the Sharanahuas, for the first time in the ten years since we had been with them, embarked on a community project. They were so anxious to have a school that they worked together as a community to put up a schoolhouse. Usually, when they did anything connected with our work they expected pay, but this time they worked willingly and freely. This was a real delight to us to see them working together on something that would benefit them and their children. Besides, it would be a lot more enjoyable to teach in a schoolhouse than in one room of our own house.

Marie taught the Sharanahua children every afternoon while

I worked on the translation. Together, every morning except Saturday we taught about fourteen men. They used all day Saturday for hunting and fishing. The men were enthusiastic to be able to learn to read and write in their own language.

The Lord was also doing other "new things" that warmed our hearts. Whenever it was time for us to leave the community for a while, we were told they were going to miss us. But usually that was the "long slow curve," which was invariably followed by, "What are you going to give me so that, seeing it, I can think about you while you're gone?" But this time old Bayacondi, who called me his son, and whom I called father, now brought us an armadillo skin that he had made into a horn and gave it to us. I thanked him and asked him how much I owed him.

He replied in a way we had never heard before. He said, "This is a gift to you. I don't want anything for it. I wish you didn't have to go."

That's the closest a Sharanahua had come to telling us he loved us. We didn't even know their word for "love" yet. We loved Bayacondi and longed for him to come to know the love of Christ and become God's child.

Then the Lord did another brand new thing for the Sharanahuas. A young couple, Jim and Marie Middlestedt of Gospel Recordings, came out to the Sharanahua community of San Marcos while we were there. For the first time, recordings of the Scriptures were made in the Sharanahua language, the language that spoke to their hearts. We appreciated the burden Gospel Recordings also had for the Bibleless language groups of the world.

Then, for the first time, in 1968, translation of the Word in the Sharanahua language had been approved for publication. The Sharanahuas would be getting a booklet called *Life of Christ* in their language. It was a compilation of verses from the four Gospels, telling of Christ's birth, ministry, death, and resurrection. Also included were passages from Acts and the Epistles, which covered Jesus' final orders, ascension, and his second coming. What a happy day that was for the Sharanahuas to receive this booklet! We, too, were on cloud nine. At last, part of the Word of God was in print for the Sharanahuas!

—29—

THE POWER IN JESUS' NAME

Marie and I had become accustomed to being called any time of the day or night to help a Sharanahua who was in need of medical attention. The Sharanahuas had many times seen the quick improvement from antibiotics or other medicine we gave them. At one point the chief said, "As long as you are with us, no one ever dies." Though I was glad he trusted our medicines, I knew there was going to come a day when, nevertheless, one of them would die.

The shaman Domingo lived next door to us and he, like the others, came to us for medical help. Marie and I had just retired for the night when he called me with great urgency. "Come quick, my wife is very sick." I quickly got dressed and hurried to his house. There were a lot of people in the house, and many of them were inside his wife's mosquito net. I got inside, too, as I had been invited to do. Suddenly, his wife Chatafundia said, "They're taking me away!" And even though strong men had ahold of her arms, she sat right up as though she was going to leave. I recognized that this was not a medical problem but demon possession. I had never dealt with anything like this before. This was during our early days with the Sharanahuas, and I realized that I was the only Christian in the net and if there was going to be any deliverance for her, I was going to have to allow the Holy Spirit to do it through me. So I did what I had never done before and said in English, "In the name of Jesus Christ I command you to leave her and leave this vicinity!" As soon as I said that, she laid right back down and went to sleep. I should not have been, but I was amazed, or at least in awe, at the result. This gave me boldness to say to the Sharanahuas that she was going to be alright now.

Her little children were sitting on the floor outside the mosquito net, crying. I told them, "You don't need to cry anymore. Mama is going to be all right. You can go to bed now and not worry about Mama."

I went home on cloud nine. As I got back in bed, I told Marie what had happened. I said, "There really is power in the name of Jesus. The demons had to leave at the command in his name. As I commanded them to leave in Jesus' name, she immediately laid back down and went right to sleep. What a powerful God we serve." As we were thanking the Lord for releasing Chatafundia from demons, we thought of what Jesus had told the disciples, "Do not rejoice that the spirits submit to you [in my name], but rejoice that your names are written in heaven" (Luke 10:20). This passage was being translated for the Sharanahuas in their language, and reading what Jesus said, they would be able to deal with demon possession themselves in Jesus' name. With that thought we were able to sleep peacefully.

Much later in our work with the Sharanahuas, Pablo, the son of our fellow translator Gerhart Fast, was out with us and had brought a generator for showing a film on the life of Christ. The Sharanahuas had never seen a movie before, and they thought they were actually seeing the real Jesus and his life while on earth. When it came to the crucifixion scene, many of them began to weep, thinking they were actually seeing our Savior crucified. I didn't have the vocabulary to explain that this was just acting, something that had never been a part of their culture. After watching their first-ever film, their chief and pastor, Gustavo, stood in front of them and said, "We heard how he suffered and died for us. We read how he suffered and died for us, but now we have seen it with our own eyes. How can we continue to sin against this one who loved us that much?"

Later, while Pablo was still there, a young Peruvian soldier, perhaps still a teenager, deserted from the military post at Esperanza. The Sharanahuas would never turn someone in to the authorities; rather, they took him in and gave him food and shelter. Basic training for servicemen in the States is difficult, but in Peru it was much harder at that time.

One day while this young soldier was there at Gasta Bala, the Sharanahuas came rushing to our house, saying he had gone crazy and had fallen down the bank to the river. Pablo and I rushed to where he lay and quickly got our army cot to get him up to the house where he was staying. He was foaming at the mouth and had a horrified look in his eyes. It seemed to both Pablo and me that this must be demon possession. We prayed for the young man and in the name of Jesus commanded the demons to come out of him. He relaxed, though completely spent, and we left him to rest.

Later he came to the house, and we had the joy of leading him to Christ. I said to him, "You have really been having a difficult time with demon activity in your life, haven't you?" He replied that he had. I asked him if he knew how it had happened that the demons were able to possess him.

He replied, "Yes, I know exactly how it happened. I was visiting my uncle in Pucallpa, and he asked me if I wanted power in my life. When I said I did, he said he was going to teach me how. He told me to invite Satan to be in control of my life, and I did. And that is why I have been having these attacks. I'm so glad that I have been delivered, and from now on I want Jesus to control my life."

Without any prompting from us or the Sharanahuas he went back to the military post to face whatever his punishment would be. Later when he was out of the army he came to visit us at Yarinacocha and told us how happy he was in the Lord and what a delight it was to him to have fellowship with other Christians at the church he was attending. What a joy it was to see this young man enjoying fellowship with the Lord and growing in his knowledge of the Word of God. Yes, there is power in the name of Jesus. All glory be to him!

—30—

THE STONE AXE PEOPLE

Sharanahuas had seen them, but they hadn't been close enough to try to communicate with them. Doubtless they had seen the Sharanahuas, perhaps before the Sharanahuas had seen them. They could have shot arrows at them but never had. They had shown no signs of hostility; rather, it seemed they were afraid to make contact with outsiders. Mestizos, too, had seen signs of these people far upstream on the Purus River. They had seen their crude shelters, just a few palm leaves thrown together. The sightings occurred during dry season when people hunted for turtle eggs, a favorite of many people in the area.

When I related the sightings to our administration and pilots told of spotting their shelters toward the headwaters of the Purus, it was decided in 1971 to survey and see if a contact could be made. It seemed likely that these people were part of the Pano language family. Because Sharanahua is in that family and geographically this indigenous group was closest to them, it was logical that I take part in the survey. And yet we couldn't know for sure that the tribe was part of the Pano language family without a contact. One thing for sure was that these, too, were people for whom Christ died, people who needed to hear the good news of the gospel that God loves them.

Since they had shown no signs of hostility, the administration considered the risk minimal in making a contact. Likely, unless we had some way of convincing them otherwise, they would run from us, as that's what they had done every time anyone had been close to them.

Pilot Ted Long, my next-door neighbor, was asked if he would accompany me. After praying, Ted readily agreed, and I was very pleased. Ted's walk with the Lord was obvious to everyone. Ted had a real burden to see people come to Christ, and he had a gift from the Lord in leading people to accept Christ as Savior. I couldn't have asked for a better companion than Ted for this survey, which would last for how long, we didn't know.

I went ahead to San Marcos, and arranged for two Kashinawas to make the trip up the Purus to try to locate these people. Because we didn't know what they wanted to be called, and because stone axes had been discovered in one of their baskets, we decided to call them the "Stone Axe People" until their real name was ascertained. The Kashinawas, Quirino and Jairo, provided the canoe with a *peke-peke* motor. The Peruvians called them peke-peke motors because they make a peke-peke sound. These Kashinawas were friendly, good-natured young men and proved to be pleasant traveling companions. My good friend Samuel, a Sharanahua, was also happy to go.

Ted arrived on June 14, 1971, bringing with him Abram, an Amarakairi. He was the only Christian tribesman to make the trip. Now the survey team was complete. It would mean six of us in the canoe, which was about 10 meters long. The equipment and six people were just about the limit for this canoe. Since we didn't have room in the canoe for more supplies, we were going to be dependent on getting game and fish while on the trip.

On the 18th Ted and I were up at 5:30, hoping to get an early start. Tribespeople always get up at the crack of dawn, so it would be no problem for them to be ready.

We traveled upstream until that evening and stopped for the night at the little stream Pintuyaco, a tributary of the Purus. Early the next morning we set up our antenna on a sandbar and called Yarinacocha. Our administrator had instructed us to call in at the close of every day to let them know that everything was alright and we were safe. It was a beautiful day. As the pilots say, it was CAVU (ceiling and visibility unlimited).

The crew is eager to start their arduous journey.

In the morning we arrived at the mouth of the Curanja River, the Sharanahua community where Marie and I had first begun our work back in 1958. We had a good visit with Chief Alfonso, Pablo, and several others. Pablo was the first Sharanahua to help me learn his language. We dispensed some medicine and treated Pablo's little baby. They wanted us to stay all night, but we thought we should keep going. When they heard we were trying to make contact with the Stone Axe People, whom they called Mashcos, they told us it was too dangerous. We thanked them for their concern but assured them that we would be careful, and since they had never been known to shoot at anyone, we didn't think there was any danger. Our God was our "Shield and Defender."

As we got underway again, the men spotted a wild turkey, and Ted shot it. That was part of our supper. Late in the afternoon we pulled up to a sandbar to spend the night. The mosquitoes were bad, and after killing several I slept quite well. When we woke up we saw the tracks of *capybaras* (the largest rodent in the world), which had come up almost to our beds.

Getting off early the next morning we soon spotted some big red howler monkeys across the river. Ted and I each got one. I had a .22 semi-automatic rifle, and Ted had a little larger one, a .30 caliber. Tribespeople eat monkeys, and we join them when we're with them. Then the men spotted a capybara a little ways upstream and told Ted to shoot it. Ted is a very good shot, and he got it, but when we got to it and Ted told them to put it into the canoe, they answered, "No. We don't eat them unless there is nothing else to eat." Ted was not a happy camper and told them not to tell him to shoot anything else unless they intended to eat it. It began to rain when we ran across a couple of Chandinahuas upstream who informed us that the Stone Axe People are 7 feet tall. Ted told them they had been misinformed. When we stopped for the night we were glad the rain had stopped too.

The next day was another hot one but beautiful. Ted shot two ducks that were side by side with one shot. That impressed the men as it did me. We arrived at the house of an Amahuaca early in the afternoon.

Later that afternoon we were soaked by a heavy rain shower. A lot of our stuff also got wet. The canoe was a muddy mess. We stopped where there were a few Amahuaca houses and dispensed medicine to them in exchange for yuca, bananas, and papaya. The Amahuacas also warned us that the Stone Axe People were dangerous. Again we felt they had decided this without knowing of any instances of hostility.

We were off the next morning early. That evening Samuel asked to hear the Word. I told him the story of how the disciples had fished all night and didn't catch anything. Then Jesus came to them and told them to cast their net on the right side of the boat, and they pulled in 153 large fish. Since fishing is a big part of the Sharanahuas' life, that was an exciting story to Samuel.

The next morning the fellows cleaned out and patched up the canoe. It was great to have a clean, dry canoe again. That day we saw several alligators and one small deer, but we were unable to get any of them. We finally shot a howler monkey, and that gave us our supper. We came to the house of one of the patrons (merchants), Alberto Gamboa, nephew of the mayor of Esperanza. He waded out into the middle of the river to invite us in for the night. As a very friendly gesture, he gave up his sleeping quarters to Ted and me. He related some valuable information on the Stone Axe People. He said he had spotted twelve of their *tambitos* (small palm-leaf shelters) at a tributary that flowed into the Cujar River where we were headed.

One week later on June 25, we arrived at a beautiful spot at the mouth of the Curiuja River and the headwaters of the Cujar River. The fellows gathered around while Ted told them the story of David and Goliath. I interpreted into Sharanahua. Hopefully, Abram, the Amarakairi, could understand some of Ted's Spanish. Ted and I were glad that we were able to have contact by radio that day with our families. Quirino, the Kashinawa who ran the motor, became sick, and I gave him an injection of penicillin.

On the 26th Samuel complained of an aching arm, Jairo had diarrhea, and Quirino had a sore throat and aching chest. With those fellows not well we decided to stay where we were for at least another day or until they were all better.

One of SIL's single women, Patsy Adams Liclan, who was working among the Culinas way downstream on the Purus River almost to the border of Brazil, had offered to stand by on her radio as long as we were in the territory of the Stone Axe People, which was reassuring to us. The respite for a day gave us the opportunity to get things dry again, wash clothes, and air the bedding. We had a radio contact with Director of Tribal Affairs Will Kindberg to bring him up to date on the trip thus far and our plans on how to proceed.

Samuel and I went hunting. He didn't want to go far as there were no trails there. Even indigenous people can get lost in the jungle if there is no trail. That night we praised the Lord for his goodness, for helping us get a pheasant-type bird, and for the fact that Quirino was getting better. As Psalm 68 says, he "daily loads us with benefits" (KJV). That night Ted told the fellows the flood story. We talked to them again about how we hoped to contact the Stone Axe People.

The next morning we waited for a heavy fog to lift, then another cloudless day, beautiful! As we continued on our way we encountered several Peruvians who had been up to a stream just ahead of us. They had seen the tracks and the palm-leaf shelters of the Stone Axe People. After we left them we shot one small alligator. Alligator tail is delicious, somewhat like chicken. We put the alligator in the canoe, thinking it was completely dead, but it wasn't, and it almost got Ted. The river was very narrow there, and it was almost dark before we could find a sandbar to sleep on.

The administrator was not too pleased that we had not called in earlier for our afternoon radio schedule, as our folks back at Yarinacocha, who were following our progress by radio, would be concerned if we didn't call in until late. He didn't realize that we were fortunate to call in at all, as we weren't able to find a sandbar before we called in. It was such a tiny sandbar that there was just barely enough room to get the antenna up to make the call. When we explained the situation, he understood why we couldn't call in sooner.

The next day when we came to a tributary, Ted, Abram, Samuel, and I started up this stream in the hopes of finding the tambitos. It was a beautiful stream, but we encountered no tambitos. I slipped off a log and fell into a pool up to my neck and both camera and gun went clear under. The camera was full of water, which wrecked the film. After a long walk through the stream, we got back to the main stream, the Cujar. About three miles farther up the Cujar we found some tambitos. We encountered my friend Olivio, a Peruvian patron, way up there. He gave us some helpful information and said that in the morning he would show us the other tambitos the Stone Axe People had left behind.

The next morning Ted, Abram, Samuel, Olivio, and his sons went to see the tambitos. I stayed to talk with Patsy on the radio. Thanking the Lord for Patsy's concern and encouragement, I closed up camp and got ready to leave. In the afternoon Ted got back with Abram and Samuel, having seen ten to twelve more tambitos upstream. Then we all left, arriving at the tambitos late afternoon. Needing something to go with the soup for supper, Ted went out and again popped two ducks with one shot. Unbelievable!

Passing through some swift rapids the next morning, we came to another tributary, which Ted, Abram, Samuel, and I started walking up. After about two hours my shoes wore out. We saw no new human tracks and just a few old ones on any exposed banks. As we walked along, with heavy brush on both sides of the stream, Ted and I realized if anyone wanted to shoot us, we would be sitting ducks. But we knew that we were in the Lord's hands, doing what we believed he wanted us to do, and so we weren't worried.

Rapids make river travel exciting.

We saw nothing and decided to start back to the main river. When we got to one of the bigger streams, we found a lot of rocks. Quite a contrast to where Marie and I had our house downstream on the Purus River where there were absolutely no rocks, only sand and dirt. The rocks were hard on my bare feet, and I couldn't go fast. Next Samuel led us across the side of a cliff where one slip would have been disastrous. We were relieved and thankful to the Lord when we got back to the main river where the other fellows were waiting for us. As usual we called on the radio to Yarinacocha to let them know we were all well.

We were now about two weeks into our journey. We walked upstream that day for five hours. I slipped in some rapids and went up to my chest in the water. Rain began to pour, and we were soaked, but I didn't mind. I couldn't have been any wetter anyway. I praised the Lord that my duffle bag didn't get too wet, and I had dry clothes and a sleeping bag. The sandbar we were sleeping on was right across the river from a good-sized tributary, and we decided to go up that one the next day.

Going up the tributary was difficult. We had to plunge through the jungle part of the way. Samuel was rather miffed that Ted and I had said that after we got to the Cujar River they couldn't use their shotguns anymore. The roar of a shotgun could scare off the people we were trying to contact, but the quieter sound of a .22 rifle could be mistaken for bamboo cracking, which was commonly heard there. And we needed the game to keep us going.

About one o'clock in the afternoon we stopped going upstream. I was having more and more trouble with my back and an ache in the groin. I had taken two Darvon pills for the pain before starting back, but it got progressively worse. Ted wanted to stop and spend the night where we were instead of going on back to the sandbar so that I wouldn't have to keep traveling. He said I looked like I had hepatitis. Tired and relieved to be back to our camp, I got into dry clothes and went straight to bed, feeling miserable all over. A toe had become infected, which was especially painful. We had walked nine hours in the tributary, sometimes wading up to our waists.

Thankfully, I felt a little better the next morning. It was the 4th of July, but we weren't thinking of "the rockets' red glare, the bombs bursting in air." I was just thinking and praying about getting over this sickness so the contact with the Stone Axe People wouldn't be hindered. I started on a course of an antibiotic, Terramycin. I read to Samuel and Jairo from the *Life of Christ* passages in Sharanahua. Sharanahua and Kashinawa both being in the Pano language family, I was hoping that Jairo, a Kashinawa, would also be able to understand most of it. It started to rain about noon and really poured for a couple of hours. In the afternoon I got on the radio and talked with Dr. Holston, then with Marie and the kids, and finally with our administrator, Will Kindberg. Will encouraged us to take it a little easier. We decided not to go up the tributaries so much anymore.

Early the next day we reported on the radio that we wouldn't be traveling that day. The river was beginning to rise. Ted and I talked things over concerning how we should proceed. The fellows moved their tambitos to higher ground about noon. The river continued to rise, and the rain was pouring down. The pains I had had on the 4th were much better. Later in the afternoon the river was only a meter from our beds and still rising. We tried to call Yarinacocha on the radio but couldn't get through.

Protected by a temporary roof, daily radio contact is essential.

Ted and I were awakened about 11:15 p.m. by Abram calling us. "Hurry! Get your things together. The water is coming in." Ted and I got packed in record time. We had no higher ground to go to. As soon as we finished getting our things into the canoe, the water completely covered where our beds had been. The other guys went higher into the jungle. We tied the canoe to some small trees, and Ted and I tried to sleep sitting in the canoe. We decided we had better move the canoe from under the trees lest it topple over as the river rose. When the river is high, it often uproots trees along the shore as it erodes the ground under them. We slept very little during the night. It was cold, and we couldn't find comfortable positions.

First thing in the morning we tried going upstream, but the current was too swift. We had to come back and set up camp on the other side of the river where the ground was higher. We knew that our Lord was watching over us and would help us to make the contact. Samuel and the two Kashinawas made camp by the river. Abram, Ted, and I went on up higher into the jungle. I called Yarinacocha and talked to Marie and was able to wish my son Steve a happy eleventh birthday. We had a supper of soup, rice, Sanka coffee, and one half of a chocolate bar.

There were lots of *izulas* around, which are large ants with a horrific sting. Even grown men have been known to shed tears when bitten. I praised the Lord that though I had to go barefoot since my shoes had worn out, I hadn't been bitten nor had any of the others. That night Ted and I heard some bird or animal that sounded just like someone sneezing. In fact Samuel yelled, "*Yoi yambawu*," which is what the Sharanahuas say when someone sneezes. It means, "Don't say it!" The sneeze could have come from a jaguar.

The next morning I packed up while Ted went down to the fellows' camp and had a radio contact. We were finally off and encountered lots of rapids, the second one very rough. Early that afternoon we arrived at a falls four or five feet high. We had to drag the canoe on dry ground around the falls. I spoke to the fellows that night to tell them how Jesus showed that he is the Son of God.

The next morning as we rolled out of bed, Ted's stomach was bothering him, and he also had diarrhea. I read James 5. Very encouraging! "Be patient and stand firm…. Don't grumble against one other, brothers…. We count as blessed those who have persevered. …. The Lord is full of compassion and mercy. … Is any among you in trouble? Let them pray. … Is anyone among you sick? Let them call the elders of the church to pray over them and anoint them with oil in the name of the Lord. And the prayer offered in faith will make the sick person well (8–15).

We didn't have the elders with us, but Ted and I were elder enough to pray for each other. We talked by radio to one of our nurses, Ruth McKennon. She recommended that I keep up with the Terramycin but to be sure to eat something with it.

It was a beautiful day with not a cloud in the sky, and the water level in the river was dropping slowly. We washed clothes and took a bath in a very cold river. Ted inventoried the amount of food we had on hand, which wasn't much. Abram chopped down a palm tree and got the heart of it. That's called *chonta*, and is very nourishing. We had a supper of rice, soup, and chonta, plus Jell-O for drink. It was a beautiful night with the moon out nearly full, shining through the trees and making a dazzling reflection on the river.

The fellows were aggravated that they were not able to shoot their shotguns, but Ted and I had to insist. It was hard for them to pass game and not shoot it. Game is so essential to their daily diet.

There was a gorgeous sunrise the next day, July 11. The fellows were getting antsy staying here, so Ted and I talked on the radio to

Will Kindberg, and he was very much in accord with our making a move that day. We pulled the canoe around a 4- or 5-foot falls. Around midday we came to some more rapids and had to get out of the canoe and pull it through. We stopped at a sandbar late in the afternoon and got the antenna up so Ted could call Yarinacocha to let them know we were safe. Abram caught a big fish called *sungaro.* That was our supper. After supper I read the story of Nicodemus to the fellows. Ted then told it in Spanish for Abram's benefit.

The next morning, another beautiful day, I woke up about 5:30 and read 1 Peter 4. Verse 10 stuck out: "Each of you should use whatever gift you have received to serve others, as faithful stewards of God's grace in its various forms." We wanted to serve the Stone Axe People. I thought, *Could this be the day we make contact?*

Passing by another tributary we came to the fifteenth rapid we had had to get through. Later in the afternoon we came to another falls. Quirino wasn't sure he wanted to go around this one, and Abram had hurt his knee on the last rapid. We were finally able to get the canoe past the falls. We were up to our chests in water part of the time. At one of the rapids we had to take a run at it four times before we made it. We finally found a good sandbar late in the afternoon, which served as our place for the night. I read the story of Zacchaeus to Samuel and Quirino that night.

The next morning while pushing the canoe, Ted fell up to his neck. This provided the fellows a good laugh. At noon we arrived at a very rough rapid, and for the first time we decided that we had gone far enough upstream and started our long journey back downstream. Just then Quirino spotted a very large footprint of a Stone Axe Person on a sandbar. We saw where he had hastily buried a turtle in the sand. We went up the tributary, following fresh footprints, and went by trail to another tributary and followed it until Abram wanted to turn back. We decided we would return to search the next day.

During the night I began to get chills and fever. Ted got on the radio and called Dr. Swanson in Lima, who thought it might still be from the infected foot and not from malaria as we had presumed. He said I should stay down until all the tenderness was gone. I had a terrific headache, and my eyes were hurting, much like episodes of malaria I had had in the past.

We had left a cooking pot as a gift at the place where we saw the footprint and the turtle. Ted and the fellows went to see if the gift had been taken. It had not, so they brought it back. They saw more evidences that the Stone Axe People were in the area as they found another tambito. In the late afternoon I had chills and fever again. Ted had given me two penicillin shots.

The next day, the 16th, I was feeling somewhat better when I awoke, but my head and eyes still hurt, and I was really bushed. I talked with Dr. Swanson on the radio, and he thought some residual infection got into the bloodstream. I wanted so badly to go with Ted and the fellows, but, of course, with doctor's orders and Ted urging me not to try it and with the way I felt, it was out of the question.

The fellows were gone all afternoon. When it got to be after five o'clock and they still weren't back, I got concerned. Patsy called on the radio to let me know she was standing by and would continue to be until the men got back. That was a consolation. When it got to be six o'clock and they weren't back, I began to wonder if they had been attacked. To my great relief they got back just before dark with exciting and yet disappointing news. They had seen the Stone Axe People.

Abram had seen that the water in one of the streams had recently been stirred up where the people had just started up a trail. The fellows started trailing them, following the scent of burning coals that the people were carrying in a turtle shell. Not know-ing that Ted and the fellows were following them, they stopped on a sandbar to rest. There was a growth of trees between them and where Ted and Abram were observing them. There were about fourteen of them—all naked.

Unfortunately, Ted had given the tape recorder and camera to Samuel to carry. Ted had no way of knowing that Samuel was afraid (I think he was remembering that big footprint and didn't want to get too close to them), so he wouldn't come up to where Ted and Abram were observing the people but stayed way back.

When Samuel didn't come up with the camera and tape recorder, Ted and Abram decided they needed to let the people know they were there and try to make a contact with them before they left. They stepped out onto the sandbar with their hands held out in front of them to show the people that they weren't armed. Just in case they spoke his language, Abram said to them in Amarakairi, "We come in peace. We want to be your friends." But they took one look at Ted and Abram and, screaming, fled, leaving behind their baskets of stone axes and wild boar tusks used as knives. In their haste to get away they even left behind their bows and arrows. It may have been that they had never seen a white, bald-headed man with glasses, and that terrified them. We will never know for sure what caused their panic.

Stone axes and wild boar tusks, the only tools these people had.

Scotty with bows and arrows left by the fleeing people.

The fellows came back with the artifacts, including some of their bows and arrows. But we later decided to take them back so that the Stone Axe People's first thoughts of us would not be that we were thieves. Ted took pictures of the artifacts, and then they returned them. Also they left a pot and a machete there for them as a gift, hoping and praying that it would help them realize that we wanted to do good to them and not harm.

To say that I was disappointed to not be in on this contact is an understatement. Had I been there with Ted and Abram while they observed the people, I think I would have been able to tell if they were speaking a Pano language. Also knowing Samuel as I did, I think I would have been able to tell that he was afraid. Knowing that, I would have had the tape recorder and camera with me, and we could have at least gotten their pictures and recorded their language. For some reason the Lord allowed me to get sick, and so we leave the disappointment with him.

Now that we had gotten this close to the people and they had fled, we knew that apart from a miracle, they would be staying as far away from us as possible. It was time to go back downstream, but we would keep looking on our way back.

On July 12 a Helio Courier was sent out to drop supplies to us. We had run out of just about everything, and the battery for the radio was very low. It was a beautiful day. The fellows were excited at the thought of an airplane dropping supplies. We were by then on a very small sandbar, downstream from where the contact had been made, the only sandbar we saw in the area. The pilot was George Woodward, with Tim Townsend, one of our MKs (missionary kids), who made the drops. They had taken the door in the back off to make it easier for Tim. George circled around the sandbar two or three times, leaned the plane over, and Tim made three perfect drops. Everything was intact. We had food and a battery again.

When we arrived back at the tributary where the contact had been made, Ted and I had prayer together and decided that the Lord would have us go up this tributary again to see if the people had taken the gifts we left. We thought it would be best to take only Abram with us this time. The other three fellows were happy with that arrangement. I carried another pot with clothes inside it to leave them some more gifts. Ted and Abram traded off carrying the knapsack. Abram took off at such a fast pace that Ted and I actually had to run for a little ways to keep up with him. We came across footprints left by the people. Then a little farther along we saw where they had made a cut with the machete we had left for a gift. We found a small sandbar and decided to stay there for the night. What a paradise! No gnats and no mosquitos. Abram cut down a palm tree to give us palm heart for supper. We slept under the stars with no mosquito net.

The next day Ted and I both felt the Lord would have us make this the last week of our survey. This 24th of July was our last hike up a tributary, hoping to make contact.

After a restful night I read 1 John 3 that morning. What a wonderful chapter. I felt I wanted to know more and more of our wonderful Savior, the Lord Jesus, and become more and more like him, to love as he loves. We informed the fellows that we would call the survey to a halt by the following Sunday and keep going downstream. They were all happy with that announcement. Also we told them that they could use their shotguns again, as we didn't expect the Stone Axe People to be nearby anymore. This was another welcome bit of news.

On July 27 we had a heavy rain. This rain sealed the decision not to go up any more of the tributaries as they would be swollen and make travel impossible. From now on it was to be full steam ahead downstream.

After 46 days on the river, on August 3 we arrived at our destination, San Marcos, to a wonderful reception. All the people came out to welcome us. It was the end of a very eventful journey.

Since we didn't make the contact with the Stone Axe People, was the trip worth it? Yes, we proved that there really were people living up there who were nomadic, people needing the Word of God, the good news. Leaving them gifts showed them that we wanted to help them, which would aid in any further contact. Was it disappointing not to have made the contact? Definitely! Yet we began that journey covered by prayer. We had asked for the Lord's leading, and we rested on that. (These people still have not been reached at the time of this writing in early 2018.)

—31—

COME UP HIGHER

It was time for a family vacation, now including Priscilla, who was born in 1971. We decided we would have a more relaxing time over the Christmas holidays if we got out of the heat of the jungle and went to Lima where it would be cooler. We could see a lot of our friends there that we hadn't seen for a while.

The one in charge of making reservations for flying from Pucallpa over the Andes to Lima told me the only flight available was with LANSA. I didn't like the idea of flying with that airline as they had previously had two accidents, one of them coming out of Cuzco with about 50 US students on board who were visiting Peru. They lost an engine, tried to turn back to Cuzco and crashed into the mountain killing almost all of the nearly one hundred people on board. Only one survived. One other accident had been in a Constellation plane. All on board perished. Though I didn't like the idea, it was the only way we could get to Lima if we wanted to be there during Christmas. So Marie and I, along with other Wycliffe folks, decided to go on December 20, 1971, trusting the Lord to get us there safely.

It was a beautiful flight in the Lockheed Electra. In the early stages of the Electra, one or two of them had come apart in the air in the US. They had all been called back to be modified structurally. Now they were considered to be one of the strongest and safest planes flying.

Once in Lima, our boys, David, 14, and Steven, 12, as well as Becky, 8, were glad to see their friends. Our three-month-old, Priscilla, was content to be anywhere, just so long as Mama was near.

On the 24th, just four days after we had arrived in Lima, five of our colleagues wanted to return to the jungle to be with their families for Christmas. The flight was to be on the same LANSA Lockheed Electra that we had taken from Pucallpa to Lima.

Nathan Lyon, son of pilot Floyd and his wife, Millie, was the same age as our David, 14 years old, and a good friend.

Harold Davis was on his way back to join his family. He and his wife, Pat, had been working in the jungle alongside Wayne and Betty Snell, translators to the Matsigenkas. Harold was bringing a little Amuesha boy with him.

David Erickson had just been out among the Sharanahuas and gone to Lima for a short time. He was returning to Yarinacocha for Christmas, to be with his sister Carol Daggett and family. After Christmas he was planning to return to the States and enter Moody Bible Institute to prepare for ministry in whatever avenue the Lord led him.

Roger and Margery Hedges had left their two little ones at Yarinacocha while they had gone to Lima to take care of paperwork to stay in the country. Roger had come to be the music director for our grade school and high school at Yarinacocha. It was their first year in Peru. Roger played the trumpet like the angel Gabriel, and he and Margery sang duets that thrilled us all.

I was asked to take them to the airport that morning. Nathan Lyon had traded flights with Pete Landerman so he could be back in Yarinacocha on the 24th for his dad's birthday. We found that the flight had been delayed because of some mechanical problem. When one of the five told me that, I said jokingly, "Better to take care of that here in Lima since there isn't much room on top of the Andes to work on it." I decided to stay at the airport for a while in case the flight was canceled and the folks would need a ride back to the Cudney Center.

While waiting I asked Harold Davis how he and the little Amuesha boy were doing. He replied he was fine but the boy was scared of flying. I remarked that he wouldn't have to be afraid very long as it was just an hour's flight. Finally, whatever the problem, it was taken care of, and the five boarded the LANSA flight 508.

When I got back to the center, I was told the LANSA flight never arrived in Pucallpa. I felt like someone had kicked me in the stomach. I didn't want to believe it. All of us hoped that the plane for some reason had taken another route and was delayed, though I'll have to admit that it didn't seem likely.

When we called our radio operator at Yarinacocha, he said they had one of the worst storms he had ever seen. The wind was so violent that it actually blew some of the aluminum sheets off of roofs. This information did nothing to alleviate our fears that the worst had happened. Then the rumors began to fly. Peruvians who lived miles apart were calling in, saying they had heard the plane at this location and others at that location, flying low over the jungle. None of the rumors produced any clue as to the where-abouts of the LANSA flight. (The company lost its operating permit a few weeks later.)

Though all of us were in a very somber mood, Mrs. Cudney reminded us that it was Christmas and for the sake of the children we must show them a happy time. After all, it was the celebration of the birth of our Savior. So we passed out gifts to our kids with a joy that at that moment we were not feeling. We reminded ourselves that if our loved ones had not survived a crash, they were spending the most wonderful Christmas ever right in the presence of our glorious Lord Jesus.

Word soon spread in Lima that the Instituto Lingüístico de Verano (Summer Institute of Linguistics) had a group home there and had access to radio contact in the jungle near Pucallpa. Right away newspaper reporters overwhelmed us, trying to find out if we had any news concerning the whereabouts of the LANSA flight. Our director in Lima, Jim Wroughton, kept busy going to the door to answer inquiries, saying we had no information.

Though our hearts were heavy, the work had to go on. Since I was on vacation, Jim asked me if I would answer the door, so that he could get back to the office and his work. Of course, I accepted the assignment.

On Monday, January 3, 1972, it was time for the flight back to Pucallpa and on out to Yarinacocha. This time I went to the Faucett office, the most noted airline in all of Peru, and was able to purchase tickets for all of our colleagues wanting to return to the jungle. I alone needed to stay in Lima to meet with the newspaper reporters who kept flocking to our door. There were three cars to take the sixteen children and four adults to the airport. Our Becky was afraid to fly since it was fresh in her mind that our friends were presumed to have perished in the flight. She thought she would never see her daddy again. It tore at my heart to see her so distressed. No doubt there were also other children who were anxious about flying and probably some of the adults, too.

I kept answering the door as reporters continued to seek information, which we didn't have. Peruvians are some of the most gracious and friendly people on the earth, and most of them were very understanding when I told them I was sorry, but we didn't have any news and that as soon as we did, if they hadn't already gotten the word, we would let them know. But one young reporter replied angrily, "You have a radio out there, and you must have some news, but you just don't want to tell us. Why don't you be cooperative and let us know the news you have?"

One of the Peruvian employees who worked at our group house heard him and answered, "If he tells you he doesn't have any news, he doesn't have any news. He is not like you. He tells the truth." End of inquiry.

Finally, on January 4, nine days after the LANSA plane disappeared, one lone survivor among ninety-one passengers and crew was found. Juliane Koepcke, a 17-year-old senior studying in a German school in Lima, had miraculously survived, having landed in the jungle still strapped to her seat.[6] Her father, a biologist working out of Pucallpa, had told her that if she ever got lost in the jungle to find a stream and follow it downstream and eventually she would come to a bigger river and people. This she did. She was flown to our center at Yarinacocha. Our colleagues were given strict orders by the Peruvian Army officer in charge of the search for the LANSA plane not to tell anyone she was there, so that she would not be bombarded with questions by reporters. She stayed in the home of Don and Jean Lindholm where she could have peace and quiet. They provided her with a German Bible to read.

Now that Juliane came out of the jungle, the search area for the LANSA aircraft could be greatly reduced. JAARS pilots aided in the search, and it was soon discovered. Parts of the plane were scattered over a wide area. Our pilots estimated by the size of the area that the plane must have come apart at about 10,000 feet. The search party saw the results of the decision to keep flying despite heavy turbulence. Since the plane had been discovered, there was no further reason for me to stay in Lima, and I returned to my family.

_____

6 See en.wikipedia.org/wiki/Juliane_Koepcke, and www.youtube.com/watch?v=rlJVIc-CPIl8.

Having discovered some parts of the plane, the search was on for the bodies of those who died in the crash. Because I had taken them to the airport and been the last to see them, I was asked to describe what they were wearing, as that would identify the bodies. I wanted so desperately to remember, but I realized how unobservant I am regarding clothing. The only thing I remembered was that Roger Hedges' trousers were bellbottoms, which was not common back then. Nathan Lyon and David Erickson were the first to be brought in. Eugene Loos, our Peru director, asked me to arrange the memorial service for everyone.

All our colleagues had been identified and brought in except Harold Davis. Marie and I knew this had to be very hard on his wife, Pat. We went over to her house that evening, asking the Lord to help us be of some comfort to her. Pat said, "I know that it doesn't make any difference to Harold now. He is with the Lord. But it would mean so much to our children and to me if Harold's body was also among the other four when we have the memorial service. He always would say, 'If something should happen to me, just bury me under one of the jungle trees.'"

On the 13th the Hedges' bodies had been identified. And the very next day Harold Davis and the Amuesha boy were found. We were all so glad for Pat and the children. Now all of our people had been identified and brought to our center, and it was time for the graveside service. Since Eugene had asked me to arrange the services, I had been asking the Lord who should bring us the message, especially for the relatives whose hearts would be heavy. In sharing my concern with Jim Smotherman, our Yarinacocha school principal, he said, "Scotty, have you thought of Russ Reinert, our personnel director? He has been a pastor in the States, and he has a compassionate heart." That rang a bell with me. Russ was blind physically, but oh how insightful he was in things of the heart.

The day of the funeral the Lord caused the rain to stop, and as we all stood together in that spot on our center where we were to bury our friends, who had so recently been alive and well and blessing us with the talents the Lord had given them, Russ ministered to all of us. I don't remember too much of what he said, although I do know it seemed to be just what the loved ones needed as well as the rest of us. One thing I do remember Russ saying was, "They belonged to the Lord, and he had the right to take them to be with him where we will all be someday."

The Sunday before they left us, for what was to be their last trip here on earth, Roger and Margery Hedges sang a duet in our auditorium at Yarinacocha. Neither they nor we realized how prophetic it was. They sang so beautifully "Heaven Came Down and Glory Filled My Soul." That's exactly what happened for all five of our precious friends December 24, 1971. The Lord said, "Come up higher. It's time to be closer to me and enjoy the glories of my home in heaven."

—32—

A TIME TO TRUST AND NOT BE AFRAID

In 1976 the leftist military government that was in power in Peru viewed with disfavor any entity with North American membership. The Peace Corps had already been ousted and then on March 15 our administration received word that our contract to work in literacy and translation among the indigenous language groups would not be renewed and that we must phase out by December 1976.

What a blow! There were so many language groups that still did not have any of God's Word in their own language, and some tribes hadn't even been entered yet. When the meeting was called at Yarinacocha to announce the decision, everyone was stunned. Tears flowed, immediately everyone in the auditorium went to prayer to our Almighty God, praying that he would give peace and allow us to get as much translation accomplished as possible before the deadline. Everyone rolled up their sleeves and devoted themselves to the task at hand.

At that time our family was on furlough in my hometown. On March 17 as we were having lunch, the phone rang. I answered it and was surprised and pleased to hear the voice of our dear friend in Peru pilot Floyd Lyon. I was shocked when he told me we had only until the end of the year to leave the country. The administration wanted me to come back to Peru as soon as possible to do as much as I could on the translation of the New Testament for the Sharanahuas. Then he said I was to come back alone without my family. That was an unexpected blow.

Getting off the phone, I interrupted the happy chatter at the table to give the news. Son Steve's sad question was, "What's going to happen to Sparky?" That was our beautiful, gentle German Shepherd dog, a favorite of everyone in Yarinacocha. We had given her to Steve for his birthday when she was just a pup. Of course, one's age makes a difference as to what is priority—he was 15 years old.

Now gears shifted in the extreme. All the things we had planned for the coming months came to a screeching halt. Marie made new plans to stay in the States with the children. For me, it was packing and making flight arrangements to return, but keeping some final speaking engagements. "Trust God from the bottom of your heart; don't try to figure out everything on your own. Listen for God's voice in everything you do, everywhere you go; he's the one who will keep you on track" (Prov. 3:5–6, The Message).

On April 2 I boarded the plane in Los Angeles for the flight to Lima and then over the Andes to Pucallpa and from there the 15 or 20 minutes over road to Yarinacocha.

Having arrived, I was told I would be staying in the Children's Home. Maybe they thought I was entering into my second childhood! Seriously, Al and Barb Shannon, dear friends of ours, had been staying in our home while we were on furlough. Someone had suggested that for me to stay in our own home would make me too lonesome for my family. So while it would have been a happy arrangement to stay in our own home with Al and Barb, I did enjoy kids a lot, so it was no disadvantage for me to be near them. Besides, our friends of many years Art and Dottie Jackson were at this juncture asked to be house parents. Art was in charge of the center maintenance, including mechanics and electrical work.

It was good to be able to share my heart with them and at the same time listen to their concerns and take all of these things to our compassionate God, knowing that our concerns are his concerns.

Right away I saw that Yarinacocha was one big beehive of activity. We had to take the government seriously when they said we had to leave the country by the end of the year. Some felt they couldn't wait until the last minute to make plans for the future. Therefore, some who were in non-translation positions took on other assignments away from Peru. Personal effects that would be difficult to take out of the country had to be disposed of in one way or another, such as household appliances and furniture. In order to cut down on the chaos of people in the vicinity constantly coming to our center to make purchases, our administration assigned Ray Parker to be in charge of sales at a designated time and place, and according to the price the owner placed on the merchandise. This kept more than one person busy all day. If we had allowed people to come anytime of the day or evening, this would have caused interruptions and cut down on our Scripture translation production, which had top priority.

Word soon got around to our Peruvian friends and others nearby that we were selling things in preparation to leave. Even those who were translators were selling some of their nonessentials. I wondered and prayed about what I should do. I didn't like the idea of selling our things without Marie there to help me make decisions about what we should keep or sell or give away. I asked my friend George Hart, who had done most of the consultant work on the Sharanahua translation, what he and Helen were doing about their things.

He replied, "We're not doing anything about our things. We don't have time. We're devoting all of our time and energy to do as much translation of the Scriptures as possible for the Chayahuitas. If in the process we lose all of our things, so be it." That sounded like the right plan to me, and so I did likewise, asking for a Sharanahua to come to Yarinacocha so that I could get right at the translation.

Nearly daily during this time, the leading newspapers in Peru were publishing articles that were maligning Instituto Lingüístico de Verano (ILV; Summer Institute of Linguistics). As God always does, he had the right man as our director at this time. It was Lambert Anderson's first year as director and what a time to step into those shoes! But for Lambert, the shoes fit perfectly, though I'm sure Lambert wouldn't have said so and didn't face this assignment in his own strength, but he was completely relying on the Lord and his wisdom. Lambert, with his wife, Doris, had made many friends in government circles, even while they continued the translation for the Ticuna people.

Lambert never answered the attacks against us in the papers but took it to the Lord in prayer. His demeanor had a calming effect on us all. He never "wrung his hands" in an attitude of worry but rather took seriously the apostle Paul's admonition in Philippians 4:6–7, "Do not be anxious about anything, but in every situation, by prayer and petition, with thanksgiving, present your requests to God. And the peace of God, which transcends all understanding, will guard your hearts and your minds in Christ Jesus."

We never ceased praying individually and collectively that our Almighty God, for whom nothing is impossible, would intervene and allow us, his children, to complete a Bible translation for every language group in Peru. Most of all, we prayed his will would be done and that we would be the testimony for Christ that we should be to our Peruvian neighbors and friends and to the Peruvian government.

The attacks against us in the newspapers intensified and continued almost daily. Let me quote from a report Lambert gave at our annual conference December 1976 well after the storm had calmed down:

On March 15, 1976, our administration received a 'reserved' official letter from the Minister of Education directing a transfer of all our work to the Peruvian State by January 2, 1977. After that, all the directors of the large newspapers were suddenly deposed and new directors were named. Then the assault on Wycliffe [SIL] in Peru began in earnest, and it was announced in the COMERCIO in the leading headline that we were leaving the country. And the Prime Minister of Peru signed a resolution that the transfer of our property and work to the State was to be carried out by January 2, 1977.

Then God stepped in. On April 26, 1976, three of the major newspapers carried a four-point declaration by sixty-six outstanding leaders of the military, academic, and professional worlds of Lima, proclaiming the positive contribution made by ILV over thirty years, and requesting that the government reconsider the official action previously taken. A week later sixty-seven more prominent backers signed their adherence to the previous declaration.

However, on June 3, 1976, some who were in opposition at San Marcos University published a declaration characterizing the 133 backers who signed in favor of ILV as being "a group of bureaucrats, intellectuals, and military personnel that put themselves at the service of a North American institution that was repeatedly questioned because of its imperialistic penetration.

One of the original signers, General Jorge Barbosa Falconí, was indignant with the declaration from San Marcos and published an extensive letter declaring his indignation at having his service to his country called into question, and he also came to the defense of ILV. He called the San Marcos group to task for insulting the distinguished members of the military and intellectuals who had signed the letter defending us. That letter, it now appears, marked the end of the major attacks against ILV. I like to think of the letter from General Barbosa as the answer that brought praise to the Lord as well as defending us.

Again, quoting from Lambert Anderson's report to us at the December 1976 Peru branch conference, he started off by quoting some appropriate Scripture:

> But because the Lord was overseeing the entire situation, our enemies did not force us to stop building (translating), but let us continue.... Ezra 8:23 reads "So we fasted and begged God to take care of us. And He did" (TLB). As far as I'm concerned, no matter what we had done or not done over the previous years, I don't believe it would have been possible (save for divine intervention) to spare us from attack. The simple fact is that a political group selected us as a target—not because of mistakes we've made, but because of who we are—and zeroed in their sights with every intention of removing us from the country.

Then, following a change in government on July 15, 1976, the Prime Minister who signed the resolution to terminate our work was removed from office. The government that had wanted our work terminated by the end of 1976 was ousted, and the new government allowed elections again in Peru. Today nearly all of the language groups of Peru, including the Quechua people of the highlands, have the New Testament in their own language. A few remain to be translated and the Peruvian government has allowed SIL to continue to work in Peru to this day.

In closing this chapter, I'd like to quote once more from Lambert's report:

I firmly believe that God intervened and performed a miracle on our behalf.... God has been good to us all as He has taken us through the fire to the point where we're beginning to see the other side. Two years ago, Jerry Elder admonished us in his report, "Trust in the Lord with all your heart; and lean not unto your own understanding. In all your ways acknowledge Him and He shall direct your paths" (Prov. 3:5–6 KJV [sic]). I believe that as we follow that counsel, God is somehow (I don't know yet in what manner or fashion) going to allow us to see the completion of the task He has committed to us—that of giving His Word to the tribal groups of this great land we have all come to love as our very own. God bless you!

And he has.

—33—

WHOOPING COUGH EPIDEMIC

In 1977 Marie and I were out with the Sharanahuas when an epidemic of whooping cough broke out. We had vaccinated most of them against whooping cough, but while we were back in the States for a year or two, the babies born during that time hadn't been vaccinated. All those little ones came down with it. The parents, not realizing that it would bring on pneumonia, would take their babies down to the river and put them in the water to bring down the fever. Then, from getting cold, the child would come down with pneumonia on top of whooping cough. Their little bodies couldn't take that much sickness, and they would die. In one month's time, no matter how much we fervently prayed or what we did to try to cure them, fifteen sweet little Sharanahua babies died.

Lord, please spare this one.

Late one afternoon two of the young men who were there helping to build an airstrip went with me to bring down the fever and pray for a little Sharanahua baby. Frank Hamilton was a premed student from Georgia, and Brian Doswald was from Clovis, California. Just before coming out to help us, Frank had accepted Christ through the ministry of our doctor's wife, Lois Dodds, at Yarinacocha. After we had brought the fever down and prayed, Frank said, "I have faith to believe the Lord is going to heal this one." I have to confess that, though I had not the slightest doubt that the Lord was well able to heal, I couldn't say I knew for sure he would. We had seen so many others die for whom we had prayed.

That night I heard wailing coming from the house where the little girl lived, and I knew she had died. I felt absolutely dejected and perhaps rejected too. That night I talked to God in a way I had never done before. I said something like, "Lord, don't you see us down here in the jungle? Why didn't you answer prayer and heal that little baby and show your power to the Sharanahuas and to that babe in Christ, the premed student?"

As I talked to God, he brought to my mind the story of Job, who suffered immensely as God allowed Satan to test him. Job's conclusion was, "Shall we accept good from God and not trouble?" And he did not sin in what he said. Later Job said, "Though he slay me, yet will I trust in him" (KJV, 13:15).

When I thought about all that had happened to Job, which he didn't understand, but he still trusted in the Lord and praised him, I said, "Lord, I don't know why you didn't heal that little Sharanahua baby. Either you're good or you're not good at all. I *know* that you are good, and so I trust you even though I don't like what happened, and I don't understand."

Sometimes we don't know why things happen like they do. Jesus knows what it is to suffer, and he can help us and sympathize with us when *we* suffer. When we get to heaven, then we will know. And God tells us in the Bible that when we get to heaven he will wipe away every tear from our eyes. There will be no more death or sadness or crying or pain for all the bad things that happened here on earth will be gone never to happen again.

Frank's reaction to the outcome was: "I don't know if I can ever believe God again." I understood how he could feel that way as a new believer. He would learn, as I had.

When all those fifteen little babies died, most of the Sharanahuas didn't know the Lord Jesus as their Savior yet, so they suffered terribly at the loss of their children, more than those who know Christ and know they will see their little child again.

The epidemic had subsided, and Marie and I were getting ready to return to our center at Yarinacocha, a 2½-hour flight from the Sharanahua community. We asked Vicente to come with us to help with the translation. As we prepared to leave, Vicente's 2-year-old daughter, Patricia, came down with whooping cough. We thought, *We're going to our center where there is a clinic with doctors and nurses. Maybe there was something more that we could have done to save those babies, and the doctor and nurses will know what to do to save this little one.*

Vicente, his wife, and little Patricia stayed in the backroom of our house. After we had been there a few days, in the middle of the night Vicente called me, "*Ochi!* (Big brother!) Come quick! My baby is dying just like the other ones did."

Even though it was about two o'clock, I called our doctor, Larry Dodds, and he said, "Scotty, we have done everything that can be done medically for that little baby. Only a miracle from the Lord could save her."

I immediately called two couples who had come to Yarinacocha as short-term assistants, Jack and Phyllis Milligan and Les and Lois Erickson. They came right over, and the six of us knelt by the hammock where the mother was holding the baby. We laid our hands on little Patricia and prayed earnestly for her healing. The Lord heard our prayers. It wasn't an instantaneous healing, but almost immediately her breathing got better, and the Lord brought her through whooping cough, a collapsed lung, and pneumonia.

When she was well, as you can imagine, her parents were beside themselves with joy. Vicente said, "I can hardly wait to get back to my people and tell them, 'Our shaman couldn't heal our little Patricia. Your doctor couldn't heal our little girl, but Jesus healed her.'"

We thought of the verse in Isaiah 42:8 where God says, "I will not yield my glory to another." Jesus didn't have to share his glory with the shaman or our doctor. He got all the glory, and he wonderfully healed little Patricia. The other little Sharanahua babies he took to himself to care for them in heaven, and the Sharanahuas heard from Vicente the wonderful power of the Lord Jesus to heal.

—34—

CAN THE LORD USE TERMITES TO SAVE LIVES?

What we so appreciated about our JAARS pilots was their willingness to help in any way they could. Butch Barkman, who later became president of JAARS in Waxhaw, North Carolina, was one of the pilots who personified that servant heart. He was scheduled to go out to the Purus River to service the translators working with the Culina. The Culinas lived just about 15 minutes by air downstream from the Sharanahuas. We were in Yarinacocha at the time, and I asked Butch if on his way to the Culinas he could stop at San Marcos. We had seen a termite nest beginning to form on one of the main poles in our tribal home. We didn't have anything at the time to kill termites. Butch readily agreed to take out a small amount of arsenic to put in the nest. The termites that hadn't eaten the arsenic would eat the dead ones who had until they all died. We were always very careful to keep the arsenic sealed and marked plainly and in a place where Sharanahuas—both children and adults—could not get to it.

When Butch landed at the airstrip in San Marcos, he was surprised that there was only one Sharanahua there to greet him. The arrival of an airplane in their community was infrequent, and everybody would always line up along the airstrip to greet the pilot and whomever might be with him. Butch asked Samuel, "Where is everybody?"

Samuel replied, "Everyone is sick." As Butch went to the houses, he found everyone under their mosquito nets. Butch got on the plane radio and called us, explaining that he had found everyone sick. A very powerful strain of flu had struck the community. In fact, it wasn't confined to San Marcos, as the seat of government at Esperanza was also struck with this flu. Other communities were also afflicted. Four Sharanahuas had died in San Marcos. Butch asked us if we had medicines there that he could give to the people. We had given him the keys to our 50-gallon drums, which we used for storage, and told him where he could find some medicine in them. The medicine wouldn't take care of the epidemic entirely, but it would help. Butch then went down to the Culinas and got more medicine from the translators there and brought it back to San Marcos.

When he got back to our center he passed on the information about the flu epidemic and soon the Peruvian army asked JAARS for a flight out to the Purus for one of their doctors to treat the sick.

The doctor, a major in the Peruvian army, arrived at our center with two or three other army officials. The doctor was going to stop in San Marcos on his way to Esperanza. I wanted to go out also to treat the Sharanahuas. Our flight coordinator Kenny Jackson asked one of the army officers if I could go out on the flight to help. He said that wouldn't be possible because the plane would be full. After the officer had said that, Kenny noticed that they were putting cases of whiskey on the plane to take out to the soldiers at Esperanza. Kenny reported this to the pilot, Tom Brewington.

Tom said, "I've never flown liquor on any of my flights, and I'm not starting now." And he ordered the whiskey taken off. Then Kenny went to the doctor, who outranked the officer.

Kenny said, "Doctor, Don Eugenio is the linguist for the Sharanahuas where you will be stopping first. Some of the Sharanahuas don't speak much Spanish, and he could translate for you." The doctor said, "Oh, by all means, he must go." So for the first time in my life I replaced a case of whiskey.

As I went with the doctor from house to house as he gave medicine, he told me what should be given to them and how to proceed. I was so glad that the Lord had made it possible for me to go. I wondered if some of the Sharanahuas were going to make it. I felt if I didn't stay to dispense the medicine daily that more would die. I hadn't come prepared to stay but to return on the same flight. I don't think there would have been room for any more baggage on the outgoing flight, anyway. When I told Tom I wanted to stay, he loaned me an extra pair of pants and a shirt he had brought along. Tom was slim, and his clothes were pretty tight on me, but by the time I left the Sharanahuas I had lost so much weight that they fit just fine.

With a radio there I could be in communication with our center. I was making daily rounds to the houses to dispense the medicine the doctor had prescribed. Two of the very sick ones were the old albino Tomas and his wife. Tomas was one person who had resisted the translated Word. He had said, "Those are dangerous words."

As I treated him and his wife I asked them, "Wouldn't you like to know that if you should die, you would go to a place where you would forever be safe and never be sick again? Jesus loves you and died for you to give you forgiveness of sins and eternal life with him." This time both of them said they wanted to accept Jesus as their Savior. They prayed, confessing their sin and asking Jesus into their lives.

One of the Sharanahuas that I was most concerned about was the chief, Andres, Gustavo's father. He was very sick and couldn't seem to eat anything. I wanted to feed him something to give him strength, so I made him a chocolate drink every day. Gustavo had been with me at Yarinacocha, working on the translation. There had not been room for Gustavo on the plane, so I reported to him every day how his father was doing. I thought after a few days that he was going to make it, so when I talked to Gustavo I told him he was doing better.

I had just gotten off the radio with him when one of the Sharanahua boys came running to me saying that Andres was dying. I thought, *Oh, no! How can I tell Gustavo that, when I just got done telling him his father was better?* I ran to Andres' house, praying on the way that the Lord wouldn't let him die. His mosquito net was full of wailing women. I got inside the net where he was lying in his hammock. I said, "*Ushto* ("Little brother"; he called me *Ochi*, "Big brother"), can you hear me?

"Yes, I can hear you, but they are taking me into the fire."

I said, "Ushto, you don't have to go with them. Jesus is stronger than they are, and he will keep them away from you. Just call on him and he will hear and answer you." He smiled and called on Jesus and was delivered. He didn't die and continued to get better.

The next morning or soon after that, I woke up aching all over, and my eyes hurt. One of the people who had had the flu came over, and I asked him, "How did you feel when you got the flu?" I didn't tell him how I felt.

He said, "Oh, you wake up and you hurt all over and your eyes hurt."

I prayed and said, "Lord, if I get sick, who's going to take care of all these others? Please show your mighty power and in Jesus' name heal me of this sickness." By the end of the day I was feeling fine. The Lord had mercy not only on me, but on all those I was treating.

Soon all the patients were getting better and I was able to leave them, knowing they were all going to make it. No more died after the four who had died before I got there. I hate to think what might have happened if Butch had not stopped to kill those termites and then told us the Sharanahuas were all sick from the flu. Praise the Lord that he knew Butch needed to stop at San Marcos and then arranged for me to go out on the doctor's flight. Praise the Lord for his mercy and compassion.

—35—

A WARNING BECOMES
AN OPPORTUNITY

"*Coca!*" ("Uncle!") The urgent call rang out about 3:00 in the morning as Marie and I lay sleeping in our thatched-roof home in San Marcos. Rushing outside I saw Conshico standing by the door with his face horribly beaten. With deep concern I asked him what had happened. He said, "My son Carlos did this to me, and I want you to get on your radio and call the police downstream and tell them to come and arrest my son."

As I mentioned earlier, turning one's fellow tribesman in to nonindigenous authorities was unheard of among the Sharanahuas, especially a member of your own family. As I got Conshico into the house and onto a cot, I told him that our radio didn't reach the authorities downstream, but if he would tell me what he wanted to say to the authorities, I would write the letter for him and see that it got sent to the police the next morning. Carlos was known for his violent temper, and when drunk he was especially dangerous. He was what we would call a juvenile delinquent.

Early the next morning we fed Conshico some Jell-O, as he was so beat up he couldn't chew anything solid. Then, as he dictated to me, I wrote the letter for him and sent his denunciation of his son. Conshico stayed with us until he was better and then returned to his village at the mouth of the Curanja River.

The following Sunday, as was our custom, Marie and I were making the rounds visiting Sharanahua homes. In nearly every home people solemnly warned us that because we had sent the letter for Conshico, the family of Carlos were blaming me for turning Carlos in and were coming to kill me. Rumors were rife on the Purus River, and we took this to be another one of them. We told the Sharanahuas not to worry about us, that we belonged to the Lord Jesus, and he was taking care of us, so we weren't worried.

That evening a boatload of four or five Sharanahua men from Carlos' village, whom we knew, arrived and came to our house. One of them was his cousin Ruani. In Sharanahua culture, often the person offended didn't personally take revenge, but one of his relatives would. As unlikely as it seems, both Marie and I had forgotten the warnings given us that day. The river was high and rising, and it was unusual for Sharanahuas to travel in these conditions unless it was an emergency. Canoes had been known to turn over in the swift current, and lives had been lost.

As the Sharanahuas sat down on our porch with their shotguns and spears, Marie brought them food to eat, and we chatted with them. I told them that since the river was high and it was getting dark, they should stay all night and continue their trip the next morning. They said, no, they would continue on downstream that night.

Then one of them asked a highly unusual question: where did we sleep. We hadn't lived there very long, so they knew little about us. At that time for the most part the Sharanahuas didn't have any walls in their homes, so they didn't have bedrooms. Their only privacy was their mosquito nets. But again, surprisingly, I didn't think anything of it and told them where our bedroom was. They finished their meal, and though I urged them again not to continue their trip that night, they declined and left the house in the dark.

When I came back into the house Marie said, "Are you thinking what I'm thinking?"

I replied, "I wasn't, but now I am."

Both of us recalled the warnings given us that afternoon and the fact that these were Carlos' relatives and from his village. The walls in our home were made of slats with plenty of cracks between them. Our little daughter Becky, about 2 years old then, slept in the crib made for her in the room next to ours. As I thought of the warnings and the question about where our bedroom was, a sudden, unreasonable fear struck me, a near panic attack. It wasn't fear for myself, but if they shot through the walls where our bed was, what would happen to our little girl?

I got out my Bible, and Marie and I read together David's words in Psalm 56: "When I am afraid, I put my trust in you. In God, whose word I praise—in God I trust and am not afraid. What can mere mortals do to me? … For you have delivered me from death and my feet from stumbling, that I may walk before God in the light of life" (vv. 3–4, 13). With these reassuring verses Marie and I went to sleep.

Nothing happened, and we will never know what the intentions of the men were and why they traveled in high water. One thing we do know, the Lord was giving us assurance and comfort from his Word and protecting us. He wanted the Sharanahuas to have his Word in their language.

—36—

BLESSED ARE THE PEACEMAKERS

As we lived among the Sharanahuas, helping them in any way we could—medically, repairing things for them, teaching them, and asking the Lord to show the love of Christ to them through us— they more and more looked to us to help them when problems arose. One role I never wanted among them was policeman. A peacemaker, yes; a policeman, no! It seemed a fine line between the two.

I remember one day when Carlos in one of his drunken outbursts had beaten the old albino Tomas severely, I was called to the scene, which was still tense. When I arrived, having prayed on the way, Tomas had a piece of cable in his hand and would have used it had Carlos come at him again. Besides Carlos, several of the men had been drinking.

I said calmly, "Look what strong drink has done! Why don't you take all this strong drink and throw it in the river, then you wouldn't have so many people getting angry and hurt."

A Spanish speaker who didn't understand Sharanahua said to me, "Why don't you raise your voice and bawl them out for what they're doing?"

My mission wasn't to raise my voice and bawl them out because they were doing something I didn't approve of. My mission was to be controlled by the Spirit of God and to translate the Word for them. Until they had the written Word in their own language, our job would be to let them see Christ, the Word, in us.

On another occasion, a young woman came running to our house and yelling, "Come quick! Carlos has attacked my partner with a knife." She was one of two women, 18 or 19 years old, from the Catholic mission, teaching the Sharanahua children Spanish at the other end of the community.

One of our mechanics, Kenny Gammon, was visiting us at the time. So Kenny and I ran as fast as we could. When we arrived Carlos was still there, and the young teacher had a spot of blood on her white blouse.

I had never used such strong words to any of the Sharanahuas before, but this time I said to Carlos, "You leave her alone. Go home and don't you ever do this again!"

He said he hadn't used a knife but had poked her with his fingernail during an argument. In this instance, I chose to believe the teacher that it was a knife, but I didn't think he meant for the knife to penetrate very deeply. I think if I had been in the habit of yelling at people, Carlos probably wouldn't have listened to me, but he did listen and went home. He never attacked with his knife again.

The Catholic priest said to me, "As long as you are here, I don't worry about the young teachers."

Another time Marie and I had just gone to bed when one of the Sharanahua men ran to our house and shouted outside our bedroom walls, "Come quick! They're hurting each other." I hurriedly jumped into my clothes and followed him. Perhaps twenty Sharanahua men there had been drinking, evidenced by a broken whiskey bottle on the ground. They had one teenager,

Ichupaya, by the hair, who was covered with blood. I'm not particularly brave, and I don't have a wish to step into someone else's fight and get hurt myself, but I had been called, and I thought I could do something to prevent any further bloodshed. The Sharanahuas had never come even close to threatening me.

I stepped between Ichupaya and those who had ahold of him. Then I took Ichupaya by the arm and said, "Let's go home and get you patched up." He went willingly, and those who had grabbed him didn't stop me from taking him away. I took him to our house, and Marie came out to bandage him.

His father came, too, and said to Ichupaya, "I told you not to go over there, and you wouldn't listen to me. Now look what's happened to you. Go home to bed and don't go back there again!"

After Marie had finished patching him up, I reiterated what the father had said and urged him to go home to bed and not go back again, telling him it was dangerous.

I had just gotten back in bed when the silence of the night was broken by the roar of a shotgun. As I leaped into my clothes again, I thought, *Oh no! What am I going to find this time? Help, Lord!*

On that beautiful moonlight night, as I ran down the path toward the sound of the shotgun, I saw Ichupaya standing there with a shotgun in his hand. I yelled, "It's me! Don't shoot!" He took off running, and I went to the house where Sharanahuas were gathered. Boiling with rage they said Ichupaya had fired into the house, and one piece of the buckshot had hit one of the men on the ear. Miraculously, no one else was hurt, and the ear injury was superficial.

I thought, *I praise you, Lord, that this skirmish didn't result in serious injury or death.*

They all swore what they were going to do when they got ahold of Ichupaya, but he had escaped, got into a canoe, and went downstream to another community. As I remember, it was two or three months before he came back. By that time tempers had cooled down, and nothing was done to him.

Years later Ichupaya would attend nearly every meeting, listening to the Word in his native Sharanahua, singing the Sharanahua hymns, and living in peace with his family.

—37—

AN UNUSUAL HOLIDAY
IN SAN MARCOS

Dia de San Juan (The Day of Saint John) is an important holiday on the Peruvian calendar, June 24. The Sharanahuas had often used this day to get drunk, as they had seen other Peruvians doing. Marie and I decided after prayer that we would introduce a functional substitute to our Sharanahua friends of San Marcos. Instead of the usual liquor, Marie prepared enough Kool-Aid to serve everyone in the community.

Then we introduced new games to add to their own. The Sharanahuas love games. They joyfully entered into three-legged races, human wheelbarrow, and one of their favorites, a tug-of-war. This is one game we had not introduced. They had their own rules, or lack of rules. It was always the men and boys against the women and girls. Accompanied by much laughter, everyone knew that the women never lost. They would drive a stake into the ground and tie their end of the rope around the stake, making it nearly impossible for the men to budge it.

The first time I joined the Sharanahua men in the tug-of-war, I didn't know what was coming. To make sure that they won, the women would get a dried palm leaf, set it on fire, and one of them would rush toward the men with the burning leaf, so the men would either let go or be burned. I probably let go faster than some of them. That was the end of the tug-of-war, and as always the women won. After the women were declared the winners, both men and women would dissolve into gales of laughter.

Everyone was enjoying the day. There was lots of laughter, lots of competition, and a beautiful day for the games. Boys, girls, and teenagers were entering in with enthusiasm. The older ones on the sideline were getting a kick out of the activities. It was a fun-filled time.

Then Carlos arrived from his village upstream. Of course, he brought with him his liquor to share with the Sharanahuas of San Marcos. One of the older Sharanahua men, Shico Lopez, called me aside and said, "Won't you talk to Carlos? If people start drinking, soon there will be a fight, and all the good feelings of today will give way to anger, and people will get injured."

Praying that the Lord would give me the right words and that Carlos would sense the concern, I went to him. I told him that I was glad to see him and that he could see the people were having a good time, but if he got them to drinking, soon there would be a fight and all the good feelings would end. Instead there would be injuries and hard feelings. I told him I liked to see him and the people liked to see him, but not bringing in liquor. I suggested that he come back again when he wasn't bringing strong drink.

In reply, he said, "I don't need you. I don't need God." With that he held up his bottle of whiskey and said, "This is my god!" And he stomped off.

I was amazed that he left because I was afraid he would want a confrontation. Not wanting him to think I had ill feelings toward him, I went down to the bank of the river to see him off. Again he said to me, "I don't need you!"

I answered, "I need you, and I hope you will come back again soon."

He got into his canoe, took his shotgun, and did something unheard of among the Sharanahuas, something men never did unless they were going to shoot. He pushed a shotgun shell into the chamber and cocked it. As he did, he said with emphasis, "*Don Eugenio Scott!*"

My sons, Dave and Steve, who were with me, because of Carlos' violent reputation and thinking he meant to shoot me said, "Get down, Dad!"

It wasn't because I'm so brave, and I didn't have a death wish, but I thought he was only bluffing with no thought of really shooting. Also I thought that if the Sharanahuas saw me running from Carlos, what would they think of my God whom I had said would protect me? Just as I thought, Carlos put down his gun without firing a shot. The Sharanahuas of San Marcos continued their festivities and the peaceful, enjoyable holiday resumed.

Later the Lord gave me the opportunity to show love to Carlos and his wife. I was in the hospital in Pucallpa, visiting a Sharanahua. I didn't know that Carlos had come in with his wife, who needed an operation. As I was walking down the hall to leave, I saw two of the hospital staff coming toward me, wheeling a young woman on a gurney. As I looked I recognized that it was Carlos' wife. She had never been away from the Purus River where she had always lived. I could tell she was afraid, and as I greeted her, she told me she was afraid. I asked her if she would like me to pray for her. She said she wanted me to do that. Those wheeling her to the operating room stopped while I prayed for her and assured her that everything was going to be all right.

As they took her into the operating room, Carlos came up. We greeted each other. I asked him where he would stay while in Pucallpa. He replied that he didn't know. I said, "Why don't you come on out to Yarinacocha and stay in the house that is right behind my house." He replied that he would like to do that. So he came, and later when his wife was able to leave the hospital, he brought her there too. It gave Marie and me an opportunity to minister to them and share the Word with them.

The next time I went out to the Purus area, though I hadn't asked him to do it, Carlos met me with his canoe and motor to take me wherever I needed to go. Love is the answer in every situation. Carlos and I remain good friends.

—38—

TIME TO CHECK THE BILINGUAL SCHOOLS

In 1981 we were living at San Marcos, the Sharanahua community farthest downstream on the Purus River. The bilingual school at San Marcos was going well, but Marie and I wanted to check on the two Sharanahua communities upstream: Santa Margarita and Gasta Bala.

Two of the young Sharanahua men, Yambarutundi (Yamba for short) and Iscofo (Isco for short), were going to take us. The day started off sunny and looked like a perfect day for the trip. As we took our things down to put in the canoe, I was concerned that it wasn't bigger than it was; both sides of the canoe tapered down a bit, not leaving much freeboard. I asked Sebastian, the bilingual school teacher at San Marcos, who was standing on the bank to

The government built schools in each Sharanahua community.

215

see us off, if he thought this was a safe canoe for us to make the trip. He assured me it was. Not wanting to second-guess those who had grown up with experience in a canoe since childhood, I accepted his judgment, though I must admit, it was with trepidation.

We four started happily on our way, all of us singing Sharanahua hymns and enjoying looking at different attractions along the edge of the river, including bright-colored macaws, some with red and blue feathers, others with bright yellow and blue. Once in a while we would see spider monkeys or an occasional howler monkey in the high limbs of the trees. Upon our approach, the alligators sunning themselves in the sand would slither off into the water. On a large branch hanging out over the edge of the river, there might be as many as five or six turtles lined up also enjoying the sun. They, too, would slide into the river at the sound of our canoe.

Isco was at the bow and Yamba at the stern, poling the canoe. We noticed that every time the fellows poled, water came over the side of the canoe, so Marie and I were kept busy, she using a teacup and I a tin can to bail out the canoe. Things were going well until late in the afternoon of the first day.

As the sun was beginning to go down, suddenly Isco yelled, "Yamba, were sinking!" Quick as a flash both young fellows jumped out of the canoe to give it less weight. I started to jump out also, but both of them yelled, "No! Stay in the canoe!" No doubt they figured I wouldn't jump out as spryly as they did, not having grown up doing it as they had. They probably thought that if I jumped out I might capsize the canoe, and they were probably right.

This situation called for something bigger than a tin can, so Marie reluctantly dumped the peanuts out of a bucket, and we started bailing like mad. With the weight of the fellows out of the canoe and our bailing, the canoe quit sinking. We were able to bring the canoe up to a sandbar and unload the canoe to sleep under the stars. I hesitate to think what would have happened had the canoe sunk with all of our sleeping gear and clothes in it. Praise the Lord, it didn't happen. As it was, we had to sleep with damp blankets.

The next morning Isco was not feeling well and was running a low-grade fever. We stayed at the community of Santa Margarita the next day, which gave him a chance to rest and get over his sickness. Marie and I were pleased as we observed the bilingual teacher Jorge teaching the children. We could see they were learning, and Jorge was teaching with skill and patience.

As the Sharanahua men there at Santa Margarita saw our canoe and heard how we had almost sunk, they said we needed a bigger, better-built canoe to make the rest of the trip upstream and for the return trip downstream. Marie and I could say a hearty "Amen!" to that. A bigger canoe was loaned. There was no more bailing and lots more room. It made for a more comfortable and safer river trip. The day layover in Santa Margarita gave our bedding a chance to dry out too.

The next day, as we headed upstream to check out the bilingual school in the last Sharanahua community, we were approaching a couple of houses up high on a ridge. We heard Pablo, the first Sharanahua I ever worked with to learn their language, calling out to us. We tied up the canoe and started up the steep incline to the houses. He was calling out to us that his little boy had been bitten on the face by a dog. Pablo had his shotgun ready to kill the dog if he could catch it. We cleaned the wound and gave him an antibiotic shot to stave off rabies in case the dog was rabid. Rabies shots would have been better, but antibiotics can help if rabies vaccine is not available. Fortunately, the dog had not torn the face, so sutures were not needed. The wife prepared a chicken so we got a good meal before continuing on upstream to Gasta Bala. On the way back downstream we could check on the little boy to make sure no infection had set in.

Again, we found the Sharanahua bilingual teacher Imbiomba doing a good job and with nearly a hundred percent of the children in attendance. They were learning. We were pleased with the progress we saw in all three communities.

The children were eager to learn.

On the way back downstream, Yamba got sick and was suffering from diarrhea. We pulled up to the edge of the river while Yamba crashed back into the jungle. While we were waiting for him to return, we heard a lot of noise across the river. Looking over there, we saw a whole herd of wild boar. Isco motioned for us keep quiet.

When Yamba got back to the canoe the herd, apparently not seeing us, had started to swim across the river toward us. It looked like there could have been fifty of them. We waited until they were close to halfway across the river, and then we launched out to meet them. I was the only one with a gun, my semi-automatic .22 rifle. As soon as we were in the midst of them I began to shoot. Sometimes when the boar was shot it sank before we could retrieve it. And with a big herd like that, it would be very dangerous to go into the water to get them. They have long tusks and could seriously maim if not kill a person. In fact I was praying I wouldn't fall out of the canoe as I was standing to shoot them. One fall into the midst of that herd could be the last mistake I ever made.

Yamba and Isco said I shot about twenty of them. I think that was an exaggeration, but at least we got three of them into the canoe. There wasn't much room for more anyway. This was going to make a good feast for the whole community—meat for every house.

Yamba was now so sick that he could no longer paddle. I took over for him, and it was just the Lord giving me the strength to match Isco stroke for stroke. As we think back on it, both Marie and I are totally convinced that the Lord empowered me to paddle like that for close to five hours. Working daily at the translation desk does not produce the calloused hands needed to paddle that long. Amazingly, I didn't even feel too tired and didn't get one blister on my comparatively soft hands. "They that wait upon the Lord shall renew their strength" (Isa. 40:31 KJV).

But as soon as we pulled up to the shore of San Marcos, I began to feel sick, and by the time we got to our house I was running a fever along with a sore throat. The Lord had allowed me to keep well until we got there. It would have been difficult for Isco to paddle the canoe alone. Marie and I praised the Lord for his goodness and strength and for providing food for the Sharanahuas. The trip to check out the bilingual schools in the three Sharanahua communities had been very profitable.

—39—

ALL'S WELL THAT ENDS WELL

The Helio Courier taxied up to the Purus riverbank at San Marcos. Pilot Doug Deming threw out the rope to tie the plane to the shore. He stepped off the float and worked his way up the steep bank to the chatter of Sharanahuas, always there to greet pilots. After delivering the supplies and enjoying a short visit with us, Doug went to the gas shed where pilots stored aviation gas to fill up for the return trip to Yarinacocha, some two hours and 15 minutes away. Much to his dismay, Doug found the 50-gallon drum empty when it should have been full. Fortunately, at the military post, Esperanza, about 10 minutes away by air downstream, there was more aviation gas stored, so Doug went on down there to refuel.

Thinking that one of the traders, who went up and down the river selling their goods, had stolen the gasoline for his motor, Doug reported the theft to the police. He hadn't told me he was going to make the report, as there was no need for me to know. Later, the police headquarters in Esperanza sent two policemen to San Marcos and called for all the men in the community to report for a meeting (I attended also). Both policemen were very polite and reported to the Sharanahuas that they had come to investigate the theft of the gasoline and wanted to ask a few questions. They accused no one, nor even hinted they had any idea of who might have been the thief. After about a half hour with the men, the policemen returned to their headquarters in Esperanza.

About a week later Gustavo received a letter from the police, telling him they wanted to have a talk with him. I think that Gustavo suspected nothing and went downstream very willingly. When he got there the officer said, "You are the thief of the aviation gasoline. No one else has a motor for his canoe there except you. You are the only one who uses gasoline. Therefore you are sentenced to time in jail." For the Sharanahuas, who in time past didn't even have walls in their homes, it was a claustrophobic experience to be jailed, to be "put between the walls."

Word very quickly got to San Marcos that Gustavo had been "put between the walls" for the theft of the gasoline. Everyone jumped to the conclusion that I had turned Gustavo in to the authorities. As was mentioned, in a Sharanahua's eyes one of the worst things you could do was turn one of them in to nontribal authorities. Gustavo's father, Andres the chief, came over to our house and asked me why I had turned Gustavo in. Andres and I were good friends, and he and I had had many amiable conversations. I told Andres that I hadn't turned Gustavo in, that I didn't even know that the pilot was going to tell the authorities. I'm sure Andres believed me and was relieved that I hadn't done it, which in their culture would have meant that I had betrayed Gustavo, even though he was guilty.

They released Gustavo after a very short time "between the walls," and he came back accompanied by one of the policeman. Marie and I saw the canoe coming from downstream while it was still quite a ways away and could see that there were people in it from Esperanza. We had a feeling there might be something coming that needed prayer. I got on our two-way radio to call

Yarinacocha and told the operator to tell the folks to pray for us, because we didn't know what the arrival of the men might portend for us. It *just happened* that this was the day of prayer at Yarinacocha, so everyone there prayed for wisdom for us and for victory in whatever was going to happen.

As the canoe pulled up to the bank and the passengers got out, we saw that one of them was an officer from the police in Esperanza. He called a meeting of all the Sharanahua men and asked that I be present also. During his time "between the walls" Gustavo had had plenty of time to think about why he was there. He concluded that I had given the report that put him there. The more he thought about it the angrier he became that I had betrayed him. He was seething with rage toward me and wanted revenge. After being released from jail he gave the police a bad report about me and also accused the very first Sharanahua bilingual teacher, Sebastian, of sexual abuse of the young women in his class.

When all the men had assembled, the officer got right down to business. He said to me that Gustavo reported that I hadn't taught them anything since I came. I replied that when we came none of them knew how to read or write, but now they did. He asked Gustavo if that were true. Gustavo replied that it wasn't true. I was not going to have an argument there in front of the officer and the Sharanahuas, so I said nothing more. The Sharanahuas knew the truth. Then the officer said that Gustavo accused the bilingual teacher of having illicit relations with the young Sharanahua women in his classes. The officer said that for that reason he would have to take Sebastian down to Esperanza to stand trial. Then he dismissed me from the meeting.

I left feeling quite discouraged. Not only did I stand accused and the reputation of our mission might suffer from that accusation, but also we were losing the first and only Sharanahua teacher who had been taught at the Teacher Training Course at Yarinacocha. When I got about 30 feet from the building where the men were meeting, the officer called me and hurried over to me.

He said, "I don't want to make things difficult for your work. What can we do?"

I said, "Well, concerning the aviation gasoline, Gustavo has already been punished. Let's drop that issue. Concerning the bilingual teacher, I don't know if he is guilty or not, but I don't think you should take him in." He decided to drop that charge also. Do you suppose all of the prayers at Yarinacocha concerning this situation had anything to do with the officer suddenly changing his mind?

Afterwards Marie and I invited the officer to our home for a meal. During the course of conversation, I showed the officer a letter that Gustavo had written to me in Sharanahua. The officer said, "Wow! That's almost better than I can write," or some such thing. With that, it became unnecessary for me to explain to him that we had reduced their language to writing, providing them with an alphabet and primers. And I didn't have to repeat what Gustavo had said about us not teaching them anything.

Later that evening, after the officer had left, Gustavo came to our house. I'm sure his father had talked to him and told him that I was not the one that gave the report to the police. As we sat down together on our porch, he said, "I have done badly. I want to read this verse to you." We hadn't translated the whole New Testament yet, but he read to me 3 John 9. I wouldn't have chosen that verse to confess to wrongdoing, but I'm convinced he thought it fit the bill. When he read "Diotrephes, who loves to be first,..." he must have thought he had been proud and wanted to be thought of as the preeminent one. What had started out to be a defeat for us and for the bilingual teacher ended up in a confession from Gustavo, his way of apologizing for stealing, and an encouragement to us to see how God was answering prayer and using his Word in the hearts of the Sharanahuas.

—40—

GUSTAVO—CHIEF AND PASTOR

He was peering into our house through the window. I had never seen him before. He had to stand tall to see in. Gustavo had come up from Chushpi, the community downstream where his father Andres was chief. Andres was one of the tallest of the Sharanahuas, but Gustavo was short like most Sharanahua men. I remember that first glimpse of him, seemingly arrogant, even at the age of around 14. Andres didn't have the bearing of a proud man. He was congenial and easy to talk with. Gustavo knew that someday he would be chief and perhaps that gave him a sense of superiority, especially since his father and mother favored him, their oldest son.

Marie and I had lived for several years in the Sharanahua community at the mouth of the Curanja River, which flowed into the larger Purus River, so we didn't often see Gustavo. Later we moved down just below Chushpi to begin a school in the community of San Marcos. Andres brought his whole community there to live close to us and be able to take advantage of the school. By this time Gustavo was in his late teens or early twenties. Though I had pleasant conversations with him, it was evident that he had a volatile temper and was easily provoked. The Sharanahuas at San Marcos had never gone to school before. When we called the men together to teach them, Gustavo was there for every class and showed a good aptitude for learning.

As Marie and I were teaching them to read and write in Sharanahua, I was also doing Bible translation with the assistance of various men, including Gustavo. He was easy to work with ... except when he wasn't. I found him very moody, and I never knew what mood he was going to be in when he came to work. In some ways it was easier to work with others who may not have been quite as sharp as Gustavo but who were never moody. I think that, as the chief's son, he felt everyone should bend to his whims.

After being at San Marcos for a few months, it was time to return to Yarinacocha. There we could analyze our findings, check them with consultants, and have some uninterrupted time at the translation desk. Over the ensuing years we spent about two-thirds of our time at the center and one-third in the Sharanahua community.

After getting settled at Yarina for a while, and having time just to spend with our children, we asked for a floatplane to go to San Marcos and bring back one of the Sharanahua men to serve as a co-translator with me. We gave the pilot a list of the names of five possible men to choose from, in the order of priority, to bring back with his wife. Gustavo was number five on the list. If no one else was available, we would take it as from the Lord that he was the chosen one, even though I didn't look forward to his moodiness. With him I always felt like I was walking on eggshells. We felt that with a list of five, surely one of them besides Gustavo could come. When the pilot arrived back, lo and behold, it was Gustavo in the plane. We had to believe that for some reason he was the Lord's choice.

There were small houses not far from our house that were made especially for the indigenous people who came to work on the translation or take part in the Bilingual School Course or for medical reasons. These small houses were made using planed lumber, and the floors were smooth. The roof was extended in front to make room for their fire for cooking. There was room inside for them to put up their hammocks. Sharanahuas are not used to sleeping any other way than in a hammock. We made sure that they had firewood and food to cook that they like: cooking bananas (plantains), yuca, and meat. Gustavo and his wife had never lived in a house put together like this one, but they seemed satisfied with their housing and their food. Gustavo's wife, Ishama, had brought along cotton and a spindle to spin in her free time, something that all Sharanahua women did. And, of course, she cooked the meals.

We spent some very enjoyable days translating, and Gustavo was rarely moody. So later we brought him to Yarinacocha to work with us a number of times. I believe it may have been the third time that I asked him one day, "Gustavo, when are you going to confess your sins and ask Jesus to forgive you and be your Owner?"

He replied, "I already have."

We hadn't seen much change in Gustavo, but we needed to remember that his people didn't have much of the Word yet in their language. Also, some of us, after accepting Christ as our Savior, don't show much of a change for a while either. He didn't have fellow Sharanahuas to encourage him. Marie and I were the only ones to give him encouragement. I urged him to share with the Sharanahuas what he was learning in the Scriptures. Gustavo was the first of the Sharanahuas to make Jesus his Owner; it would be a number of years before we saw another make that decision.

Eventually, while we were there in San Marcos, they built a house to be their church. The people would get together in the evening with their kerosene lamps made from coffee cans with cotton for the wick. Gustavo would share with them what he was learning from the Word. We had translated some hymns into Sharanahua, and they liked to sing those songs of praise

229

to the Lord. Sometimes, after Gustavo had spoken, I would share something with them from the Word also.

One day we were translating the book of Acts and had come to the fifth chapter, about Ananias and Sapphira. At the end of the previous chapter it had told how Barnabas (which means "son of encouragement") had sold a piece of property and brought all of the proceeds to the apostles. No doubt Ananias and his wife, Sapphira, saw this and probably heard the other believers talking about what a wonderful thing Barnabas had done and what a good man he was. Perhaps they thought they would

Gustavo was chief
and pastor in Gasta Bala.

like to have people talking about them like that. So they sold a piece of property also and brought it to the apostles. They gave only part of the proceeds to the apostles, but they wanted everyone to think they had given it all, just like Barnabas had done.

We got to the part where Peter says to Ananias, "Ananias, how did Satan get you to lie to the Holy Spirit and secretly keep back part of the price of the field? ... The money was yours to do with as you wished. So what got into you to pull a trick like this? You didn't lie to men but to God" (Acts 5:3–4, The Message). When Peter said that, Ananias dropped dead.

I hadn't made any comment on the verse, but when Gustavo heard that Ananias dropped dead, he said, "Wait! Wait! Wait! I have to pray." He began to confess all the sins he could think of. It seemed that he thought if he didn't get things right with the Lord immediately, he was going to drop dead right there at the translation desk.

I thought, *How powerful is the Word of God when it is given in the language that speaks to the heart, in the mother tongue.* I had just witnessed the truth of Hebrews 4:12–13: "For the word of God is living and active. Sharper than any double-edged sword, it penetrates even to dividing soul and spirit, joints and marrow; it judges the thoughts and attitudes of the heart. Nothing in all creation is hidden from God's sight. Everything is uncovered and laid bare before the eyes of him to whom we must give account."

Gustavo came to Yarinacocha shortly after the whooping cough epidemic, which claimed the lives of fifteen little children 2 years old and younger. He brought with him, besides Ishama, his younger sister, Yawaosho, and her children. His sister needed medical attention. They were living in the small house behind ours. I had the impression that both Gustavo and I looked forward to our translation sessions daily.

It was almost time for Gustavo and his family to return to their village when I got a call from one of our doctors, Larry Dodds. He said, "Scotty, I'm sorry to have to tell you, but Gustavo's sister's little boy has whooping cough. So they shouldn't go back to their community for another three weeks to make sure he's over it and won't infect his community."

Shortly before we were scheduled to go to the translation center where we worked, I told Gustavo what Larry had said. He exploded. He had been looking forward to getting back to his people, and he didn't want anything to deter that. I said, "Gustavo, you remember how those fifteen little babies died out in your community? You wouldn't want more of them to die, who might catch the whooping cough from your nephew."

He wouldn't listen to reason and said, "My nephew doesn't have whooping cough. He just has a bad cough."

I reminded him that our doctor knew the difference between a plain cough and whooping cough and wouldn't tell us that it was whooping cough unless he was sure. That didn't pacify him one little bit, and he replied, "You just want to make me stay here to work more on translation."

I didn't tell him that, as a matter of fact, Marie and I were looking forward to their departure so that we could take a vacation in Lima. We would have sent him and his wife back, without his sister and children, but it was a long, expensive flight, and we just couldn't afford to pay for two of them.

With this said, we went up to the translation center. Gustavo scowled; it was evident he didn't have his heart in translating. I knew we were not apt to have a good translation session.

I said, "Gustavo, we can't translate God's Word if we're angry."

He retorted, "I wasn't angry before, but now I am! There isn't another tribe that has to put up with a linguist such as you. I'll never come back here again." And with that he slammed his key to the translation center down on the desk.

I wanted more than anything to continue with the translation and have a good one for the Sharanahuas, but now it seemed impossible to continue. The hopelessness of the situation hit me, and I said to him, "I don't know what to do." And the tears came unbidden.

I think when he saw the tears he realized I wasn't trying to make things difficult for him but rather to keep any more of his relatives from dying. Then he, the strong chief, began to cry also. I had a box of Kleenex there and put it between us. The translation rooms all have a small window in the door. I thought anyone going by and looking in would think, "They must be translating the saddest verses in the Bible."

After we both had wept for a while, Gustavo said, "I need to pray now." And he poured out his heart to the Lord, telling him that he had been thinking wrong and was sorry for his attitude, and he asked him to help him translate his Word correctly.

After that we had one of the best translation sessions ever. When it was time to have a break for lunch, without saying anything, he picked up his key from the desk and put it in his pocket. He said nothing more about his nephew not having whooping cough, and we continued to make good progress until it was safe to take his nephew back.

After Gustavo had been helping me for a few years with the translation, he called the tribe together and said, "We need a pastor. Whom shall we choose to be our pastor?"

Right away someone said, "You know the Word better than any of us. You be the pastor." Immediately, everyone agreed that Gustavo should be the pastor. He may have felt that they would choose him. There was not one dissenting voice. So he accepted their choice.

Then I told the Sharanahuas, "You have chosen Gustavo to be your pastor. Now you need to listen when he speaks to you from God's Word and obey God's Word. You need to pray for him."

Then we prayed for Gustavo, and he was recognized by the Sharanahuas of his community as their pastor. Then deacons were chosen to help Gustavo. He told his people, "Some of you don't know how to read. You can't grow in knowing Jesus and his Word if you're not putting his Word into your innermost. I'm going to be up here every night telling you God's Word, so if you don't learn his Word, it won't be my fault." Marie and I didn't suggest they meet every night; that was Gustavo's idea, and no one objected.

I have mentioned before that Gustavo had a tendency to be moody. After we come to Christ, some of our unChristlike characteristics don't disappear right away; so it was with Gustavo. And just as any pastor, Gustavo sometimes went through times of discouragement.

Gustavo, like many of God's servants before him, some of whom are mentioned in the Scriptures, such as Elijah, have had high points and low points. Sometimes I shared in his low points as I did in his high points.

Here is a letter I got from Gustavo while we were on furlough in 1989, which was such a joy to me:

It is I, Gustavo, Father. I am sending writing to your land in order that you know. I am not sick; I am well. I heard about you that you haven't gotten well yet. I miss you very much. I am habitually praying to our Owner [Lord] Jesus for you that you will be like you used to be. I very much want to see you but you live so very far away. My people are all well. I'm going to cause you to know about me now. My work remains telling God's Word habitually. I am the pastor at Gasta Bala. Every day I keep on telling God's Word. I will never put my Owner behind me. I only want to do what God commands us to do. My dear father died the 7th of February. Just before he died, my father said, "I'm going to arrive to God," he said. Thus hearing that, I cried. I cried for two days. Thus later my heart was made to be at peace. I am delighted! Now I am telling you, Father, that on the 18th of July I am going to Yarinacocha to have my wife's teeth caused to be put in. Then on the 2nd of August I will return to Gasta Bala. As the Peruvians say, I am sending you greetings. Greet Aunt Yambacora [Marie] and Tutu [Becky], Cafi [Priscilla] and Fuco [Steve]. Fosho [David] we really love. He was among us for two weeks recently. Every day he got together with us to hear God's Word. Thus that is all of my words. It is finished what I am writing to you. That is all.
Fahuino [Gustavo]

All these years Gustavo has remained faithful as a pastor.

—41—

ON WINGS AS EAGLES

It would have been absolutely impossible to accomplish the work among the Sharanahuas without the aid of JAARS, what was then called the "aviation and radio service arm" of Wycliffe Bible Translators. How many times Marie and I thanked God for the faithful pilots, mechanics, and radio technicians, who contributed so selflessly to giving God's Word to the Sharanahuas.

God had blessed the work of JAARS. Though the pilots and mechanics were skilled, they and we knew that it was also the protection of the Lord that kept them safe. After nearly sixty years of flying over some of the most remote and rugged terrain in Peru's Amazon basin, there has never been a fatal accident. Every effort was taken to make flying safe. JAARS pilots never put on board the plane one kilo more than the safety requirements called for. Weather reports were constantly being given to the pilots from the center of operations, Yarinacocha, as well as from the location where they were going or from a nearby location. Translators working in tribal areas en route to the pilot's destination would also give weather reports. They had been given lessons in how to report the weather —the cloud coverage, the altitude of the clouds, which direction the clouds were moving, the direction and speed of the wind on the ground, the tendency of the weather, and if there was rain in the area. The airstrips, which were adequate but marginal, were kept in good condition so that landings and takeoffs would not be hazardous.

One morning when a floatplane was to arrive to take us back to Yarinacocha, as was our custom, Marie and I read from *Daily Light on the Daily Path*, a Scripture devotional book. One of the verses was Genesis 22:8: "God himself will provide..." With Don Weber as our pilot, we took off from the Purus River. The weather was ideal, but on this particular route, there was no station to give us a weather report.

The arrival of a JAARS plane was a big event.

About an hour into the flight, the weather began to deteriorate. There was no river in the area big enough to land on. Soon we were into the clouds, and the plane was beginning to dance around from turbulence. Fortunately, there was no thunder or lightning. Don said, "Keep your eyes peeled, because we don't want to cross over the Urubamba River. There are some pretty high hills on the other side."

Just before we got to the Urubamba, a small hole opened up in the clouds. Don skillfully brought the plane down, and the Urubamba below us was a welcome sight. When Marie and I thought of that hole in the clouds, we remembered the verse the Lord had given us that morning, "God will provide." Yes, again our Lord was looking out for his own and making sure that nothing would hinder taking the Word to another of the tribes in Peru.

In the first years of our work with the Sharanahuas, it was a 4-hour flight in an Aeronca floatplane from Yarinacocha to our location on the Purus River. Halfway out to the Purus River we had to land to refuel. At that time pilots flew without the aid of a GPS (global positioning system). For navigation they had their compass and a map of the area, and they followed the rivers, observing checkpoints on the way. Clouds would sometimes make it difficult to keep the river in sight. The pilots never got completely lost, but I think that all of them at one time or another became disoriented before picking up the route again.

It always amazed me how the pilots could cope with this flight to the Purus, arriving in the intense heat of the jungle, and then dealing with clouds of gnats during the day. The pilots would roll a 50-gallon drum of gas to the airplane, and then the gnats would swarm around them as they gassed up the plane. I never heard one of them complain about this. After the strenuous work of gassing up the plane, they had to take off from a straight stretch in the river. This called not only for alertness, but the strength to get the floatplane "on the step" (the tail up) and get it off the water and fly between the trees until there was enough altitude to lift it above the jungle. We praised the Lord for the pilots and their skill and stamina.

All of our pilots were a blessing to Marie and me. One of our favorites was Bernie May, who went on to become the president of JAARS and later Wycliffe Bible Translators. Like the other pilots,

Bernie enjoyed helping the local people when he could. On one of his flights to service us, the chief brought a huge turtle and asked me to ask Bernie if he would take the turtle downstream to Esperanza where Bernie was headed. The chief wanted to sell it to someone there at the army base. Bernie told me to ask the chief if the turtle would bite. The chief assured us that it wouldn't bite. Bernie put the turtle behind a Peruvian passenger on board. The seats on the Aeronca were like canvas lawn chairs. During the 15-minute flight the turtle that didn't bite bit the passenger severely. Fortunately, it bit the passenger and not Bernie, or he might have had a difficult time landing.

Another time I was flying out to our location with Bernie in a floatplane. As always, Bernie had to fly by compass and visual. As we were getting close to our destination, a cloud coverage made it difficult to see the rivers below. There were the headwaters of two other rivers close to the one we wanted to follow. As we broke out of the clouds, Bernie asked me, "Scotty, do you recognize anything down there?"

I replied, "I'm sorry, Bernie, but everything looks the same to me from the air."

Then Bernie said, "This heading isn't right. I'm going to land on this river where those thatched-roof homes are to find out where we are."

We landed and found out that we were at a community of Kashinawas in Brazil. They had named this community California. When Bernie found out where we were he knew which way we should head back. As we were taking off, here came a boatload of Brazilian soldiers. Bernie said, "I don't think we'll go back and greet those fellows." Though it couldn't be helped, we were in Brazil without permission. It might have proved costly if the Brazilian authorities had impounded the plane due to being in Brazil without documentation. Bernie then skillfully flew us directly to the Sharanahua community on the Purus River in Peru.

Time and time again we witnessed the Lord's hand on the pilots and the airplanes that were in his service to bring his life-giving Word. The very first airstrip made on the Purus River, with the exception of the one at the military post at Esperanza, was built near the mouth of the Curanja River. With the help of about thirty Sharanahuas and our friend Kenny Gammon, a mechanic, the airstrip was completed. This was accomplished using only picks, axes, machetes, and gunnysacks made into stretchers to move the dirt from one place to another. Then armed with thick, heavy poles around 5 feet tall, all the Sharanahuas lined up on one end of the airstrip and marched to the other end, tamping down the airstrip to make it firm enough to land on.

On the day the airplane was to make the initial landing with pilot Ralph Borthwick, who had served in the Royal Canadian Air Force, it poured down rain for an hour or two before the plane was to land. Marie and I were very concerned that the airstrip with no grass on it was going to be a sea of mud, and that the plane might slide off the end into the river. The airstrip was about 5 or 10 minutes by canoe downstream from the village. As the estimated time of arrival was near, Marie and I, with the Sharanahuas, went down by canoe to the freshly completed airstrip to meet the plane. Imagine our surprise and delight to find that while it had rained heavily all around it, not a drop fell on the airstrip. Thank you, Lord! The Sharanahuas thought our God must be powerful to keep that one spot in the jungle dry.

On another occasion, Marie and I were scheduled to return to Yarinacocha. A couple of weeks or so before the scheduled flight, there was an epidemic of flu among the Sharanahuas. The flight was scheduled for a Monday, but bad weather set in and the pilot, Bob Hettema, had to cancel. He tried to come Wednesday, but again the weather would not permit.

That evening a canoe-load of Sharanahuas arrived from downstream, most of them sick with high fevers. We were thankful we were still there. We used up all the antibiotics we had left, giving shots. Had Bob come on Monday, at the scheduled time, we would not have been there to save the lives of the gravely ill Sharanahuas.

The next day, Thursday, was not what the pilots would call CAVU (ceiling and visibility unlimited) weather. Bob waited to see if the weather would clear enough to make the trip. He decided that if he had a 2,000-foot ceiling he would come ahead in the floatplane. For the whole trip, that was almost exactly the altitude of the clouds. We were thankful that before we left, the Sharanahuas were almost all over the flu, and that those who had arrived the night before were given antibiotics, which we prayed would keep them from getting worse.

After arriving back at Yarinacocha late that afternoon, Marie and I had to spend time preparing for the trip we were scheduled to make the next day to Lima. As we were still packing late that night, Marie went by our daughter Becky's crib and heard her labored breathing. Becky was about 2 years old at the time. Marie called me and though we hated to do it at that hour of the night, we decided we better call our doctor. Dr. Swanson came over on his motor scooter. He listened to her breathing and checked her over. I told him that we hated to "press the panic button," especially at that hour of the night.

Dr. Swanson replied, "You didn't press the panic button. Becky has pneumonia, and at her age it sometimes doesn't take long for complications to set in. A child that age could quickly become dehydrated with dire results. Keep a close eye on her the rest of the night, and you had better cancel your trip to Lima tomorrow as it would be dangerous to take Becky over the Andes in her condition."

It was with great praise to the Lord that we could stop packing and that pilot Bob had come to get us that day. If he had not, we would have been stuck out in the tribe with no more antibiotics for Becky, and we might have lost her. If he had come on the day originally scheduled, we might have lost the very sick Sharanahuas who had come the night before. They all survived. We believe the Lord was the one rearranging the flight schedule.

—42—

TRIAL THROUGH FLOOD

It's not unusual in one night for the Purus River to rise over 20 feet. Many smaller streams feed into the Purus, and in the rainy season the Purus becomes swollen, filled with fallen trees and other floating debris that have come from the eroding banks of the river. On this particular day in 1982 we took note of the rise in the river but were not alarmed as we had seen this many, many times. But around noon we noticed that the river seemed to be coming up even faster than usual. When I mentioned my concern to the Sharanahuas, their reply was, "There's no cause for worry. It never gets as high as the airstrip." So about 4:30 that afternoon as we were having the last check-in with the radio operator back at our center, I mentioned the rise in the river but repeated what the Sharanahuas had told me: "It never covers the airstrip."

About five that afternoon, the "never before" happened. The water covered the airstrip. Still the water had quite a ways to come uphill to get to the houses. As evening and darkness came on, so did the rain and the rise in the river. The water finally came into our yard, toppling our beautiful coconut tree.

Then, to the distress of the Sharanahuas, a house a short distance from ours collapsed as the river rose to flow under the house.

All of the houses in the community were set on heavy stilts to keep them off the ground and give them some protection against snakes and other unwelcome creatures. The river had eroded the dirt and sand into which the stilts were driven. Most of the people now had gotten into their canoes and gone to higher ground. So now all the canoes were gone—either taken by people or the flood had swept away.

As the rain continued to come down and the river to rise, the waters were soon a rushing torrent under our house (the floor was about a meter above the ground). One of the young Sharanahuas waded through the water to our house, saying, "Our house is about to collapse. May we come to your house?"

"Come quickly," I replied.

Then after midnight I heard slosh, slosh, slosh, coming toward our house. I went out onto our porch and shined the flashlight into the darkness and saw our neighbor, Nahuuruco, wading knee-deep in the rushing current with a look of terror on his face.

He said, "My house is ready to fall over. May we come to your house?"

I told him, too, to hurry over with his family. Then as I saw the river was getting dangerously close to coming into our house, the thought came to me: *Maybe we should try to walk to higher ground while we still can.*

When I expressed this to Nahuuruco, he replied, "Oh no! We can't. The river is too swift. We can't see the holes and ditches in the ground, and we would fall into them and get swept away and drown."

So much for that thought. By this time we had exhausted any hope of being able to escape this unheard-of flood.

It was pitch black and still raining as the river continued its upward, unrelenting course. On the back of the radios, radio technician Jim Baptista had devised a button that if activated would alert one of our radio technicians, who would keep a two-way radio in his home in Yarinacocha to receive an emergency call at night.

As I looked at that button, which we sometimes referred to as the "panic button," I said to Marie, "Do you think it's time to press the button?"

She said, "If ever there was a time, I think this is it."

I pressed the button and immediately Wes Swauger answered. I relayed to Wes what we were facing. I said, "Wes, we have a huge flood out here. Houses on both sides of ours have collapsed as the water has eroded the ground around the *orcones* (heavy stilts). It's still raining. We have fourteen Sharanahuas in our house, the children sleeping on the floor, and parents have hung their hammocks. The water is 4 inches from coming into the house. Don't call our children; we don't want to alarm them, but please call our prayer partners and explain the situation to them so they can pray for us."

After talking to Wes, Marie and I took out our Bible, and the Lord turned our attention to Isaiah 43:1–5: "This is what the Lord says—he who created you, Jacob [Marie], he who formed you, Israel [Gene]: "Do not fear, for I have redeemed you; I have summoned you by name; you are mine. When you pass through the waters, I will be with you; and when you pass through the rivers, they will not sweep over you. ... For I am the Lord your God, the Holy One of Israel, your Savior; ... Since you are precious and honored in my sight, and because I love you.... Do not be afraid, for I am with you."

With those heartwarming, encouraging words from our Lord, I was able to sleep. Marie didn't sleep as well, as she was hearing the water rushing under our house, and right under our bed. Each time she was awakened by the river surging under our house, she would think of those verses we read from Isaiah, and her heart was calmed.

At the crack of dawn, villagers who had escaped the evening before returned in canoes to take us to higher ground. The water was just touching the bottom of the floor but had not come into the house. The children on the floor had stayed dry.

The canoes took us, along with our radio, translation and linguistic materials, and some clothes, to a home on higher ground, the only one that was not flooded. After we had gotten situated with other families there, I asked one of the Sharanahuas if he would take me back to our house in his canoe so I could check on things again. When we arrived, the water was already ankle-deep inside our house.

Before the river crested, the water rose to about a meter inside our house, the current knocking over our 50-gallon drums, which contained our books, papers, and other things we wanted to keep safe and dry.

All was lost.

In the high-ground house with the Sharanahuas now, there was barely room for us. Even so, as there were no walls in the house, it made it easier to move around and to hang our mosquito nets. The ever-resourceful Sharanahuas did something they normally would never do. They put mud on the floor of the house to build a fire for cooking, as there was no dry ground elsewhere.

It was easy for the Sharanahua men to get game, as the flood forced the animals to what higher ground there was. Wild boar, deer, and other animals were plentiful. That was just about the only positive thing about the flood.

Gustavo, the chief, went to higher ground and shot a wild boar. As he was returning through the water, he stepped into a deep hole that he couldn't see. As he went down, he didn't want to let go of his gun and he didn't want to lose the boar that he had over his shoulder. He said that he called out to the Lord, "Save me!" The Lord answered his prayer, and he was able to get out of the hole and not lose either his gun or the boar.

The vegetable gardens of the Sharanahuas were ruined. Their staples of yuca, bananas, and corn were gone. As we stayed in the only Sharanahua home not covered by water, Marie and I were just two more mouths to feed where food was at a premium. We were so thankful that no one was sick. We told the people that if they wanted us to stay, we would, but if they would prefer, we would ask for a plane to come get us as we had been scheduled to go back to our center of operations soon anyway. If we did decide to go back, we would ask the pilot to load the plane with sacks of rice for them, since their gardens were ruined. In this case, they chose the rice.

We were able to get the radio antenna up and call for the plane. Pilot Doug Deming arrived with the sacks of rice, as many sacks as the plane's weight allowance would permit. Doug never had an easier time getting the plane tied up close to the house! We practically stepped out of the house into the Helio Courier for the flight back to Yarinacocha.

Later one of the teachers from Yarinacocha, Frank Johnson, came out with me to see what was salvageable. What was once a thriving Sharanahua community now looked like the landscape of the moon. Nothing but gray sand everywhere we looked. The Sharanahuas had moved to higher ground to build another village. Now it would take a Noah-sized flood to reach them.

—43—

"KEEP ME TRANSPARENT, LORD!"

Marie and I were fortunate to have one of the houses on the Yarinacocha lakefront. Every day we enjoyed beautiful sunrises coming up over the still, peaceful lake. This day, however, as I walked alone on the lakefront path, my heart was not at rest. I lacked that peace that every child of God should be experiencing. I was inwardly disturbed. Oh, I hadn't committed any gross sin, as some people count sin, but my thought life wasn't always what it should be and that to me and to God was gross. No one knew of my inward struggle but God and me. I hadn't even said anything to my dear wife. As I recall, I said to the Lord, "Please, Lord, I need that peace that only you can give. I can't be effective for you here in the jungle of Peru as I am. I need you to do a new thing in my heart. I confess to you that I haven't had that zeal for you that I should have. I feel a failure. I'm not what others think I am. If they knew my inward struggles, they would probably ask me to leave Peru."

It was shortly after that walk that our director Jerry Elder came early one morning to our house. Jerry and his wife, Evie, had come to Peru about the same time as I had. They, along with Dave Farah and I, lived in the same home in Lima to learn more Spanish. I got to observe Jerry and Evie while I was there. I had always looked up to them, but now, seeing them more closely, I admired them and their walk with the Lord even more.

We had elected Jerry as our director while he was on furlough in California with his wife and children. When Jerry got back to Peru to take up his duties, he shared something personal with us all. While he was preparing to return to Peru, he was driving down the freeway, talking to the Lord, and said, "Lord, I feel as dry as dust. You have to do a new thing in my heart. I can't return to Peru like this." He said the Lord met with him right there in the car. He sensed the presence of the Lord and experienced wonderful joy. When he came back to Peru, though it had been obvious that the Lord was in his life before, it was also very evident now that the Lord had done a new thing for him. One of his biggest concerns as director was that the spiritual life at Yarinacocha be healthy.

When Jerry arrived at our house early that morning, after a few pleasantries, he asked me if I would serve on our Yarinacocha devotional committee. I decided to be perfectly honest with him— in front of Marie—and told him some things that were going on in my life that I didn't think were pleasing to the Lord. Therefore, I didn't feel I was worthy to serve on the committee. When I finished telling him, he said, "Praise the Lord!"

I thought, *He didn't hear anything I said.*

He went on to say, "Now the Lord can use you."

We prayed together, and I confessed to the Lord the things I thought were displeasing to him. I think all three of us shed some tears; I know I did.

After Jerry left, I went to a translation workshop on 1 John, the book concerning the love of God. Each of us translators would give a back translation: a word-for-word translation in English of the passage in the local language. After giving our English translation of a verse, others in the workshop could give their opinions on whether it was good or not. Often these back translations were helpful to other translators in their search for appropriate wording.

One man there always sounded so dogmatic, as if the way he had translated a verse was the only way. Though I never said anything, I could hardly stand it when he gave his back translation. It grated on my nerves. Now that morning, I may not have agreed with his translation of the passage, but I found myself loving him. I wanted to shout "Hallelujah!" because I knew this had to be the Lord giving me this love. "God's love has been poured out into our hearts through the Holy Spirit, who has been given to us" (Rom. 5:5).

After the workshop was over, I felt like I wanted to tell someone what the Lord had done for me that morning when Jerry was at our house. Helen Larsen, whom I admired for her walk with the Lord, was lingering after the workshop session. I told her how the Lord had worked in my heart that morning and that during the workshop I had sensed his love in a deeper way. She said, "Oh, you should have shared that this morning with the whole group. After all, the whole book of 1 John is talking about the love of God."

Later that morning, the very one who irked me so saw me and said, "Scotty, have you got a few minutes to come into my office and talk with me?" His wife was in the States at that time.

I answered, "Sure, I have time."

As I sat across the desk from him, he began to pour out his heart to me about some issues over which he was finding it difficult to find peace. If he had asked me to meet with him before Jerry had met with Marie and me, I wouldn't have been able to help him, but now I felt that love of the Lord for him, and we were able to pray together over his needs.

That afternoon I wrote down the things I felt had been hindering my walk with the Lord, and I confessed and asked his forgiveness again. Then I took a red pen and wrote "1 John 1:9" over each sin: "If we confess our sins, he is faithful and just and will forgive us our sins and purify us from all unrighteousness."

I was asked to bring the message one Sunday in Yarinacocha. I had been reading in the book of Nehemiah and felt the Lord would have me apply it to my own testimony. In the book it tells about Nehemiah's friends having just come from Jerusalem and telling him the sad news that the city was in ruins. Jerusalem was supposed to be the place that God met with his people. The glory of the Lord was supposed to be there. When Nehemiah got that news from his friends, it made him feel so bad that he wept for days and fasted and prayed.

Nehemiah was the king's cupbearer, an important position in the palace. The king looked on him with favor and gave him permission to go to Jerusalem to rebuild it. When Nehemiah got to Jerusalem, he tried to enter at the gate, but the rubble was piled so high he couldn't get in. How sad.

I thought, *We are the temple of the Lord and he wants to reside in us and display his glory through us but, like the rubble surrounding Jerusalem, sometimes we let sin pile up so there is no room for our Lord to show his glory.* It seemed to me that the Lord was saying, "Would you be willing to be transparent before your fellow missionaries and share with them about the list you wrote out of your sins with '1 John 1:9' written over them?" I didn't want to make myself vulnerable and perhaps lose the respect others had for me. Then I thought, *What is more important, my pride or obeying the Lord?* I told the Lord I would do it if he wanted me to.

That morning, before I got up to speak, Paul Friesen, a dear Mennonite brother, sang one of my favorites hymns (by Thomas O. Chisholm):

Oh! to be like Thee, blessed Redeemer,
This is my constant longing and prayer;
Gladly I'll forfeit all of earth's treasures,
Jesus, Thy perfect likeness to wear.

Oh! to be like Thee, full of compassion,
Loving, forgiving, tender and kind,
Helping the helpless, cheering the fainting,
Seeking the wand'ring sinner to find.

Oh! to be like Thee, while I am pleading,
Pour out Thy Spirit, fill with Thy love,
Make me a temple meet for Thy dwelling,
Fit me for life and Heaven above.

When Paul finished singing with that beautiful voice God had gifted him, we could sense the presence of the Lord. I felt that the Holy Spirit just took over as I spoke to my fellow missionaries from the book of Nehemiah. When I got to where I was going to share the things that God had been dealing with me about, I didn't see the list among my notes, and in my mind I thought, *Lord, maybe you didn't want me to share that after all.* But when that thought crossed my mind, I looked again, and there was my list.

Instead of the reaction that I thought some might have, several of the fellows came to me afterward to tell me that some sin I mentioned was the very thing they were battling, and they had wondered if they were the only one. So the Lord used it.

I felt now that whenever Satan came against me, "the accuser of our brothers and sisters, who accuses them before our God day and night," I could say, "Accuse all you want because I've already confessed that, and now 'there is no condemnation for those who are in Christ Jesus.'" That's the way I want my life to continue— transparent before him.

—44—

"COME, RELIEVE THEIR MINDS"

A company was hiring Peruvians to explore for oil near the Manu River. Many men jumped at the chance to make good wages and volunteered for the job. Some of those who enlisted were not from the region; some were from the Andes city of Cusco, situated at 11,000 feet, or from other places in the mountains. Jungle living would take some getting used to, but they were willing to acclimate themselves in order to make good wages.

Having read or heard stories of "wild Indians" who would attack, the men from the mountains began to get nervous as they began living in the depths of Amazonia. After a while their imaginations began working overtime. If they heard a limb or twig fall to the ground, they were convinced it was an Indian spying on them and getting ready to attack. These fears began to affect their work. Some complained to those over them that precautions weren't being taken and even threatened to leave their jobs if more wasn't done.

The Peruvian government decided that ILV had more experience in the jungle than any other group, so they asked our administration if they would send out a couple of linguists to check things out and relieve the minds of the oil workers. The director of

Tribal Affairs asked Dick Hyde and me if we would spend a week or so with the oil workers, checking out the area to make sure no hostile tribal people were near them. Dick and I took Abram, the Amarakairi, with us.

The oil company sent a small plane to transport us out to their airstrip in the Manu area. After we left Yarinacocha, the young pilot never touched the radio again. Here we were, flying over the jungle with no communications should the plane have trouble. We weren't used to that, as our JAARS pilots would call in every 15 minutes to give their exact location and heading. Observing this pilot's lack of safety precautions, Dick said to me, "I'm not going back to Yarinacocha except in a JAARS plane." He wanted to make sure he would see his wife and baby again.

Arriving at the oil camp we were greeted warmly by the man in charge of the oil exploration. He was from Columbia, and I liked him immediately. Oil companies, at least this one, spare nothing to make sure their workers remain satisfied. Those involved with the exploration are treated handsomely. The sleeping quarters at the main camp were comfortable, and the food was excellent. Noon meals usually consisted of steaks flown in and other good staples. A large generator kept the food refrigerated and drinks cold. It also provided light at night.

Dick and I were introduced to three helicopter pilots who had served in the US Air Force in Vietnam and were now working for the oil company. They were excellent young pilots and friendly. My only concern with flying with them was that often they would stay up quite late playing cards and then have to be out flying around seven in the morning. I wondered how they could be alert with those kinds of hours.

From this main camp, Dick, Abram, and I were flown out to where the men were working deeper into the jungle. A small aluminum boat was provided for us to navigate the river, stopping now and then to investigate the surroundings to see if anyone besides the oil workers had been there. Of course, Abram, having grown up in the jungle, was excellent at detecting any sign of people having been in the area. He saw no footprints or any other evidence of people having been near. Daily we would investigate and then return to the main camp to report our survey to the administrator. Our conversations with him were always cordial, and he seemed to enjoy talking with us, as we with him.

I became friends with the pilots and had some lively conversations with them. Once in the evening, as they were ready to start playing cards, one of them said, "Come on, Scott, get in the game."

I replied, "I'll have a game with you if you'll have a Bible study with me." They never invited me to play with them again.

One of the pilots while in Lima was led to the Lord by an American missionary. Being a new Christian, he had a lot of questions. One day he handed me a *Playboy* magazine, pointing out an article by a man who had been brought up by strict parents. He had been turned off by their legalism and thus rejected Christianity. The pilot asked me if I would read it and tell him what I thought. I hoped no one would take a picture of me with a *Playboy* magazine in my hand. I kept my eyes from looking at anything else in the magazine and read the article and discussed it with the pilot. I told him that being a Christian wasn't a matter of dos and don'ts but rather accepting Christ as Savior, reading and meditating on God's Word, enjoying fellowship with Christ in prayer, obeying his Word, and living daily in his grace and forgiveness.

Dick, Abram, and I were back again in the boat the next day to check out other places. Then one of the pilots set the helicopter down close to us and motioned to come over. He told us to get in, that some workers had reported evidence of people being close to us. We flew to where the rest of the men and one of the administrators were. The administrator, who had been flown out to talk with the workers, asked me if I would speak to the men and try to calm their fears. He said they were near to panicking.

Praying that the Lord would give me the right words, I stood on an elevated place to speak and try to reason with the perpetrators of the rebellion, because that's what it had now become. I told them that we had covered nearly all the surrounding area for a week and had found nothing to indicate that there were any other people in the area. I told them that Abram had grown up in the jungle and knew it like the back of his hand. He would have seen footprints and other indications if there really were other people coming close to them. I told them that I had a wife and children back at Yarinacocha that I fully intended to see again. I didn't have a death wish and if I had any suspicion of hostile people close to us I would certainly tell them, not only for their sakes, but also for our own. So I asked them to please not listen to any more false rumors that would cause them fear. I could absolutely guarantee that they were in no danger and that there was nothing to fear.

When I finished, the leader of the rebellion told the men not to listen to me, that I had no way of knowing that there weren't people out there waiting to kill them and that the best thing for them was to leave immediately while they still could. The mood was growing ugly, and the ringleader told the administrator that he would not be allowed to fly out unless *all* of them could fly out to the main camp. The administrator responded, "So this is a boycott."

The helicopter arrived and was starting to set down to take the administrator back to headquarters. The administrator could see the trouble brewing. He got on the radio and told the pilot not to land, that he was afraid of what the men in their ugly frame of mind might do. The pilot then took the helicopter back to the main camp and reported to the Columbian head of the operation.

The rebels told the administrator they were going to walk out and that he had to go with them. He was overweight and not use to hiking in the jungle. I knew it was going to be terribly hard on him. I even feared he might have a heart attack or not be able to make it. I knew I was in much better condition than he to make this long hike. I called the administrator aside and told him to please tell the head of the rebellion that I would like to go in his place. I was used to hiking and would be able to take it much better than he could. He thanked me but told me that these men wanted someone from the administration and wouldn't hear of me taking his place. It pained me to see him leave with the rebels. It was too far to make it to their destination that day. They would have to sleep on the trail. He had no net to protect him at night when mosquitoes would be out in full force. It was going to be one miserable night for him.

Then the Columbian director of the exploration called on his radio to the Peruvian authorities, who sent policemen or soldiers to the edge of the river to await the arrival of the rebels. I don't know how many of them were arrested. The administrator made it, but I'm sure he would never want to repeat that hike again.

After the rebels had left, the helicopter came back and took Abram, Dick, and me back to the headquarters. We had done all we could. I was so sorry that the ones leading the rebellion wouldn't listen to us and had disrupted the work. The next crew that the oil company hired, I'm sure, was questioned thoroughly to make sure they wouldn't disrupt the work as these men did.

After some quality time with the three helicopter pilots and our Columbian friend, a JAARS pilot arrived to take Abram, Dick, and me back to our homes. Dick and I didn't have to worry about the pilot not following safety procedures. It was an experience I wish had ended in a different way, but at least we had done what we were called to do and no one was hurt. I was also glad for the time I had talking about the Scriptures to the helicopter pilot who had just accepted the Lord. Again, as always, it was good to get back to Marie and my children.

—45—

BONDING FRIENDSHIPS

Those working under SIL in Peru were sometimes referred to as the "happy branch." One of the reasons was that Wycliffe's founder, William Cameron Townsend, was with us for the first nine years of our work in Peru. I can still hear him saying as he often said to us in the auditorium: "Beloved, remember that we are to love one another. Yes, we are to speak the truth, but the Scriptures tell us that even that has to be in love." And he certainly demonstrated that to all of us. His joyful, friendly example was contagious. Another reason we were happy stemmed from the close, enduring friendships that developed there. Marie and I counted everyone on our center as friends, but, as in any community, some friendships become closer than others.

Cecil Hawkins was not only the center administrator and one-time flight coordinator but was also the one who started, along with his wife, June, the work among the Sharanahuas. I don't think I ever met a person more generous than Cecil, not only with his things, but also with his time. Once while Marie and I were out in the village, Cecil decided to varnish the floors in our house at Yarinacocha. He never told us he was going to do it, so when we arrived back in our grubbies and looked inside the house at the shining floor, we almost felt it was too beautiful to walk on. Another time when we were away among the Sharanahuas, he and our friend Art Jackson decided it was time to paint the exterior walls of our house. Again we had no idea they, out of the generosity of their hearts, were going to do that.

Our dear friend Kenny Gammon, along with Art, was responsible for center maintenance—keeping the generator and the vehicles running. Kenny went out with us to help build the first airstrip among the Sharanahuas. He rigged up a small lamp so that we could see to read in our mosquito net at night. It was too dangerous to use candles, our normal means of lighting, under a net.

Along with those who helped us in tangible ways were those who helped us through prayer. Every Tuesday evening our colleagues gathered in different homes on the center to pray for those who were out in the tribes, as well as their own needs.

Then on Thursday nights a few would gather together in one of the homes to praise the Lord, sing hymns or choruses, and pray for any particular personal needs. At these times we could share anything we felt needed the attention of the Lord and know these people loved us no matter what. We knew that the personal things we shared there stayed there, not to be talked about to others, but only to the Lord. Sometimes I was too tired to go, but I always went anyway and was so glad I did. We sensed the Lord's presence and the love of the group. We left feeling refreshed and renewed for the work ahead. It was such a joy to be with our friends for whom we cared deeply: the Mishlers, Smiths, Shannons, Dodds, Hudsons, and sometimes others.

It was our joy to have Bill and Ila McIlvain as neighbors at Yarinacocha. They were teachers who had come from Cheyenne, Wyoming, to teach the children. They became more than just neighbors. Our kids and their kids became best of friends and visited back and forth. They didn't even have to knock; they could come right into the house just like it was their own home. Early one morning about 6 a.m. the McIlvains' son Mark, who was 2 years old at the time, came into Bill and Ila's bedroom. They told him, "Why don't you go up and visit Uncle Scotty and Aunt Marie?" We were always glad to see Mark, even at that hour, as he came chattering into our bedroom with his cheery greeting. One morning we woke up to find Mark and Becky side by side in our rocking chair having a great time rocking back and forth together.

Once Bill and Ila took care of our boys when we went to be with the Sharanahuas, and our boys had to go to school. We felt like we were leaving Ila with a real handful to mother with their four plus our two. Then one day we got a message over the radio that Ila had broken her foot, and we wondered if we should return to take our boys back. She would not hear of it. She said she was getting along just fine on her crutches. She wouldn't let a broken foot slow down the progress of Bible translation. So she and Bill had six children to care for, each in a different grade at school.

Speaking of school, when children at Yarinacocha were approaching high-school age, parents had to make a decision. Did they continue the work the Lord had called them to in Peru and send their children home for someone else to take care of them, or did they leave the work to go home with their children and give them the home and guidance they would need as teenagers? We had a center-wide meeting as parents to discuss the problem. Some said they would have to go back to the States to be with their children. Bill suggested an alternative. Why not put out the notice that teachers for high-school-age children were needed at Yarinacocha and have our own high school. Bill's suggestion carried the day. Yes, we realized that there might be some school activities in the States that we would not be able to provide in Yarinacocha.

But over time, the Lord surprised us. Our teens had chemistry labs, sports, drama, and music—nearly everything a US high school had to offer, and the Lord always supplied excellent teachers.

Jim Smotherman, a former semi-pro baseball player and also an excellent teacher, came and served as the high school principal. As you can imagine, he was one of the favorites among the kids. I counted Jim as one of my best friends.

I never heard any of the kids say they regretted spending their high school days in Yarinacocha instead of their home country. For many, the bonds the children made, not only with their peers, but also with their teachers, continue today. Our youngest daughter, Priscilla, who, like our other three children, grew up in Yarinacocha, said to us recently, "I don't expect to find another place like Yarinacocha until I get to heaven."

Our front lawn hosted the Easter sunrise service each year.

Another highlight for those of us who lived as friends and neighbors at Yarinacocha was our Easter morning sunrise service. Our front lawn was chosen as the best spot to have this heartwarming celebration of the resurrection of our Savior, the Lord Jesus. People brought blankets and lawn chairs to sit on. We sang songs of praise and remembrance of our Lord's resurrection. Sometimes just as we sang "Up from the grave he arose," the sun would appear on the horizon over the lake in all of its glorious splendor. It was like an "Amen!" to the triumphant song of his resurrection. Then one of the men would give a short message, remembering the glorious victory our Savior accomplished over death, hell, and the grave.

It's true that sometimes a friend sticks closer than a brother. And the friendships bonded at Yarinacocha continued over the years. The happy family atmosphere at Yarinacocha lingers on. We were one in Christ, and that relationship will never be forgotten.

—46—

A DENTAL CLINIC FOR THE SHARANAHUAS

Like any other people, the Sharanahuas often had dental problems. They grew their own sugar cane and liked to chew and suck on it, which accentuated their trouble with decay and toothaches. Not having any dentist in the area, the Sharanahuas often suffered much pain from toothaches. It was a happy day for the Sharanahuas when Dr. Dan Hodges, a dentist from Atlanta, volunteered to have a dental clinic out on the Purus River.

Dan arrived at our location with a willing assistant from Yarinacocha, Bud Giles. Bud was actually a plumber at Yarinacocha, which didn't help him any in learning dentistry, but he wanted to expand his horizons, observe, and learn all he could. Dan was glad for his help. My part was to translate for Dan.

Dan was busy from dawn till dark pulling teeth and relieving pain. We traveled to three Sharanahua communities to set up his clinic, which was not easy in the primitive conditions. While he pulled teeth, a swarm of gnats kept him company, and if he went on after dark, mosquitos replaced the gnats.

On one occasion, we were going upstream in the canoe when it began to rain. One of the Sharanahuas, old Conshico, who was not a believer, said to me, "If your God is so good why does he let it rain on us?" Dan asked me what he said, and when I told him, Dan said, "Tell him that it's because the Lord lets it rain on both the believer and the unbeliever, so we're both getting it." I'm not sure Conshico thought it was funny, but Bud, Dan, and I did, and it gave Conshico something to think about.

On another day as we traveled upstream in the canoe, it wasn't raining, but the sun was beating down on us. Bud was sitting there without a hat. The Sharanahua Zacarias said, "Tell your country-man to put a hat on."

So I told Bud and he said, "I don't like to wear a hat," even though his hair was rather thin. I told Zacarias what he said, and he replied, "Tell him to put one on anyway." I repeated that to Bud, and he still didn't put a hat on.

So then Zacarias said, "Tell him to quit being disobedient or his eyes are going to start spinning." (This got a laugh out of Dan.) To get Zacarias to quit bugging him, Bud, who didn't have a hat, put a shirt over his head. This probably saved him from getting sunstroke and having "his eyes spinning," as the tropical sun is no respecter of persons.

When we arrived at the Sharanahua community of Santa Margarita, all the Sharanahuas turned out to greet us as usual. Among them was Fushna, the widow of the shaman Bidisario. She could be stern if someone was mistreating one of her animals, but also she had a sense of humor like we had never seen in any other Sharanahua woman. As soon as we arrived, she told me, "Tell the dentist what I tell you to say."

I said, "OK."

"Tell him I want to marry him."

I knew she was joking, but Dan didn't. And when I told him what she said, I believe he must have turned several shades of red. After a moment's silence, he said, "Tell her I'm already married."

I told her, and she said, "Tell him that's alright. I'll be his traveling wife and cook his meals and wash his clothes." I relayed this information to Dan who turned redder yet.

After collecting himself, he said, "Oh, tell her that I don't know how to hunt."

At this Fushna said, "Oh, what a pity. I guess it won't work." And Dan was off the hook.

When he got back to Yarinacocha he told his wife, Linda, about the incident. She, with a mischievous smile replied, "What! She offered to cook meals and wash clothes and you turned her down?" Whenever we see Dan and Linda we still get a good laugh out of Fushna's proposal.

After Dan had finished the dental clinic and taken care of many Sharanahuas and relieved a lot of pain and discomfort, we headed back downstream to the community of San Marcos where the plane was to take Dan and Bud back to Yarinacocha.

On the way, a large puma was crossing the river ahead of us. The Sharanahua, steering the canoe with the Briggs & Stratton 9 horsepower engine, headed straight for the puma. The albino Sharanahua Yoshi, in the bow of the canoe, had a long pole in his hand. We kept getting closer and closer to the puma.

Dan said, "Scotty, tell the guy steering to be careful and not get too close."

That advice fell on deaf ears. When we got close enough Yoshi took the long pole and hit the puma right across the back—for the fun of it. The puma rose clear out of the water with his fangs showing and claws bared. Fortunately, he couldn't touch the bottom of the river to leap closer to us and jump into the canoe as we veered away from him.

Dan said, "What a set of teeth! And I didn't have my camera ready to get a picture of him." We did get a picture of him crossing the river, but that wasn't nearly as exciting as that leap. I think

National Geographic would have been glad for that picture. We'll always be thankful that the Sharanahua steering the canoe hadn't gotten any closer to the puma.

The Sharanahuas will never forget Dan and all he did for them while he was in their community. Though he couldn't speak their language to give them his testimony without a translation from me, his message of the love of Christ came through loud and clear as he ministered to their physical needs.

—47—

AURORA—FRIEND AND HELPER

We heard a knock on our door in Yarinacocha. On the other side of the screen stood a lovely young Peruvian woman. She said, "My name is Aurora Isuiza, and I was wondering if I could work for you. I played volleyball with your daughter Becky, and I thought how much I would enjoy working for her parents." As Marie invited her in, she was immediately struck by the friendliness and politeness of this young woman. It was also a plus that Aurora liked our daughter Becky. Marie had been praying the Lord would lead her to the right woman to help her. In answer to her prayer, the Lord brought that woman to her.

To have a maid in the US is a luxury that only the rich can afford. In Peru nearly everyone has one. Hiring a young woman not only helps her and her family financially but also frees our women colleagues to do or help language and translation work. Marie wasted no time in inviting Aurora to work for us. It was one of the best decisions we ever made in Peru. What a God-send she was and is, as she continues to minister to the Sharanahuas.

It didn't take her long to catch on to how Marie wanted things done. Aurora was always diligent. Like most of the Peruvians who lived close to Yarinacocha, Aurora's family didn't have much of this world's goods. We tried to not put temptation in her path, but we need not have been concerned. Sometimes, I would forget and leave money in my pants' pocket. Whenever Aurora washed clothes she would always return the money to me. We soon learned that she was a Christian and wanted to serve the Lord by helping us.

Aurora was also an excellent cook. Though she could not *speak* English she could read enough to follow the recipes in Marie's cookbooks and do a good job of it. Even today she makes and sells special occasion cakes. (See the photo of the birthday cake she made for Marie.) We never tired of the Peruvian dishes she put before us; *aji de gallina* (chicken stew in a spicy, nutty cheese sauce), *lomo saltado* (marinated beef steak strips with onions, tomatoes, French fries, and other ingredients, served with rice), and *sopa criolla* (beef noodle soup with carrots and zucchini) were among our favorites. On Friday Marie would hand her a list of menus for the week. Then on Saturday, on her own time, Aurora would go to the market, buy everything needed, and bring it to our home to store in the refrigerator.

Aurora's husband, Juan, didn't know Christ as his Savior. One day he was in my office at the translation center. We enjoyed one another's company, and it was easy to joke with him. After a while the conversation turned more serious, and I asked Juan if he had

No, that's not a hat; it's Aurora's culinary art.

ever asked Jesus into his life. When he said he hadn't, I asked him if he would like to. When he answered in the affirmative, I led him in a prayer, and he confessed his sin and asked Jesus to save him and come into his heart as his Savior. That was a wonderful day! Now not only Aurora walked with the Lord but Juan, too, had joined the family of God. Like the rest of us he had some growing to do in the Lord, but the Holy Spirit was present in his life to cause him to grow.

After a while Aurora meant more to us than just a maid. We began to call her *Hijita* (Dear Daughter), and she called Marie *Mamita* (Dear Mom) and me *Papito* (Dear Daddy). Her kids and Juan also called us by endearing names.

Not only did Aurora become like a daughter to us, but she became a very close friend with the Sharanahuas. When we were out in one of the Sharanahua communities, we could call Aurora on our two-way radio system and give her an order for the Sharanahuas: pants, shirts, dresses, pots, shotgun shells, and various other things. She would go into Pucallpa and buy what we had ordered. Then she would mark each bundle with the Sharanahua name we had given her. It made it so easy to pass out the trade goods without having to look for each individual item while others looked on. Often the pilot had to watch the weather and try to make it back to Yarinacocha before nightfall, so he really appreciated what Aurora had done to speed things up. We were finally able to get room for Aurora on one of the flights, so she could visit the Sharanahuas whom she had been helping over the years. They made her feel welcome.

Ever since our work among the Sharanahuas finished, Aurora has continued to help them. She and Juan have taken sick Sharanahuas into their Pucallpa home and taken care of them. Though Juan and Aurora don't have much themselves, they see that visiting Sharanahuas have enough to eat and a place to stay. They often take Sharanahuas to the hospital for treatment and see that their bills are paid. They have talked with them about the Lord and have prayed with them too.

Seeing Aurora and Juan reaching out to help the Sharanahuas, I think that someday the Lord will say to them, "I was hungry and you gave me something to eat, I was thirsty and you gave me something to drink, I was a stranger and you invited me in, I needed clothes and you clothed me, I was sick and you looked after me, I was in prison and you came to visit me. ... Whatever you did for one of the least of these brothers and sisters of mine, you did for me" (Matt. 25:35–36, 40).

We love Aurora, Juan, and their children, and we can never thank the Lord enough for bringing her to our door many years ago. She is a Proverbs 31 woman and many Sharanahuas "will arise and call her blessed."

—48—

MORE THAN ALL WE IMAGINE

We had been almost twenty-five years among the Sharanahuas by 1983. Translation was progressing, but we weren't seeing the fruit we longed for. We wanted to see a vital church, a growing group of believers. It seemed that nothing much had changed since our arrival. Oh yes, a bilingual school had been established. They were learning to read and write, but it seemed nothing, or very little, was happening spiritually. We went home on furlough just "plumb discouraged."

Ray Ortlund, a man of God, had left a very successful pastorate in Pasadena, California, as he felt the Lord leading him to a different ministry, which he called Renewal Ministries. Ray, and his wife, Anne, and their team believed that the Lord was calling them to a Barnabas-type ministry to encourage pastors, missionaries, and Christian workers. Ray and Anne came to speak at our conference in Yarinacocha. In answer to prayer, the Holy Spirit graciously ministered to us through Ray's messages. Hurts were healed; sin was dealt with and cleansed. We experienced a wonderful renewal among us as missionaries. It seemed we couldn't get enough of the Lord, and love for one another in even a larger measure than we had ever known before was flowing throughout our center.

Some years later while we were on furlough in my hometown of Centralia, Washington, we received a phone call from Ray. He said he had just returned from Peru and that he was going to be in Seattle speaking to a group of Baptist Sunday school teachers. He wondered if we could come up to see him. He wanted to tell us what the Lord had done during this time in Peru. We jumped at the chance to see our dear friend and arrived in Seattle in time to take in one of his sessions.

He said to the teachers, "Maybe some of you have been teaching the Word for a number of years and you haven't seen much response. Maybe you haven't even seen anyone come to Christ. You have become discouraged, and you think nothing is going to change. You think, 'I'll keep teaching, but I guess there aren't going to be any results.' Perhaps you have completely lost the vision of what Christ wants to accomplish through your teaching. How much do you think the Lord can do? How much have you asked him to do? The Bible says he 'is able to do immeasurably more than all we ask or imagine, according to his power that is at work within us'" (Eph. 3:20).

Marie and I didn't know what the Lord was saying to those teachers, but he was speaking loud and clear to us. We asked the Lord to forgive us for having lost the vision and to do "immeasurably more than all we ask or imagine according to his power that is at work within us." After that, wherever we spoke, we asked people to pray, especially for Gustavo, now the chief among the Sharanahuas.

Upon our return to Peru I received a letter from Gustavo telling me they wanted an airstrip in Gasta Bala, so that JAARS planes could land there even when the river was too low for a floatplane. He asked if I would come out with a pilot and check out the place they had chosen and let them know if it was suitable.

So one of the JAARS pilots and I went. When we arrived, there was hardly a man in the village. They had all gone downstream to

Esperanza to get supplies. Late that afternoon we heard them coming in their canoes. As they approached, they were shooting their shotguns. Immediately, I knew they were drunk. A Sharanahua never wasted a precious shotgun shell unless he was drunk, or to announce the birth of a child.

As the canoes arrived at the shore, Gustavo staggered up the steep bank. It seemed to me the Lord was saying, "I want you to love him just as he is, not to wait until he is what you want him become. Love him just like I loved you before you accepted my Son Jesus as your Savior." When he made it to the top of the bank, I took his hand and told him I was glad to see him. I wasn't glad to see him drunk, but I was glad to see him.

That night Gustavo was too drunk to talk with us, but the next morning he showed us the site they had chosen. Although the pilot agreed that it was a good spot, he said it would take a lot of work to make it usable.

The next day we returned to Yarinacocha. A couple of weeks later a plane was out in Gustavo's area and returned with a letter from him. He wrote in Sharanahua, "I was so ashamed when I thought about how you had seen me drunk. I had to get out my book of Romans (they didn't have the entire New Testament yet) to see if God could really love someone like me."

A couple of weeks later when Marie and I returned to Gasta Bala, I asked Gustavo if he would serve as co-translator for the books of Matthew and John. He readily agreed and, as we translated, day after day the Holy Spirit was using his Word to speak to him.

One day without telling us what he had in mind, he called the whole tribe together. As they gathered in anticipation of what their chief was going to tell them, Marie and I also wondered what it was all about. He said, "I have been the poorest excuse for a chief to all of you. I have not only been getting drunk myself but bringing strong drink in to you so that you, too, could get drunk. I've been living in immorality." (He wasn't telling them anything that most of them didn't know already. In a community of two hundred people everybody knows nearly everything that's going on anyway.) Though they knew, he felt he must confess before them. He continued, "I don't want to live that way any longer. From now on I want Jesus to be my Owner." Having said that, he bowed his head and prayed a very humble prayer, telling the Lord how sorry he was for the way he had been living, and asking him to forgive him and be his Owner. After he had prayed, two of his brothers prayed similar prayers.

About a week after that, Gustavo called all the people together and again we didn't have any idea what he wanted to say. He told them, "I see from God's Word that if you are really serious about following Christ, you must be baptized. Next Sunday I'm going to be baptized." I called our dear friend Wayne Snell on the radio. Wayne and his wife, Betty, translators to the Matsigenkas, had worked with them longer than we had been with the Sharanahuas, and many of them had come to Christ.

I asked Wayne, "What did you do when the first Matsigenka wanted to be baptized?"

Wayne replied, "Well, you can do one of two things. You can baptize the first one yourself to show them how it is done, or you can explain baptism to two of them and have them do it themselves." I chose the latter way and explained to Gustavo and his younger brother Luis the significance of baptism.

The next Sunday the whole tribe turned out and stood on the bank of the muddy Purus River to see what their strong chief was going to do. He walked halfway down the bank and turned and looked up at his people. Then he did something we had never seen any Sharanahua man do in public, except at the time of death. The tears came and he said, "I have so hurt my Owner over the years,

278

and I don't want to ever hurt him again but give him my life." Then he continued on down the bank into the river. Luis, waiting to baptize him, said to the Sharanahuas, "This is not really me who is doing this. I'm doing it on behalf of the Holy Spirit."

They didn't follow exactly the pattern I had given them, but I was totally convinced that the Lord was very pleased with this first-ever Sharanahua baptismal service. It's so wonderful when the people speak from their own hearts and not just parrot whatever the translator has told them they should say. During the rest of that month while we were there, many other Sharanahuas followed their example and were baptized.

The Sharanahuas gathered together every night to sing hymns in their language, to listen to the Word, and pray. Every night for a whole month, at least one Sharanahua confessed his or her sins and asked Jesus to be his or her Owner. One night one of the women got up and began to tell about a canoe trip she had taken. Another of the women interrupted her, saying, "Never mind all of that, just confess your sins and ask Jesus to be your Owner." The joy that the Sharanahuas were experiencing was wonderful to behold.

One night when they had met at our house, there were too many to fit on our porch, so some of them were sitting on the ground in front of the house. When the meeting was over, Marie and I stepped off the porch and felt it sprinkling. We were amazed because Sharanahuas never sit outside when it's raining. They were so engrossed in praising the Lord, singing to him, listening to his Word, accepting Christ as their Savior, and praying, that evidently they hadn't even thought about the drizzle.

The meetings went on nightly, as the people spontaneously met together. Marie, I, and our daughters were like spectators looking at what the Holy Spirit was doing. At the end of the month every adult Sharanahua in Gasta Bala, with the exception of five people, had prayed, confessing their sins and asking Jesus to be their Owner. It was a glorious time. We wished our sons could have been there, too, to witness what God was doing. Always our kids had been anxious to leave the village and return to our center, to be back with their friends and be away from the gnats, but not this time. Becky and Priscilla were excited about what God was doing among their Sharanahua friends. We were witnessing the Lord doing "immeasurably more than all we ask or imagine, according to his power at work." What an encouragement!

Several months after we returned to Yarinacocha, I received a letter from Roy Hoyle, one of three brothers engaged as traders of supplies among the Sharanahuas and others living on the Purus and Curanja Rivers. He wrote that Gustavo had arrived at their home to buy some supplies. As usual he offered Gustavo some Brazilian rum.

Gustavo replied, "No gracias, Don Roy, I have asked Jesus to be my Owner and his Word tells us we are not to get drunk."

Roy thought this was just a phase Gustavo was going through and that he would get over it. A few months later Gustavo returned to Roy's house. Roy said that again he said to Gustavo, "Let's sit down and have some rum together."

Again Gustavo said, "No gracias, Don Roy. Like I told you before, I don't drink that anymore. I've made Jesus my Owner. I'm obeying God's Word that tells us not to get drunk. We don't want strong drink in our community

Sharanahuas eager to hear the Word.

280

anymore, and we wish you wouldn't bring it when you come to visit us."

Roy said to me in the letter, "Don Eugenio, I've never seen such a transformation in anyone in my life. I need that kind of a transformation in my own life."

I thought, *Isn't it something that the Lord would use one that many would call a lowly Indian to be a strong witness to a man who was a graduate of the most prestigious university in Peru.*

Again the Lord was doing "immeasurably more than all we ask or imagine, according to his power" working through Gustavo as he obeyed God's Word.

—49—

DOES THE WORD OF GOD
MAKE A DIFFERENCE?

On January 8, 1956, five young men were slain by Waorani spears on the Curaray River in the jungle of Ecuador as they attempted to make a peaceful contact with the people group, then known as Aucas (a disparaging name). After months of prayer and preparation, the men had flown into Waorani territory and landed their Piper Cub airplane on a sandbar at the edge of the river. I was in Lima recuperating from hepatitis when the news came. Shortly after that, someone came from the States and brought a copy of *Life* magazine to our group house. I remember reading in the letters to the editor: "Why don't the missionaries leave those native people alone? They're happy the way they are."

I remember thinking, *Only those who have never lived in a community where the people have never known the good news of the Scriptures could say a thing like that.*

When we first went to the Sharanahuas they had no concept of God, they had never heard of Jesus Christ, and they had not one verse of the Bible translated into their own language. Their language had never even been written down. We saw how "happy" they were. Marie and I can never forget one heartrending sight, indelibly fixed in our minds, of the young Sharanahua man, Basho, standing in the grave dug for his 2-year-old daughter, holding her lifeless body in his arms, wailing piteously. He had never heard that Jesus loves little children and that he said, "Let the little children come to me, and do not hinder them, for the kingdom of heaven belongs to such as these" (Matt. 19:14).

Basho thought he would never see her again, that sweet, precious little baby of his. As was their custom, one of the Sharanahuas came over and tenderly took the lifeless baby out of his arms while another Sharanahua gently helped him out of the grave and led him to his house as he continued to wail loudly. His wailing, along with his family's, would go on for days, weeks, and even months. This same anguish of soul applied to any of the Sharanahuas who lost a loved one. They had never heard in their language that "God so loved the world that he gave his one and only Son, that whoever believes in him shall not perish but have eternal life" (John 3:16). They thought that death was the end and they would never see that loved one again. To them there was no hope. Happy the way they were? Hardly!

As we mentioned earlier, during our first years with the Sharanahuas there was no doctor or nurse in the area. What medical attention they received came from us. Whenever they were hurt or sick they came to us. Often it was a wife who had been beaten by her husband, not just beaten, but beaten unmercifully. Some of the atrocities committed against wives were unspeakable. Always the wife would come to Marie and me afterwards to receive some balm for her wounds.

When a wife felt she could stand it no longer, sometimes she would run away. Then the whole village would go out hunting for her. When she was found, as invariably she was, the husband would beat her. One teenage wife ran away from a particularly cruel husband. When they found her, the husband got a big board and began to beat her. Their house was close to ours, and we could hear the loud Whack! Whack! Whack! as board struck soft back. Usually, I tried to stay out of marital problems and other family or tribal issues. I hadn't come there to be a policeman over their disputes or fights but to give them the Word in their language, which would bring peace and a Christlike attitude. This time I could stand it no longer, as I knew that soon we would be treating the lacerated back, and I wanted it to stop, not just so that we wouldn't have worse wounds to treat, but also so that the poor, young wife's pain would stop. I walked over to the home and said to the husband, "That's enough!"

He replied, "She's not worth anything." The husbands had never experienced Christ in their lives and didn't know that his Word says: "Husbands, love your wives, just as Christ loved the church [his people]" (Eph. 5:25). They didn't know the Word of God says, "Let this mind be in you, which was also in Christ Jesus" (Phil. 2:5 KJV), and again, "In your anger do not sin," "Get rid of all bitterness, rage and anger, ... along with every form of malice. Be kind and compassionate to one another, forgiving each other, just as in Christ God forgave you" (Eph. 4:26, 31–32). They didn't know those admonitions, and so they suffered. Happy the way they were? Hardly.

Many nights I heard it coming from the other end of the community: men chanting as they sat on a log, drinking *ayahuasca*, a hallucinogenic drink made from the stem of a vine. The Sharanahua men drink it while grasping their spears or some sort of weapon. When it began to take effect, the men hallucinated and chanted. To me the rhythmic, guttural chant sounded demonic. Along with the hallucinations comes violent vomiting. It would go on for hours, and it was always difficult for me to sleep. I never got used to it.

The men saw all kinds of visions. One man even said he saw my father, who, of course, he had never seen before, not even in a picture. Sometimes they would see snakes and be afraid. I remember one young man having joined in the ayahuasca drinking for the first time. He had a very bad reaction. I don't know what he saw, but he had crossed the river and was hanging onto the canoe as though he was being attacked. He said it scared him so badly he would never drink ayahuasca again. Those drinking the drug always ended up weak the following day. Happy the way they were? Hardly.

As the Sharanahuas began to accept the Lord Jesus as their Savior, without any prompting from me or Marie, they quit using the drug. Finally, much to our joy and theirs, during the last several years we were there, we never heard them drinking ayahuasca again. They would turn out in the evening to sing songs of praise to the Lord and listen to God's Word instead. To them hearing and reading the Word of God in their own language has made a difference.

One little girl, Facuni, who was about 6 years old, heard that Jesus loved her, and she believed it. I don't think I ever saw a happier little girl. She had a million-dollar smile, which was on display all the time. She had a glow about her that was contagious. When she walked into a gathering, her smile just seemed to light up the place. Everyone liked Facuni.

While Marie and I were at Yarinacocha, Facuni became very ill. Someone told Gustavo, who was the chief and also the pastor, that he better go see Facuni.

Facuni always had an infectious smile.

As Gustavo approached her hammock, in typical Sharanahua fashion, he said to her, "Little sister, are you going to die?"

She answered, "Not if you will pray for me." Gustavo prayed for her, but she did die. As the people gathered at the burial, Gustavo said, "We prayed for little sister that she would be healed. She died, but now she *is* healed. She is in heaven with Jesus where she will never be sick again." Though I missed Facuni, I was glad I wasn't there when she died. What Gustavo said at the graveside did not come from any suggestion or teaching from me. That was the Holy Spirit revealing to him that as his Word says, in heaven we will be like Jesus, and be completely whole. There was no prolonged wailing. Yes, they missed Facuni, but she was with Jesus, and if they, too, accepted Jesus they would see her again.

Did the Sharanahuas want to be left alone and never hear about Jesus and eternal life through reading and hearing the Word of God in their own language? They would say how thankful they were for having the assurance of heaven through seeing and hearing the Word that speaks to their hearts. To them hearing and reading the Word of God in their own language has made a difference.

Do the Scriptures in their own language bring about changes in their lives? Yes, they do; changes for the better. In a million years Marie and I could not have persuaded the Sharanahuas to turn from customs that were harmful to them. But the Holy Spirit through his Word could bring about these wonderful changes, bringing them to faith in Christ and the peace that only he can give.

About forty years ago Yambafacu, which means "without child," gave birth to a girl. After the birth, her mother said, "You already have a daughter. You don't need another. I'll bury this one." That's what some of them used to do if they didn't want the new-born. So the grandmother took the little baby, dug a shallow grave, and buried her alive.

Another Sharanahua woman, Chatafundia, saw the grandmother bury the baby and said, "No! That's not right. We heard that God's Word said we shouldn't kill." And she went immediately and uncovered the baby, taking the dirt out of her mouth and nose, and the baby breathed and lived. Chatafundia took the little baby home to nurse it. Someone said, "She has been taken out of the ground, so her name is Maishato, which means "hole in the ground."

Later Maishato's mother was sorry that her mother had buried her baby and asked Chatafundia if she could have her back. Chatafundia gave Maishato back to Yambafacu, who loved her little girl and took good care of her, but the name Maishato stuck, and that's what everyone still calls her.

Later Yambafacu accepted Jesus as her Savior. And then when Maishato became a young woman, she also asked Jesus to be her Savior. If the Sharanahuas had not had the Word of God in their own language, Chatafundia would not have known that it wasn't right to kill and probably she would not have dug Maishato up and saved her.

Yawandi was the daughter of Chief Andres and Gustavo's older sister. She came over to Yarinacocha ill. I took her to the Clinica Amazonica where the doctor did an exploratory operation. He told me she was full of inoperable cancer. There was no hope, and he just sewed her back up. Yawandi was a radiant Christian, always smiling. She never learned to read, but she listened and was at every meeting to hear the Word. She had a simple, childlike faith in Christ. As she didn't speak Spanish, it became my responsibility to tell her and her daughter what the doctor had told me. I told her that apart from a miracle from the Lord Jesus, which he was able to do, she would not live very much longer. Yawandi didn't shed any tears when I told them, but her daughter did. A few months later as Yawandi was nearing death, she said to her people gathered around her, "It's alright to wail for a little while to show that you miss me, but don't wail for a long time because I'm going to be with Jesus, and I'll never be sick again."

Were the Sharanahuas happy the way they were before they had the Word in their own language, to hear of Jesus and his promise of eternal life? They would tell you they weren't. They would tell you, "We're so glad that we finally have God's precious Word in our language and can hear and believe his promises. He has given us victory over the fear of death and evil spirits and the joy of knowing we can spend eternity with Jesus."

—50—

THE BLESSING OF VOLUNTEERS

Word of the Sharanahuas' need for an airstrip at Gasta Bala reached our dear friends from Cheyenne, Wyoming, Bill and Ila McIlvain. They wrote asking if some of the young men from their church could help build it. Marie and I were thrilled that they wanted to help. Their two sons, Larry and Mark, had been like sons to us when they lived next door to us at Yarinacocha. Bill and Ila's son-in-law, Brian Kopsa, was another. To complete the four, Sam Saur also volunteered his services. Along with these, our friends Willie and Kay Gesch with their four children—Sam, Jennifer, Aaron, and Amy—

The Gesche family completed the crew (from left): Sam, Aaron, Willie, Kay, Amy, and Jennifer.

asked to help. Priscilla was excited to have her friends from Yarinacocha with us out on the Purus River, and it was always a joy to Marie and me to have our close friends and prayer partners Willie and Kay with us.

Marie and I were already out in Gasta Bala working on the translation when the four from Cheyenne arrived in a JAARS float-plane. When Brian got out of the plane and unfolded his 6-foot 8-inch frame, the Sharanahuas were awestruck, oohing and aahing. They had never seen anyone near that size. Sharanahua men rarely get as tall as five feet ten inches. Being the friendly people they are, they quickly went down to the edge of the river to warmly greet the four husky young men. They were going to need all their strength for the task that lay ahead of them.

They arrived on a Friday and were gung-ho to get out to the airstrip and start. I suggested they just take it easy during the weekend and start working the following Monday. But they wanted to get right at it and asked me to take them to the site to have a look at it. While I appreciated their zeal, I still wanted them to get used to the surroundings and the heat before tackling the job. Reluc-

Cheyenne, WY, volunteers (from left) Larry McIlvain, Bryan Kopsa behind Mark McIlvain, Sam Saur.

tantly, I honored their wishes and took them to the airstrip, a walk of 15 minutes or so. The Sharanahuas had already cut down the trees on the 300 meters where the airstrip was to be built. When the four fellows saw all of those stumps that would have to be dug out, roots and all, the formidable task they were facing suddenly struck them. Though they said nothing, I could see it on their faces.

I think they were glad after all to have the weekend to prepare for what awaited them on Monday.

When the Gesch family arrived, we became one big happy family, all thirteen of us. The Gesch family lived in our home, except for Sam, who joined the four fellows and lived in Rombu's house. Rombu was Gustavo's younger brother. He and his family moved out so the fellows could live there. All of the houses had thatched roofs. I don't think Brian was ever able to stand up straight in that house. Kay Gesch did the cooking for all of us, so that Marie could work on Sharanahua literacy materials while the girls helped with household chores. Willie and his two boys joined the Cheyenne foursome in working on the airstrip. Aaron was too young to wield a machete or an axe, but he was anxious to help where he could.

As in building the airstrip at San Marcos, the fellows freed me to devote all of my time to the translation. While I wanted to be out there with them, I was told that one of the reasons they were there was so that I wouldn't have to take time away from the translation.

Monday dawned and the fellows were off to the airstrip to work alongside about twenty Sharanahua men. There were no chainsaws or heavy moving equipment available that one might associate with building an airstrip. Their tools consisted of machetes, picks, axes, shovels, and gunnysacks made to look like stretchers with poles on both sides of the sack. The dirt was piled onto the gunnysack, which then was moved from one place to another to make the ground level or fill in holes. Where the stumps had been removed, deep holes had to be filled in and tightly tamped down. The work could not have been more strenuous, accompanied by oppressive heat and hordes of gnats. Never once did I hear a word of complaint from the fellows. At the close of the day, it was down to the river to enjoy soaking in its coolness, getting rid of the day's dirt and sweat.

In the evenings the Sharanahuas gathered together, singing God's praises, listening to his Word expounded, and praying—

all in the Sharanahua language. Though the fellows and Kay and her girls could not understand Sharanahua, still they enjoyed being with these newly made friends as they worshipped. I think it caused them to realize that the work they were doing on the airstrip would help in speeding the day when there would be a Sharanahua New Testament.

At night there were no electric lights to dim the glow of a full moon or, on a clear night, the beauty of the myriad stars spread over the entire sky. No traffic, motors, or other sounds to interfere with the stillness. Oh, it wasn't completely silent. There were crickets, owls, and other jungle sounds but nothing compared to city noises.

I remember especially one beautiful night standing out under the stars with Brian, Larry, and Mark. The night was cool, but the fellowship in the Lord was warm. We were really enjoying each other's company. I'll never forget, and it meant so much to me, when Larry McIlvain said, "Uncle Scotty, you are like another father to me." Wow! I could bask in that expression of love for a long time from this young man whom I loved and admired as I did his father and mother and the other two young men. In fact, it still brings sweet memories to me when I think of it.

After the refreshing evening and a night's rest, it was back out to the airstrip. Once the formidable task of getting all the stumps out, digging down deep enough to get the roots out too, they waited for the felled trees, bamboo, and brush to become tinder dry to set on fire. Afterwards they had to clear all of that off the airstrip and level it stretcher-full by stretcher-full of dirt.

Finally, it was considered level enough to tamp the dirt down. Heavy poles 4 or 5 feet long were prepared. Then everyone lined up across the airstrip and started down the full 300 meters, tamping as they went. Some of the strong Sharanahua women joined in too. They started off together tamping the dirt with the blunt end of the pole, which was 5 or 6 inches across. Up and down the airstrip they went until it was considered firm enough for a plane to land on. We didn't want any soft places, which could make the plane's wheel sink and cause it to flip or damage the strut. The pilot instructed us to use a sharp pole to test it, which should not penetrate more than 2 or 3 inches into the ground before it could be considered hard enough for the plane to land safely. Finally, I thought the airstrip was firm enough to have the plane make an initial landing.

All the Sharanahuas with our guests, along with Marie, Priscilla, and I lined up on the sides of the airstrip as pilot Dave Ramsdale skillfully made two or three soft touchdowns without stopping completely. As Dave was letting down for the final approach, I was standing next to Gustavo the chief and heard him talking to the Lord, "Set it down easy, Lord, set it down easy." Dave made a beautiful landing and pronounced the airstrip fit for use. This was music to the ears of the Cheyenne four and to Willie and his boys, as well as to the Sharanahuas. The rest of us were rejoicing, too. The airstrip would only get harder as time went by. For all those working on the airstrip it was a job well done.

The airstrip in Gasta Bala quickly became lined with homes.

—51—

ZACARIAS—
A HUMORIST COMES TO FAITH

The Sharanahua Zacarias was one of the strongest men I had ever seen. Once, when he, I, and some other people were going downstream in a fully loaded canoe, the canoe hit a snag just under the surface of the water and got stuck. Quick as a flash Zacarias leaped out of the canoe and into the water about up to his chest. I started to get out, too, but he said, "No, no! Stay there!" He put his shoulder under the canoe and, in spite of the weight of the Sharanahuas plus me and all of our gear, he lifted the canoe and on we went. He liked to help others, and I liked him very much.

Zacarias could always make me laugh, and he made the Sharanahuas laugh too. One day we were sitting together on a bench on our porch, he on one side of me and children on the other. He would quietly reach around behind me and flick the young one on the ear and then sit there acting innocent, hoping the child would think someone else did it. But he couldn't help but break out in a grin and a laugh, and the kids loved it. In some ways he was the town clown. Zacarias learned a few phrases in Portuguese and loved to use them with traders from Brazil, who often came across the border into Peru to sell their wares. The Sharanahuas laughed to hear his Portuguese.

Zacarias liked to give people nicknames. One pilot liked to talk with the people in Spanish. They didn't understand everything he said, but appreciated that he was so friendly and talkative. Because of the way he talked, Zacarias gave him the name *Kai*, which meant "macaw," because macaws sometimes sounded like they were talking, and they went on for a long time.

Zacharias was still joking in his old age.

After we had been a good while with the Sharanahuas, they decided it was time to take us into their kinship system. Zacarias gave me the name of one of the older Sharanahuas as his hair reminded him of mine. So I became Fasanahua. Whatever that man's relation was to other Sharanahuas, that's what I became to them. So to some I became *Upa*, Father, to others, *Ochi*, Big Brother, to others, *Coca*, Uncle, to others, *Raisi*, Father-in-law, and to some *Ania*, Brother-in-law, etc.

They gave Marie the name of Fasanahua's wife, Yambacora, and whatever relationship she had with others, that's what Marie was called. Our children were given the names of Fasanahua's children: Steve was Fuconahua, Becky was Tutu, and Priscilla, Cafi. Since they had been calling David Fosho since he was a baby, Fosho meaning "white-haired one," they didn't want to change his name. Our children were, like us, addressed by their kinship names and seldom referred to by our given names. With that, thanks to Zacarias, we were incorporated into their kinship system.

The only thing I didn't like about Zacarias was that he made fun of anyone who listened to God's Word or believed in Jesus Christ.

One day we heard Sharanahua women coming down the trail toward our house. They were all wailing very loudly. I ran outside to find out what was the matter. I heard one woman scream, "Zacarias has been bitten by a poisonous snake." We had no anti-venom with us. Quickly, I got on the radio and called our doctor. I said, "Doc, this man has been bitten on the leg by a poisonous snake. I have no anti-venom. What can we do?"

He said, "Get his leg in the coldest water possible," So I had Zacarias go down the bank of the river and sit in the water, which was cold but not very. All this time the women continued to wail in sympathy so loudly I could hardly hear myself think.

Suddenly, Zacarias did something unheard of in the Sharanahua culture. He shouted, "Quiet!" The women were shocked, but they all stopped wailing. Then Zacharias said, "Ania (Brother-in-law), pray for me."

It was easy for me to pray for Zacarias. I loved him and didn't want to see him die without knowing Christ. After I prayed I said, "Zacarias, now you need to pray yourself." He had never prayed in his life. I think he prayed about a two-word prayer: "Help, Lord!" Sometimes that's all you need to say, and the Lord hears you. The Lord heard Zacarias, and he got better.

Nights later, as I was standing outside the church, Zacarias came up to me and said, "Ania, can God forgive anything?"

I replied, "Yes, he can forgive anything."

"Can he forgive murder?" The Sharanahuas had told me that many years before Zacarias had killed someone, perhaps from another tribe.

"Yes, he can forgive murder. He can forgive anything."

He replied, "Then I'm going into the church this evening and confess my sins and ask Jesus to be my Owner."

And that's exactly what he did. After that he never missed a meeting in the church. He never learned to read, but he could listen. He lived right across the Gasta Bala airstrip from us, and nearly every evening he would be singing Sharanahua hymns and praying out loud.

One day a Sharanahua who hadn't yet accepted Christ as his Savior was going by Zacarias' house and heard him praying.

He asked, "Who are you talking to?"

Zacarias replied, "I'm talking to God."

"Well, he doesn't hear you."

"Oh yes, he does. He always hears me."

And now Zacarias is with Jesus and not only gets to talk with him but is looking into his face and enjoying all the bliss of heaven.

That was one of the great privileges we had in translating the Bible into the Sharanahua language: to see the change in lives like that of Zacarias, as they accepted the message of the Bible and learned that God could forgive anything. They could hear in their own language that "God so loved the world that he gave his one and only Son, that whoever believes in him shall not perish but have eternal life."

—52—

FIRST CONTACT WITH THE YORA

The Yora lived way upstream on the Mishagua River, a tributary of the Sepahua River. With no one near for many miles around, deep in the heart of the Amazon jungle, the Yora kept to themselves. They had no contact with people outside their territory. If anyone came close, they would shoot to kill with bow and arrow. One time a crew of Peruvian men was working close to their territory. Two Yora men crouched down, hidden in the jungle ready to shoot the workers as soon as they got close enough. One of the workers spotted them and advised his employer. The employer, a Peruvian Christian and a very benevolent man, told his men to capture the Yora but not to harm them. Sneaking up on them, the Peruvians overpowered the two and brought them back to their employer. They couldn't speak Yora, but they tried to get through to them not to shoot at them anymore. The Yora wore no clothes, so the workers gave them some, which they gladly accepted. After giving them more presents and something to eat, they let them go.

Later in 1985 Wayne Snell received word that a couple of the Yora had ventured into a mestizo community. Then they went back to their people, taking with them a very severe strain of flu. Living deep in the Amazon jungle, there was no medical help. They began to die from this flu for which they had no resistance. By the time Wayne was able to send word to our administration at Yarinacocha, many of the Yora had already died. The Peruvian government asked SIL to send medical aid. So Wayne went out with Kim Fowler to make a contact.

When Wayne and Kim came back to Yarinacocha, they brought with them two Yora who were very sick—a young man and his wife. The Yora language is in the Pano language family as is Sharanahua. The two languages are very similar, so we were able to communicate with them. They were put in a small house behind ours. It was providential that there was only one person in the house when the Yora arrived. He was a Yaminahua, whose language was also in the Pano language family, so he was a big help.

This Yora couple were like fish out of water. They had never been out of their community before, and everything was new to them—our cars and motorcycles, our strange customs, our type of food. When they first arrived, the woman had a temperature of nearly 105 degrees. It was easier to put up with our ways as long as they were so weakened and needed our medical assistance, but when they began to get well, they became very antsy to get back to their home.

One day while I was at the translation center I got a call from Ray Parker, the center director, saying, "Scotty, did you know that the two Yora are heading down the road with their duffle bag?" I certainly didn't know that. I jumped on my cycle and went to Ray's home, where he picked me up in his car. We took off to intercept the Yora. Fortunately, we got to them just before they arrived at the nearest Peruvian town, also called Yarinacocha. I say fortunately because they were dressed just like they would have dressed in their own community. The young woman had nothing on from the waist up, and the young man had nothing on from the waist down. We had put a small potty in the house for them in case they needed it. They didn't know what that was for, or didn't believe it when we told them. So the Yora young woman decided it would make a good hat, which she was now wearing. Can you imagine the response of the citizens of the Peruvian community if they had seen these two in their state of dress, or better put, their state of undress? They probably would have laughed hysterically, which would have frightened the Yora even more.

As Ray pulled up next to them, I said, "This trail doesn't go to your house. Please get into the car." Fortunately, they got in, perhaps thinking that we would take them to the right trail, when in reality there was no trail to get to their community. They could only get there by air. I told them that they weren't completely well yet, and as soon as they were well we would send them back in our airplane.

The following day a neighbor called and said, "Scotty, the Yora are leaving again." I jumped on my cycle and this time caught up with them after they had gone just a short ways. I took their duffle and went back to their little house. This time I felt we had better send them back. They were well enough and not contagious, so it was safe to send them.

I told them, "Tomorrow we will send you back to your home."

The woman answered, "You lie."

The Yaminahua man, who was standing there, said, "No! He never lies. You can believe his word." I was very glad for this word of confirmation.

The next day we sent them on their way, and this was really of the Lord. That very day after they left, a Peruvian policeman and a newspaper reporter came to our center. They were taken to the director of Tribal Affairs Jim Daggett's office. The policeman told Jim, "We have it on good authority that SIL is holding two indigenous people here against their will." Evidently, someone had seen them trying to leave and us making them get back into the car and had jumped to the wrong conclusion.

Jim answered that they had been staying behind our house and invited the men to go ask me. I explained that these two people, who had never been out of their isolated community, had been brought in terribly sick and probably wouldn't have made it without medical attention, which our clinic provided for them. Naturally, they were anxious to get back to their own community and their own customs. We felt they were sufficiently over their sickness, and we had sent them back that very morning. The policeman was satisfied with my explanation, and the newspaper reporter lost his story. The Lord's timing had been perfect.

—53—

MEDICAL EMERGENCY
AMONG THE YORA

Following Wayne Snell and Kim Fowler's contact with the Yora, a team was assigned to go treat the sick. Not one person among the Yora was well. The team included Dr. Cal Wilson; a nurse, Julie Schwandt Brasher; and a linguist working with the Yaminahuas, Lucy Eakin Lindholm. Jim Daggett asked me to go out also with Kim because I could interpret for the nurse. Carolyn, Kim's wife, would follow sometime later as she and Kim were assigned as linguists to the Yora.

Kim and I went out in the floatplane, a Helio Courier, with pilot Ray Kingsley. Before we left Yarinacocha, Ray instructed me on how to drop boxes out of the airplane. We were going to first fly over the place where the Yora and Dr. Wilson, Julie, and Lucy were and drop them some sorely needed medicines. I was in the back seat securely strapped in. The stream that Ray flew over to get there was picturesque and very narrow. In some places the overhanging branches completely obscured it. We could see that it was rugged country that Kim and I were going to have to hike over to get to the Yora. Ray made several passes over the village before we were ready to make the drop. He told me to keep my eye on him and when he tilted his head forward I was to push the door open sufficiently to let the package drop. To make the drops the plane got down as low as possible and still be safe. We made eight or nine passes, and all the packages dropped were eventually found.

After the drop was made we flew back to the Matsigenka village of Nueva Luz. Kim and I had a day and a half there, waiting for a couple of young Matsigenka fellows to take us upstream on the Mishagua River as far as they could in their 11-meter canoe.

While we were waiting, a Shell Oil Company helicopter sat down on the small airstrip. One of their representatives very kindly offered to fly us into the Yora community, thus saving us the rugged hike. He was a very gracious man, and if Kim and I had gone by our feelings we would have taken him up on his offer. However, we knew that to have a helicopter land where the sick Yora were would scare them half to death, and the backwash from the propeller might easily blow over some of their flimsy shelters. So we thanked him, but turned down his kind offer, explaining why.

After being used to the Purus River with its hordes of gnats in the daytime and mosquitoes at night, the very lovely Mishagua River was a paradise. We didn't even need a mosquito net. The river is a fisherman and hunter's dream too. Also an ornithologist would not have lacked for beautiful birds to study. Parrots and many other colorful birds, including the large-beaked toucan, are everywhere. Though I had lived nearly thirty years in the jungle and seen lots of birds, I had never seen anything to compare with these.

The macaws, some deep red and blue, and others blue and gold, flew in large flocks at times. Once we came around a bend in the river and were approaching a cliff. On the side of that cliff it seemed that there must have been nearly two hundred macaws sunning themselves. When they heard the sound of the motor they all took off at once. The sky was filled with red, blue, and gold. It was a sight that would have thrilled *National Geographic* photographers.

Traveling by canoe, you never know what awaited you around the next bend in the river or even on a straight stretch. Sometimes many black turtles lined up, sunning themselves on a fallen tree over the river. As the noise of the 9 horsepower engine got closer, the turtles would all dive off the tree into the water. Occasionally, we saw alligators sunning themselves on a sandbar. Again at the noise of the engine they would slither swiftly and silently into the water. We saw black spider monkeys swinging through the trees. Then there were red howler monkeys. The first time I heard one, it sounded like a lion. Their roar can be heard up to 3 or 4 miles away. On rare occasions one of the largest animals of the rainforest, the handsome jaguar, might be seen crossing the river or walking beside it. They won't attack unless trapped or are very hungry and come

This tiny shelter gave relief from the sun.

Kim Fowler is eager to learn the language and culture of the Yora.

307

across someone unguarded and can sneak up on the person. The gray tapir, with its curved snout, weighing between 500 and 800 pounds and standing about 29 to 42 inches tall is typically a nocturnal animal, but we did see a couple of them, which hurried to get out of our sight. What a ride!

As we journeyed along in the canoe, once in a while we would stop at a sandbar, build a leaf shelter to keep the sun from beating on us, and cook our meal there.

We encountered the first Yora early one morning, about a half dozen of them. The men were naked except for monkey tooth belts. The women wore abbreviated skirts of bark cloth. They were nearly all very sick and suffering from malnutrition. I gave three of them penicillin shots, telling them that the shots would make them get better. It was good to be able to communicate with them and to think that never having seen us before they would submit to being stuck with a needle and accept my word that it would do them good. We knew that Cal Wilson, the doctor, was on his way toward us on his way back to Yarinacocha and could check these people if they needed something more to be done.

At about noon we met Dr. Wilson coming downstream. It had been a highly emotional five days for him among these indigenous people who had been isolated for so long. On every hand were the sick and dying, and he longed to be able to communicate the gospel to them. At least he could minister to them physically and pray that one day they would hear the good news.

During the few minutes we had together he told us about one very sick Yora man to whom Lucy was able to tell a little bit about the Lord using her grasp of Yaminahua, which is also close linguistically to Yora. The man said, "That's good. I want to hear more." The doctor got choked up telling us about it because it meant so much to him to know that the very first time a Yora man heard a little bit of the gospel, he had responded positively. He told us that the hike had taken him five hours, most of it being not on a trail but walking through shallow streams. He then got into the canoe with the two Matsigenkas for the trip downstream, and it was our turn to take the hike.

Trail was a word almost too good for the route that we took to the Yora shelters. How glad we were to have the Yaminahuas and Amahuacas to guide us to our destination. Kim and I might still be lost if we had tried to make this trip without guides. We were forced to hold to a fast pace to keep up with them. Occasionally we had to go under fallen trees that weren't touching the ground. We often don't think of the jungle as being hilly, but in places it was. We came to a sparkling waterfall with a crystal-clear pool at the bottom. It looked so inviting that Kim and I dove in and had a refreshing swim.

Choro, the Yaminahua who used to live near us on the Purus River, was with us and had had a lot of contact with the Yora. He told us that whiskers were repulsive to them. So Kim and I shaved so we wouldn't look any stranger than we were. We camped all night near the waterfall. It was a restful night except that it was pitiful to hear the groans of sick Yora who had joined us unexpectedly on the trail.

The next morning at 6:30 we got underway with Pascual, a Yaminahua whom I had known when he lived on the Purus River, taking the lead. The pace was brisk at the outset. Kim and I both felt as good as we had felt since we left Yarinacocha. I had read Psalm 41 that morning, a great encouragement to me. I believed that God was going to give me the strength for the rugged trip ahead. I had about 30 pounds in my backpack, while the tribespeople were carrying at least twice that much. The sick Yora brought up the rear. Kim and I felt bad for them and wondered if they could make it. Some of them walked along slowly using a pole to keep from falling, a heartrending sight.

It was uphill and downhill, over logs and under logs, through thick brush, and occasionally fording shallow streams. At one point my legs cramped up. I just could not go on, but we had to go on to keep up with our guides or be lost in the jungle. Kim prayed that the Lord might touch my legs and take away the cramps. The Lord quickly answered prayer, and I was able to continue the hike on to the Yora village, which we reached just before noon. We were greeted by Julie and Lucy. In all of my years in Peru I don't suppose I had ever seen a more isolated place than this one, situated on top of a ridge.

I could hardly believe my eyes at the sight of these suffering Yora people. Little flimsy lean-tos of a few palm leaves were scattered here and there. The pain in the eyes of the very sick touched my heart. But there was no time to dwell on our own sadness, as we had to make the rounds. Julie prescribed the medicine needed for each one, be it an injection or pills. At each lean-to home there was a small fire built inside, so we had to be careful not to step on it or on hot coals.

These were people who had never had medicine before, and some were very hesitant to take it. One woman told us that she wasn't going to take it. I explained to her that she couldn't get well if she refused it.

Finally, she consented, "Alright, but I'll take only one of those two pills."

Julie told me, "Tell her that one won't do any good. She has to take both to get well."

She hesitated again, but finally took them, and then with a look of resignation, said, "Now I'm going to die" ... but she didn't.

None of them had ever had an injection before. They must have thought, *I'm already sick. Why are they sticking me with a needle?* But as I explained that what the needle was putting inside of them would make them well, with much fear and trepidation they submitted.

The Yora had never swallowed pills before, and some found it hard to do. They were used to chewing food before swallowing. In one case I decided to show one of them how to do it. Without thinking, I swallowed a vitamin using the same unclean cup we were using to give medicine to the sick.

Julie, shocked, exclaimed, "Scotty, do you know what you just did?" As soon as she said it, I knew what I had inadvertently and foolishly done, but the Lord saw to it that I didn't get sick. God knew the Yora needed all the help they could get, as well as someone who could understand them.

Choro had made Kim and me a flimsy shelter before we got there. Lucy and Julie had a shelter next to ours, which wasn't much sturdier, though a bit bigger. They had no table. They had their meals outside, sitting on banana leaves on the ground and also using banana leaves for a table. As Kim and I sat there with them for a meal, Lucy jokingly said, "My mother used to say, 'I wouldn't do this for love or money.' We had better be doing this out of love, because there isn't much money in it." Kim and I had their roof extended and had a table made for them so we all could eat more comfortably, keep things off the ground, and have a place somewhat more sterile to keep the medicine.

The Yora community was spread out over an area about six city blocks square. When we arrived, there were between eighty and ninety people, nearly all of them too sick to go very far from their houses. For most of the time, we had to make three rounds a day to make sure the people got the proper amount of antibiotics or whatever medicine they needed. That accounted for most of our day. When we weren't preparing shots, what little time left was used to prepare meals or take a bath or wash clothes.

The people seemed to be divided into clans. In each house or lean-to shelter, always without walls, the people laid in hammocks. Under each hammock, or almost under it, was a small fire.

They never let the fires go completely out. We gave names to the various dwellings. About 15 yards from our shelter was Big House, filled with sick Yora. About another 15 yards from there was Crawl-through House, so named because the leaves of the roof came clear down to the ground on all sides and on both ends you entered by crawling through a small opening. About 50 yards from Crawl-through House was Knob Hill. This house was set up higher than the others. Then down the hill about 20 yards was Chief's House. About another 20 more yards on down the trail was On the Trail Shelter. From there we had to go about the same distance down to the stream and about 50 yards up the stream to Across the Stream Shelter. And finally crossing the stream once more, End of the Trail Shelter.

When it was time for Lucy and Julie to return to Yarinacocha, Carolyn and Nurse Joan Lemke Oien came to take their places.

Here's a quote from a letter Joan wrote in September 1984:

A flu epidemic had hit the recently contacted Yora Indians. Many had died from pneumonia. Many more would have died if the Lord had not made it possible for medical teams … to go in to them. The first team included visiting doctor Cal Wilson, Nurse Julie Schwandt, and linguist Lucy Eakin. Dr. Wilson had to come out to meet other deadlines, and Eugene Scott and Kim Fowler replaced him. Because it was such a high-stress situation, Julie and Lucy were soon replaced by Carolyn Fowler and me. The Lord gave strength in a situation that was both physically and emotionally very intense.

At 9 p.m. one night a Yora man's axillary temperature was over 105 degrees. He was shaking so severely that he could not talk or swallow pills. Linguist Eugene Scott and I administered several injections and were using cool cloths to help bring down his fever. We worked hunched over in the dark because the grass roof was too low to stand up straight and the hammock very low to the ground. Around us were forty other hammocks of sleeping people. Each hammock had at least one fire by it. Smoke burned our eyes and coals our feet if we were not very careful where we stepped. Cockroaches swarmed everywhere. It had been a long hard day, preceded by many other long hard days. At times we asked ourselves, 'Is it worth it all?' After half an hour the patient's fever was still 105 degrees, but the shaking was letting up. He started mumbling and sounded angry. He was trying very hard to talk. With his ear down very close to the patient's mouth, Scotty was finally able to hear the man say, 'You made my shaking stop. I'm so happy! Thank you.' It was this kind of expression of gratitude on the part of the Yora that makes them unique from any other groups we have worked with in Peru. When you are bone-tired it goes a long way in making you feel that yes, indeed 'It is worth it all.' We have linguists who can communicate with these people! What a blessing to have that kind of help in a first contact amidst a raging epidemic. The gospel was shared and we know of six who 'took Jesus as their Owner.'

It wasn't so bad in the shelters that were more open, but in Crawl-through House especially, the smoke was so thick from all the fires that we could hardly see to give the medicine and the shots. Since it was so dark inside we had to use flashlights to be able to see. Once in a while we just had to get out of the house for a few minutes because our eyes were stinging so much from the smoke that we literally could not see anymore. How the Yora put up with it day after day and night after night, I don't know. After stepping outside for a few minutes, we could then get back in to try to give the shots before we were overcome by smoke again. We liked to get the shots in before dark, because the smoke was always worse at night. And in Crawl-through House there was another problem: cockroaches. They especially came out at night, and every leaf, every pole, and it seemed every square inch of ground was covered with little cockroaches. To get into the house it was almost impossible not to brush up against a leaf, which caused what seemed like a bushel of cockroaches to cascade down on us.

It was pitiful to see the condition of the Yora. Some of them were so emaciated that it was hard to find enough "meat" to give a shot. Coughing was almost constant. Despite their condition we were all of the same opinion that we had never seen such an affectionate people. For me it was a blessing to be able to communicate with them and interpret for the others. When I told them we had come to make them well they said, "*Aicho*," which means something like, "I'm delighted," or the closest thing to our "thank you." Often after we had given them a shot or some medicine they would say, "Massage me." They had been in their hammocks a long time and were sore. The Yora wanted to be touched; they wanted to know that you cared for them.

It was obvious that some of them, apart from a miracle, weren't going to make it. Time seemed to be against us, and I wanted to share the good news about Christ with them. In every house I told them of Jesus' love. Of course, they had never heard of Jesus. I related to them about the One who had created everything they could see and about his Son Jesus. After that, how much Jesus loved them, so much that he died for them and for me and for everybody. Then I told a little bit about the joys of heaven, how that where Jesus is no one is ever sick again, no one suffers, no one is ever hungry or thirsty, no evil spirits (of which they were deathly afraid) can be where Jesus is, and that Jesus loved them so much he wanted them to live with him forever. A group that had just arrived, when they heard this, clapped their hands and said, Aicho!" One woman said, "That's why you have come. You have come to tell us these good words."

Two days after Kim and I had arrived, we were distributing medicine and giving shots in Big House. One man named Shomba looked like a living skeleton. He was so full of phlegm that he could hardly spit it up. It was difficult for him to sit up without help. I wondered if he would make it through the night. I began to tell him about Jesus. He said it was so good to hear those words. When I told him that Jesus loved him, he put it in the imperative, "Oh, love me!" I asked him if he wouldn't like to make this Jesus his Owner and have him care for him forever. I told him that if he really wanted to I would teach him what to say to Jesus, that he could talk to Jesus just like he was talking to me and that Jesus would hear him. Shomba was the very first Yora to pray and ask Jesus to erase his sins and be his Owner. After he had prayed I told him that he was now God's child, that Jesus would never abandon him. He said to Jesus, "Aicho! Don't ever abandon me. Love me!" Nearly every day during the month we were there, I told them about the love of Christ for them.

One woman we called Chichi (which means grandmother) lived in Crawl-through House. She was a sweet old grandmother, though she was nothing but skin and bones. It was difficult to find a place to give her a shot, but she always managed to roll over so that we could give her an injection in hopes that her poor, tired body could yet respond to the treatment. Chichi would hold my hand as I told her of Jesus' love for her and the joys of heaven, and she was reluctant to let go. One day when we entered Crawl-through House it was obviously useless to subject Chichi to any more painful injections, as she could no longer respond. A few nights later Choro came over to our shelter in the middle of the night to tell me that Chichi had just died. He said that before she died she was talking about the things I had told her about Jesus. Then she said, "I'm going now," and died. I believe we'll see her someday in heaven.

One evening as Joan and I were treating the people in Big House, we came to a young man who was skin and bones. He was so congested that I didn't think he had long to live. I shared the gospel with him and asked him if he wouldn't like to ask Jesus to be his Owner and have his sins forgiven and live forever with Jesus

This Yora man is happy for the medical help given to his people.

where he would never be sick again and be completely healthy. He said he would, and so I led Chayka in a simple prayer of asking Jesus into his life. The next morning as Kim, Carolyn, Joan, and I were eating our breakfast in the little shelter without walls, to our amazement, we saw Chayka in his emaciated condition coming up the trail toward us, leaning on his staff. When he got to us, he stopped. We could hardly believe our ears when he started singing softly, "Thank you, Father God, Thank You, Father God. Thank You for sending your Son Jesus to be my Owner. Thank You, Father God." I felt we were witnessing a miracle right before us: that one who had never heard the gospel before would in less than twenty-four hours, by the Holy Spirit, sing a song of thanksgiving to the Father and Jesus. It was almost more than we could take in and brought such joy to us as I shared with the other three the words that Chayka was singing.

The Yora chief was called Shanuifo which means "owner of the house," their word for chief. Very friendly, he called me Shanuifo too, probably because I was the oldest one there and the only one who knew his language after Lucy left, and thus was doing most of the talking to them. One qualification of a chief in their minds was to "know how to talk."

He told us they wanted us to stay. Like many of the other Yora, he told us not to abandon them. One day he gave me a bunch of bananas to take home for all of us. He said, "I am the chief, and this is what the chief does for you." Later on that same day he brought us some papaya, and another man brought us some more bananas.

One of the most touching things the chief did was offer me an old axe head and two machetes that he had made himself from steel, which he had discovered someplace. These were precious items to him, but he wanted me to have them to show his gratitude for what we were doing. I had asked him earlier if I could trade for a stone axe like those of the people we had tried to contact on the headwaters of the Purus back in 1971. He didn't know anything about stone axes, so he offered what he had. Their custom is to bury valuable things with their loved ones who die. He had buried this axe and the machetes with his mother when she died. Later thinking how much he needed them, he dug them back up again. I hated to take them from him, but he urged them on me, and I didn't want to offend him. After we left, we sent out some new axe heads and machetes for the people, in appreciation for Shanuifo's gracious and sacrificial gifts to me.

Another man gave me something like a flimsy skirt, which was worn by men. It was almost like a hula skirt, but just rope-like material dangling down one or two inches apart. In order not to offend, I accepted it and thanked him. Of course, I didn't wear it like they do with nothing under it. I put it around the trousers I wore. It probably looked strange to them wearing it that way, to say nothing of how it looked to Kim, Carolyn, and Joan, but at least I was showing the man I appreciated it.

One of the most difficult things we faced while living among the Yora was that when we would just about be getting on top of things medically, with most of the people responding to the medicine (except for the very elderly women), then more very sick ones would come from villages farther away. On one day eighteen came, on another day twenty-seven, and at the last, we could hardly believe it, forty more came. It wasn't that we didn't want to treat the sick; that's why we were there, but sometimes we wondered when it would ever stop. At the same time we were glad we were there to give the medical help they needed. They came slowly, some of them so sick they couldn't walk and were being carried on the backs of others—a pitiful scene. They had no houses to go to, so they continued to overcrowd the houses already there or build quick shelters, which weren't much protection against the rain and wind.

I said earlier that when Kim and I first arrived, there were between eighty and ninety people. When we left, nearly two hundred total had arrived. Choro, who had traveled to some of the outlying communities where we had not been, estimated that in total forty-one people died from this epidemic. Only four died where we were. The rest died in other communities or on the trail, trying to make it to us.

—54—

"LOVE US, OH LOVE US!"

Of all the people groups I lived among during my nearly fifty years in Peru I never saw one yearning to be loved as the Yora. On one of our rounds to dispense medicines, four or five young Yora men were sitting on a log looking dejected. Like nearly all of them, probably they had lost loved ones and weren't feeling well themselves. My heart went out to them, and I began to tell them words they had never heard before: the good news about Jesus and his love for them.

When I mentioned God loving them, they all jumped off the log, beat on their chests and said in the imperative pleadingly, "Oh love us, Oh love us!" Here were people oh so ready to hear that someone loved them, and to hear that it was the Creator himself who loved them. They needed to have their physical needs met, but also their spiritual needs.

As we continued to dispense medicine, on some days it was very hot, and being on the top of the ridge with no trees, there was no shade to cool our shelters. The sun had no mercy on us.

On August 25 at about one in the afternoon as we were finishing our lunch, the wind began to whip up and the rain was coming down by buckets. Kim's and my shelter didn't have as good a roof as that of the women. We had only a piece of plastic over ours. We could see the wind was lifting it up, so we ran over to secure it. The rain kept coming down harder and the wind was getting stronger. It was so loud we could hardly hear one another. I was trying to hold down the plastic, all the while the wind was blowing the rain right in on the bedding. It looked like a losing proposition, and I imagined we could end up standing there all afternoon holding that plastic before the rain let up. So I let go of it.

About then I heard Kim calling me in desperation. I stepped around the corner of our shelter and could hardly believe my eyes. Joan and Carolyn's shelter had blown down almost flat to the ground. I saw Carolyn, but Joan was trapped under it. Both had been inside when it blew down. It knocked them to their knees, but Carolyn was close to the edge and was able to crawl out immediately. At first when Joan called for help nobody responded because the noise of the wind and rain kept Kim and me from hearing her, and Carolyn must have been dazed and unable to answer.

Here's Joan's testimony: "While with the Yora a very heavy wind and rain suddenly hit us. Our main shelter collapsed—on top of me. The next day when we were digging out our stuff, I saw that the very spot where I had been thrown was the only place where serious injury would not have occurred. A bench had caught three main poles, stopping the full weight from hitting me. The Lord gave protection."

When I saw what had happened and heard Kim calling for help, the adrenalin really started flowing. The three of us lifted up one corner of the shelter and Joan was able to crawl out on her stomach, suffering only a bruised leg. Besides not wanting to see Joan hurt, the Lord knew that without her we would have been hard pressed to know how to treat all the Yora. She was under the shelter not more than 5 minutes, but she was suffering from claustrophobia, and not getting any response to her calls for help, it must have seemed like an eternity to her. We were all thankful that no one was seriously hurt.

A few minutes later Kim's and my shelter was also blown over by a frio. It blows over the Argentine pampas and across the jungles of Bolivia and Peru, generally lasting not more than three or four days. This time the temperature got clear down to the high 40s, which in the jungle is extremely cold, as many of the houses have no walls to keep out wind.

Except for our belongings wrapped in plastic, everything was soaking wet. The storm came up so abruptly that we had had no time to prepare. So we salvaged what we could. Fortunately, the medicines were stored at the edge of the shelter and hadn't been broken. The place looked like a disaster area. Because all the Yora houses were full with sick people, we didn't even consider moving in with them. Miraculously, none of the Yora houses or shelters blew down. The poles for their houses no doubt were dug deeper into the ground.

There was one small cookhouse that wasn't being used. Since there was no floor there, we put down banana leaves and put a sheet of plastic over them. We also tried to put up some banana leaves for walls to protect us from the wind. We had one dry blanket between the four of us. Joan slept on one side with Carolyn next to her, Kim next to Carolyn, and I was next to Kim on the other side. Plastic is not the warmest thing to sleep on, but banana leaves are colder yet. If none of us moved too much we could all four stay on the sheet of plastic. And if nobody pulled the blanket we would all have a little piece of it to cover us.

I do believe it was the coldest, most miserable night I've ever experienced. We were right next to Big House, and every time we would hear a fresh gust of wind all the sick Yora would moan in unison because they knew they were about to get colder yet. In the middle of the night, when probably none of us had slept, Kim said,

"Hey gang, think how funny this is going to seem a month from now." When we all got done laughing we wondered what the Yora would think about us laughing when it was so cold and we didn't have a fire under us like they did. And besides, we were sleeping on the cold ground instead of in hammocks … but they didn't have any clothes on! So we figured it probably was about even.

The next day being Sunday, we called Yarinacocha on the radio and talked to our administrator about our situation. He assured us of their prayers, and said the frio had gotten to Yarinacocha also. Marie later told me that that morning for church everyone came with their warmest clothes on and some even brought blankets and sat as close together as possible. The next day a Helio Courier flew out to us and dropped sleeping bags among other things. Our 1½-inch foam rubber mattresses were so wet that we still slept on the ground, but warm, dry sleeping bags never felt better.

Choro, for some reason, didn't relish the idea of us sleeping another night in the cookhouse, so he and his son brought in palm leaves and poles and put up a couple more hastily built shelters. This time we asked them to please sink the corner poles deeper than just three or four inches into the ground and to put in a few more supports.

All the Yora had been so sick that no man was well enough to go out and hunt meat for them. Finally, one man thought he was well enough to go. Later in the day he came back with a *maquisapa* (spider monkey) over his shoulder. After he had shot the monkey he thought it was dead and took it by the tail and threw it over his shoulder. The trouble was that the monkey was not dead. As the man walked away, the monkey bit him severely on the leg. Then he made sure it was dead and brought it on in. He showed us his badly bitten leg. Joan took quite a while patching him up. Some of the Yora enjoyed one of their favorite meals.

At this point our director talked to me about coming back to the center, but he felt it was more important to have someone there who could communicate with the Yora.

Later, Joan and I knew that our time there was drawing to a close. Soon another nurse, Carol Sagert, and another linguist, Mary Ann Lord, who had been learning Yaminahua, were due to replace us. We needed to know the right time to leave and return to our work. On September 3 some of the Yora who were well, and some who weren't so well, left the top of the ridge to go down to the headwaters of the Mishagua River to make their gardens and start a new community where game and fish were more plentiful. They made a new house there for Kim and Carolyn.

It was hard to leave, even though I was anxious to be back with Marie and Priscilla and to get back to the translation of the Sharanahua New Testament. After a time of prayer with Kim and Carolyn and having made the medical rounds one more time, Joan and I got away with the Yaminahuas guiding us.

After spending a night at the place being prepared for Kim and Carolyn, we got an early start by canoe, instead of trail. At one point we came to a place where the river had gone down enough to leave a small pond on the sandbar. There was a school of fish in it like I had never seen before. It was so shallow that the fish were plainly visible, probably a foot or a foot and a half long. The men could hardly believe their good fortune and jumped out

Carolyn Fowler (left) wonders where they will put their things in their new home.

323

of the canoe and began to swing their machetes and a sharpened pole. By the time they were done they had between thirty and forty fish to salt and take home to their families.

At 1 p.m. we stopped on a sandbar so the men could cook up some of the fish, and all of us ate. Just at that moment our replacements, Carol Sagert and Mary Ann Lord, arrived, being brought upstream by a couple of young Matsigenkas. We gave them a quick orientation as to what they could expect when they arrived at the Yora location.

After we had talked with them for a while, we put up the antenna on the sandbar and called Yarinacocha to let them know we had made contact with each other. Our director of Tribal Affairs, Jim Daggett, answered and was very concerned about Kim and Carolyn. Choro's teenage son had gotten on the radio when Kim and Carolyn weren't around, having heard us call Yarinacocha so many times he knew how to do it. When the operator answered, he told him that the Yora were planning to kill Kim and Carolyn that evening. Not knowing the situation, Jim had no way of knowing it was a hoax. When I was told about it, I knew immediately that it was a teenage prank. I assured Jim that the Yora loved Kim and Carolyn and depended on their continued medical treatment and would never think of killing them. When Kim and Carolyn got on the radio I told them to get Choro so I could talk to him. I told him what his son had done and to scold him severely and tell him never to do that again. I don't know how much he bawled out his son, but it never happened again. I think perhaps teenagers are the same the world over—they like a little excitement.

After the conversation with Carol and Mary Ann, Joan and I continued downstream with our Yaminahua friends. About 11:30 that night, I was half asleep in the canoe, trying to stretch out over a couple of duffle bags. All of a sudden I felt a terrific whack on the side of my face, like a boxer had given me one of his left jabs. I thought at first of a low-hanging branch that I hadn't seen in the darkness. Instead it was a large fish that had jumped out of the water, gave me a glancing blow, and then I saw it fall back into the water on the other side of the canoe. It cut the inside of my mouth a little. Choro told me that the same thing had happened to him one time, but the fish had spines and hit him right in the chest and caused him to bleed quite a bit. I was thankful that this fish had only scales.

At the crack of dawn we started off and got to our destination, the community of Sepahua. I radioed Yarinacocha to let them know we had arrived and to report the weather for the pilot. The Peruvian army had a post at the top of the bank with a guard on the lookout for terrorists. The guard very obligingly let us put up our radio antenna there. After a quick breakfast we called Yarinacocha again at 9:30 and found out that the plane was to arrive at the airstrip at 9:50. I quickly took down the radio antenna, and we piled back into the canoe one more time to go upstream some 10 minutes to the airstrip. There I had a short visit with the lieutenant governor to tell him what we had been doing and what the situation was. He was a very friendly young fellow. He took down my name, and I invited him to visit us anytime he happened to be in Pucallpa.

What a welcome sight to see our pilot, Dave Ramsdale. He greeted Joan and me with cold cans of Pepsi. I don't think a drink ever tasted better. Dave was not only a good pilot and friend, but he was also a very thoughtful one. We took off at 10:25 a.m. and arrived at Yarinacocha at 12:10 p.m. A lot of our Yarina folks were there at the airstrip to greet Joan and me. I hadn't been able to wash clothes or shave for several days, so I don't know when I've looked grubbier ... or thinner. I got clear down from 170 to 150 pounds. Despite the dirty T-shirt and the dirty me, there were a lot of *abrazos* (hugs). Joan was wearing the one clean blouse she had left, so someone said that compared to me, she looked like she had just stepped out of Madison Avenue.

It was great to be back with Marie and Priscilla, although I felt like I had left part of my heart with the Yora. I knew I could never forget them and would be praying much for them and for Kim and Carolyn. I thank the Lord for all he let us do during the month we were with them, for all the answers to prayer, for the many people he allowed us to see come back to health, and for the privilege of being able to share the good news about Jesus Christ.

—55—

"I'M HERE FOR YOU, DAD"

In 1987 on the way up to the clinic to get something for a sore throat, I thought, *I don't remember ever feeling this tired.* Joy Congdon, both the doctor practitioner and administrator of our clinic at Yarinacocha, took a blood sample and sent it off to the laboratory in Pucallpa to be analyzed. A couple of days later, as I was working in the translation center, I got a call from Joy telling me I should go home to bed as I had typhoid fever. I wondered how it could be typhoid when I didn't have a fever. Later it was determined that this was a misdiagnosis, as more and more of my colleagues came down with the same symptoms as I had. This mysterious malady was no respecter of age as children also were complaining of the same tiredness. One boy about 8 said, "I feel like a puppet with the strings cut." That was a good description of our energy levels. I found that even prolonged conversations were tiring for me. As I have always been someone who enjoys fellowship with others, that was one of the more difficult parts of this sickness. Physical exertion was almost beyond me.

At the height of the outbreak there were about twenty on our center who were affected. Dr. Ralph Eichenberger, who had formerly worked with us in Peru, made a study, but could not find any common denominator to explain why so many of us were succumbing to this sickness. Since we didn't know its cause or name, we called the sickness "It." The Centers for Disease Control and Prevention in Atlanta finally gave it the name chronic fatigue syndrome. Much prayer went up for those of us affected. One translator who worked among the Quechuas had been afflicted with this for years, and no one knew how to help him. Now some of us knew how he must have felt all those years. Even as I write, some have never gotten over it. For me it took away much of my energy for ten years. If so many of us had not come down with it at the same time, I would not have been able to accept my inability to accomplish anything of value.

During this time our son David had graduated from Le Tourneau University in Texas as a mechanical engineer. He came down to visit us. Since Marie kept a diary I can say that it was on June 25, 1987, when, much to my surprise, David said, "Dad, I want to take all the responsibilities for the Sharanahuas off your shoulders except for the translation. While they're here at the center to help with the translation or to take the Teacher Training Course or for medical treatment, I want to serve as their helper and interpreter. I want you to conserve all your energy for the translation and have that as your one concern. No more going to Pucallpa to run errands for them, no more helping the bilingual school teachers, no more helping them with their problems.

A Sharanahua boy helps Dave bring supplies from Pucallpa.

To say that I was amazed and, oh, so thankful is an understatement. I was so used to doing all these things for the Sharanahuas that sometimes I would forget about David's offer, and when a Sharanahua would come to me with a problem I would start to help him. Then David would remind me by saying, "Dad, if you're going to do it, what am I here for?" Soon the Sharanahuas realized that they were to go to David with their needs and problems and that my job was to work with them solely on the translation. I never would have asked David to interrupt his own plans to do this but, since he was so sure it was the Lord's will, I wasn't going to argue with that.

The Sharanahuas had known David since he was a baby, and he was accustomed to their culture and to their language. David had a burden to help them. Since he is a mechanical engineer he was also a Mr. Fixit. He helped them with anything mechanical (which wasn't my forte). He helped them repair their peke-pekes, their 9 horsepower Briggs & Stratton engines that powered their canoes up and down the river. The Sharanahuas were delighted to have David's help. Of course, Marie and I were glad to have him back in our home. What a blessing he was to our work among the Sharanahuas and the translation of the Scriptures.

Several times over the years Marie and I had asked for help with community development among the Sharanahuas. But no one was free to help us. So we had to "grow our own." David helped not only with things mechanical, but when Sharanahuas needed documents, he took them into Pucallpa to the different offices to help them understand the official talking to them, as some of them knew very little Spanish. When Sharanahua men needed repairs to their 16 gauge shotguns, David took them in and made sure they were fixed properly and returned to them. If they were sick and needed more than our clinic could provide, David took them to the hospital in Pucallpa and stayed with them until they were seen by the doctor. There were a myriad of things he was doing for them.

If we were ever going to finish the New Testament translation, I had neither the time nor the energy to do all these things.

A sawmill was given to us free of charge. David had about six Sharanahuas come to Yarinacocha to show them how to operate it. He warned them of the danger of operating it without proper instructions and supervision and taught them safety precautions and how to maintain it. He warned them to never let children near it. After several days of instructions, and then letting each one operate it under his supervision, he was satisfied they were ready to run it on their own. Then they drew up a contract that each one signed, saying they wouldn't sell the sawmill without the agreement of the whole community. This was to prove a boon to the whole Sharanahua community.

Once the Sharanahuas had built an airstrip at Gasta Bala, they all moved their houses there, building on each side of the strip. Our house had to be moved also. So David went out, taking our director Wayne Howlett's son Jason with him, to oversee the move. It was a formidable task on the steamy Purus River, complete with its cloud of gnats. David and Jason piled right in and with the help of many Sharanahua men got the walls and the thatched roof up. They finished in three weeks' time.

When David first arrived in Peru to help us, he said that as soon as the Sharanahua New Testament was completed he was going to return to the US and see what the Lord had for him there. But the Lord had a nice surprise for Dave. Julie Mishler, who had also grown up in Yarinacocha, came to teach in the school there. During their school years, she was a few classes behind Dave, yet he had not particularly noticed her then. But now she was a beautiful young woman wanting to serve the Lord. The attraction was mutual and in a couple of years she became Mrs. David Scott. As time went on they felt the Lord's call to join our mission and settled down in Yarinacocha until the completion of the New Testament.

Marie and I are totally convinced that without David's help the translation of God's Word into Sharanahua would have been delayed for years. To be allowed to work exclusively on the translation was a blessing neither Marie nor I ever expected. We praise the Lord for a son who was burdened for the Sharanahuas to have the Scriptures in their own language and was willing to do what he could to make that happen.

Julie is a wonderful addition to the team.

—56—

OUR CHILDREN

Not only David, but all four of our children have been an integral part of our lives and ministry. They have blessed Marie and me in more ways than they ever could have imagined. They blessed the Sharanahuas also, who took pleasure in our kids. The children's identification with the Sharanahuas' culture enhanced our own ministry to the people. Our kids fit right in with the Sharanahua children. They often went down to the river with the other children to swim. Our boys loved to go on a hunt accompanied by one of the men of the community. The women took delight in painting the faces of our children with red or black paint. The adults were pleased to see them getting involved in everyday life in the tribe. Life with the Sharanahuas was not dull for our children. They took in stride this culture so different from that of their parents.

Becky (left) and Priscilla happily adapting to the culture.

Let me introduce you to our children.

David was born on August 1, 1958, in our clinic at Yarinacocha. As I mentioned before, David had planned to return to the US when the Sharanahua New Testament was completed, but he and Julie decided to stay. He later replaced his father-in-law, John Mishler, when he retired, and Julie replaced her mom as hostess at the Lima guest house.

Today David continues to serve under Wycliffe Bible Translators, using his God-given talents to encourage and counsel colleagues in Peru through occasional visits and by Skype. He and Julie now live just 10 minutes from our home in Waxhaw, North Carolina. They have two sons and one daughter-in-law.

Our second son, Steven, is the only one of our children born outside of Peru. Steven made his entrance into the world in Auburn, Washington, on July 6, 1960, on our first furlough. We took Steve to Peru when he was only 6 weeks old. I think his siblings would agree that Steve is the most studious of our children. He, too, has a heart for people, especially for those in developing countries. He married a lovely lady from Honduras, Leila Odeh, whom he met while serving in that country under World Relief. Leila later was appointed ambassador from Honduras to Spain. In order to serve with Leila in Spain, Steve left the factory in Honduras that he had established to help the unemployed in Honduras. Steve and Leila now reside here in the Waxhaw area where they continue in the business community and serving the Lord through their church and in personal encounters. They have three children.

Becky, our first daughter, was born in Yarinacocha on the May 2, 1964. To our delight, Becky loved music. From the time she was tiny she gravitated to the piano whenever there was a free minute.

In 1989 Jim Mottola was helping in a building project under Wycliffe Associates in the city of Huanuco, Peru. Jim and those working with him were encouraged to visit Yarinacocha before returning to the States. They were brought to our house for a meal, and that's when Jim met Becky, and a romance budded. They were married in Church on Red Hill in Tustin, California, one year later. Jim is now a vice president of a large medical supply company in Salt Lake City, Utah, where he and Becky make their home. Becky holds a Bible class for young women in her home once a week, where she teaches and encourages them in their walk with the Lord. She has also been very burdened for girls who are trapped in a very ungodly sect in that area. One of the girls escaped, and Jim and Becky took her into their home as a daughter and adopted her.

Lacie soon accepted the Lord Jesus as her Savior and has fit right in with the family. After having three boys, Becky finally got her daughter.

I had always wanted two boys and two girls for our family, but it looked like the Lord was going to let us be satisfied with just three children. Lo and behold, the Lord gave us a "PS" to our home when Priscilla was born at the clinic in Yarinacocha on the September 30, 1971. She has been a

Steve loves his baby sister, Priscilla.

delight to the family. Like Becky with the piano, Priscilla took to the violin like a duck to water. Our music director in Yarinacocha, Willie Gesch, recognized that Priscilla had an outstanding talent and encouraged her to spend a summer at the Interlochen Arts Camp in Michigan to see if she would want to make music her career. The Lord supplied the funds for her to go, and she had a great time, but her life took another course when in 1992 she married Philip Rutherford, serving with the US Army. Army life has had many challenges, but Priscilla has grown spiritually through them.

Priscilla is now involved in taking a course in massage therapy and hopes to use that skill in relieving pain for others. Philip retired from the army and is employed in a civilian capacity at Fort Bragg in North Carolina. That puts Philip and Priscilla and their three children about 2 ½ hours from us.

At various times while we were home from Peru on furlough, someone would say to us, "Aren't you afraid to raise your children down there in the jungle?" And to be honest, it was scarier for us to bring them to the States. After each furlough they were anxious to get back to Peru and out to Yarinacocha. There they had all their friends, a big lake to swim in, and Christian teachers who had the best interest of each child at heart. Folks at Yarinacocha were like family to them: we lived together, prayed together, laughed together, cried together, and shared one another's burdens. I never heard one of the many children who grew up in Peru express a regret that they were brought up at Yarinacocha instead of in the States.

Priscilla (left) and Becky: The jungle was the children's playground.

Each of our children in his or her own way has given us wonderful memories, and we're so thankful every time we can get together. We never get tired of remembering the events that make us all laugh.

This was no laughing matter, but David, our firstborn, like all the other children at Yarinacocha, liked to jump off the bank into the lake. On one of his jumps his foot caught on a root, and he fell headfirst, not into the lake, but onto the side of a canoe, laying open his lip. Marie and I weren't there, but adults seeing it happen were afraid he might have injured his back or neck. So they all told him not to move until they could get him on a stretcher and up to the clinic. After 10 minutes or so lying there, he said, "Can I move now? The ants are biting me." He had to have ten stitches in his lower lip. We're so thankful it wasn't worse.

Marie and I decided we would try to never show anxiety to our kids concerning finances. One summer we were assigned to the staff of the Summer Institute of Linguistics at the University of Oklahoma. I don't know if our finances had ever been lower. On our way there, one of us must have expressed some anxiety. From the back seat David, who was about 8, said, "What are we going to do?"

Realizing we had made him afraid, I tried to make up for it by saying, "Don't worry, David, the Lord has everything we need."

To which he replied, "I know the *Lord* has it, but *we* don't."

On one of our vacations in Lima, we were invited to stay in the home of a missionary with Youth for Christ while he and his family were on vacation. Steve, who was 4 at the time, was upstairs in the bathroom. He locked the door from the inside and then came out and shut it. There wasn't a key to get it open; if there was, I didn't know where. Fortunately, I was much thinner in those days. I had to scale the wall to get into the bathroom. I could barely squeeze through the small window. After unlocking the door, I said, "Now, Steve, don't lock that again," and I went back downstairs. I had hardly sat down when I heard, "Click!" Oh no, he didn't; but he had. So I scaled the wall and went back through the window again. This time getting back in I broke something made of glass. When I got the room unlocked again, I took Steve and said, "Steve, Daddy told you not to lock that door again, but you went ahead and did it. So now I'm going to have to spank you." He had a boil on his seat. Not wanting to touch that, I said, "Which side is the boil on?"

"Both sides, Daddy," he replied.

I don't remember if I was able to keep back the laughter after that answer.

When Steve was 12 years old, I hadn't spanked him for a long time. In fact, I rarely ever had to spank my kids. I didn't enjoy doing it, but sometimes it was necessary … and scriptural. Afterwards we would have what we called a "love session."

One Saturday I got a call from the center director, telling me that Steve and his friend Doug had stolen the sweet rolls in the dining room that were intended for Sunday breakfast the next morning. I said, "Well, being a son of Adam and a son of Scott, it's possible that he did that, but let me check with him when he comes home."

When he walked into the house I confronted him, "Steve, were you and Doug up at the dining room?"

"Yes."

"Did you go in?"

"No."

"Did Doug go in?"

"Yes."

"Did he take the rolls?"

"Yes."

"Did you eat some too?"

"Yes."

No remorse whatsoever, just straight answers. So I said, "Steve, when you ate those rolls you were as guilty as Doug. We just can't have a thief in the Scott house. I hate to do this, Steve, but I have to punish you for this." So I gave him a few swats and made him go back to the dining room and apologize to the dining room manager.

When he got back, I said, "Steve, I hated to spank you, but I'm sure you will never steal sweet rolls again."

He said, "Dad, I didn't steal any sweet rolls."

I was shocked and said, "But, Steve, you said you did."

"No, Dad, you said rolls, and the cooks gave Doug the leftover rolls. They weren't sweet rolls"

Oh, the bottom fell out. I wanted to tell him it was his turn to punish me.

Years later I was reading an article by Jamie Buckingham, a pastor and author who had visited Yarinacocha. He said his father had punished him for something unjustly and for years he was bitter toward his dad. He decided to get his children together and ask them if there was anything he had done for which he needed to ask their forgiveness. That sounded like a good idea to me, so I got our children together to ask them. Silence. I said, "Steve, how about that time I spanked you and made you apologize to the dining room manager for something you didn't do?"

He said, "Dad, I know that I didn't deserve it that time, but there were other times you didn't know about, so I figured it kind of evened out."

Children pick up languages quickly. They aren't embarrassed to make a mistake and just plunge in using what they know. One day I was talking to the Sharanahua chief, Alfonso. Becky, who was 3 or 4 years at the time, was playing near us. I got stuck for a word. Alfonso pointed at her and said, "Ask Tutu (Becky's Sharanahua name). She'll tell you how to say it."

From the time Becky was little, she liked to help with the medical work. One of Marie's and my favorite pictures is of Becky with the shaman Luis when she was 3 or 4. He was cutting the grass with his machete and cut his toe. Becky asked her mother for a Band-Aid and ran out to play nurse for him. In the photo he is looking at her with such a look of affection and a slight smile on his face, while she is all business getting that Band-Aid on his toe. Later, when she was in her teens, she would get the syringe ready for me to give injections.

Becky tenderly bandages the shaman's toe.

Becky, like the others, provided us with many happy and fun times. When she was about 4 or 5 years old, she was outside our home at Yarinacocha. She saw the clouds parting and ran into the house announcing, "Mama, get ready to hear the trumpet!" She thought Jesus was coming at any moment.

Another time when she was about 4 we took her to an outside amphitheater in Lima to hear a symphonic orchestra. The acoustics there were ideal. The orchestra was playing softly, building up to a crescendo. Suddenly, they came to a grand pause in the music—a silence where you could hear a pin drop. In that silence a little child's voice, our Becky's, could be heard by all, "It didn't work!" Then the orchestra began again in pianissimo, building up to fortissimo again. As the volume was increasing, again a little child's voice broke through, "It's coming; it's coming!" I'm not sure how many in the crowd appreciated Becky's remarks, but we have an unforgettable recollection from our precious little girl.

Priscilla, as did our other children, enjoyed going to Sunday school at Yarinacocha. When she was about 4, she was coming home from her class where the teacher, pilot Doug Deming, had been teaching on Revelation 3:20 to the children: "Behold, I stand at the door, and knock: if any man hear my voice, and open the door, I will come in to him, and will sup with him, and he with me." (KJV). Someone heard her quoting the verse as she was coming up the path. Priscilla's version was a bit different: "Behold, I stand at the door and knock. If you don't open the door, I'll huff and puff and blow your door down."

When she was 6 or 7, she was going with a group to the airport in Pucallpa. It was evening, and the young man driving the car came up behind a car whose tail lights were not on. Not seeing the car in time, he ran into it, and Priscilla was thrown into the dashboard. She wasn't hurt badly but was stunned. While the driver got out to talk to the driver of the other car, he forgot about Priscilla.

From left: Becky, Steve, Priscilla, and Dave in 2012.

She got out and began to walk on the side of the dangerous highway. Fortunately, a couple of our colleagues came by in another car, and seeing Priscilla, took her in with them.

Shortly after that we were in Lima. I was driving, and Priscilla was sitting on the front seat beside me. I could tell she was nervous, so I said, "Don't worry, Honey, Daddy is going to be very careful."

She replied, "I know *you're* careful, Daddy, but I don't know about the others."

Yes, there's never a dull moment when you have children, and we wouldn't have had it any other way. What an asset they were to our translation work with the Sharanahuas! Besides that, we love them dearly. They have provided us with pure joy.

—57—

THE COMPLETION OF THE SHARANAHUA NEW TESTAMENT

"You'll never finish!"

I'd heard that voice before. He's sometimes called "the accuser." I think he could also be called "the insinuator." If there's one thing the enemy of our souls wants to hinder, it's a people group having the Word of God in their own mother tongue, in the language that speaks to their hearts.

Many translators have found as they near the completion of a Scripture translation that the enemy steps up his attempts to slow down the work or bring to a halt. He attacks through sickness of the translators or their children, problems in the family, problems in the lives of the mother-tongue translators or their families, which draw them away. Discouragement is another of his chief weapons. We heard his diabolical voice, saying, "Why don't you give it up? You've translated enough. You're too weak from this virus to be able to stick to the translation. You'll never be able to finish anyway. Nobody would blame you for throwing in the towel at this point."

As we neared the completion of the translation of the New Testament for the Sharanahuas we faced such problems. It was during those times we sensed the love and prayers of our team in

Peru, as well as of those of many in the States who had prayed us through difficult times all during our journey. Also, our children were part of our rooting section, cheering us on and doing all they could to help us make it to the goal. Marie and I realized that we never could have made it without the "effectual fervent" prayers and encouraging letters of our prayer partners.

Sharanahuas came to Yarinacocha as co-translators and day after day we applied ourselves to the translation of the Scriptures. While others sometimes filled in, the main co-translators were Gustavo Melendez and then later Jaime del Aguila (better known as Cuscopindi). He is probably the most gifted of the Sharanahuas. He not only is the best at learning the meaning of the Scriptures, but he is also talented in repairing motors or radios. He loved to share the Word of God with his people and was one of the first Sharanahuas to share the gospel with the Yora people.

Finally, on October 17, 1995, at 9:45 a.m., Cuscopindi and I finished the final revision of the New Testament in Sharanahua. The horn was sounded on the center, and everyone gathered at the translation building to celebrate with us. There was an air of festivity. Even school was dismissed so the children could also join in. As Cuscopindi, his wife and children, along with Marie and

I, came out of the building and were joined by David, Julie, baby Michael, and Aurora, everyone cheered for us. But we felt those cheers belonged to the Lord and also to the ones cheering. They, too, had played an important

Cusco and Scotty finish the last verse of the New Testament.

part in this great milestone. What a day of rejoicing! To God be the glory!

Our dear friend Willie Gesch, teacher and music director, led us all in some hymns of praise, followed by several prayers of thanks to the Lord for enabling us to reach this goal. Then we went into the translation center for cake and hugs. As soon as possible, I left the gathering and went home with a 101 temperature, sore throat, and coughing. The Lord enabled us to finish the revision before succumbing to this cold or flu. Marie came home a bit later not feeling well herself but went back up to the translation center in the afternoon to put together the corrected verses. Again we felt that a huge "Praise the Lord!" was due our Savior, the Lord Jesus. It was a day neither Cuscopindi and his family nor Marie, David, Julie, and I would ever forget.

Was that the culmination of readying the Sharanahua New Testament for printing? No, there remained a lot of work yet to finally say, "This is it. Now we're ready to send it off to be printed."

The next step was a "read-through" of the entire New Testament with a committee of Sharanahuas to check for comprehension. We chose a diverse group: a younger man, an older man, and a middle-aged one. Among these was one from each of the three main Sharanahua communities. The older one couldn't read, but he could tell us if he didn't understand, or if he thought of a better way it could be said, that would make it more understandable. Also the committee would decide what they thought was best grammatically and semantically (meaning-wise) for various expressions or sentences. Since we had gone over it so many times before, the committee didn't make a lot of changes.

Finally, we came to the last, and one of the most tedious steps, the proofreading and layout of the New Testament. This included a consistency check of key terms such as *synagogue, redemption, angels*, and many more, the spelling of proper names and other words. The skilled help of our dedicated computer experts saved us many, many hours of work. Marie and I went over each verse to check the spelling and catch any other mistakes.

Marie with computer expert Bill Dyck did the layout of the New Testament. Bill loved doing this kind of work, and no one in our mission did it better than he did. At that time Marie wrote, "Bill and I found it challenging, exciting, and fun to do; not drudgery at all."

Cecil Hawkins is happy to carry the New Testament plates to Dallas.

While Marie and Bill were working on the layout, Janice Loewen and I were checking to make sure that nothing was left out, that the verse numbers were all there and other features were consistent. Janice was another one who was gifted in what she did and loved it. Praise the Lord for computers and for those who are expert in using them! Janice's skill helped cut off months of what was formerly painstaking and time-consuming searches for words and phrases. Also we chose the pictures and Holy Land maps to be included in the New Testament.

After the final proofreading and corrections were done, the Sharanahua New Testament was ready to be taken to Dallas, Texas. How providential that Cecil Hawkins, who had begun the work with the Sharanahuas, happened to be visiting in Lima at the time. He was thrilled to be the one to take the camera-ready copy to the SIL print shop where plates were made and sent to South Korea for printing.

Marie and I then went to the States for a short furlough. We planned to stay there until the New Testament was printed. This could take anywhere from six months to a year. Once they were on their way to Lima, we would return to Peru to have a dedication service and then out to the Purus River to distribute the precious cargo.

—58—

AWAITING THE ARRIVAL OF
THE NEW TESTAMENT

In April 1997 the happy news came to us that the Sharanahua New Testaments had arrived at the dock in Lima.

Our son David was at this point an assistant to his father-in-law, John Mishler, who was director of Lima Services. David was given the happy assignment of going to the port to fill out the necessary documents to have the New Testaments released into our custody for shipment to our storeroom in Lima.

On April 8, 1997, we got a phone call from David. We eagerly anticipated he would tell us the Sharanahua New Testaments were now at our headquarters in Lima. Imagine our shock when David said, "Dad, the customs officials say that a new law went into effect while the shipment was on its way from South Korea. As a result the New Testaments arrived with the old, and now improper, paperwork. That means they are illegally in the country and will have to be taken out of the country."

I could not believe my ears. "David, that is absolutely ridiculous. These are New Testaments in a native language. What possible harm could result from New Testaments being in the country? They aren't some kind of contraband. They don't pose a threat to anyone.

Anything that will benefit the Sharanahuas shouldn't be considered illegal. Surely, you can speak to the head of the custom officials and get an exception to this law and keep them in the country."

He replied, "Dad, we have tried, and they are adamant that this law cannot be broken, even for New Testaments."

I was completely stunned. I implored David to try again to get the officials to listen to reason.

This just couldn't be happening. It seemed like a bad dream. The date for the dedication out on the Purus River among the Sharanahuas and then later at Yarinacocha had already been set. What kind of a celebration would that be without any New Testaments to show? We prayed earnestly and fervently, but on April 18, while we were visiting the JAARS headquarters in Waxhaw, North Carolina, David called again. "Dad, we tried, but again the authorities were adamant. To not comply could risk a fine and other actions against us, so I have had the New Testaments shipped to Waxhaw."

There it was. We could do nothing more about it. Now was the time to follow the advice that Paul gave to the Philippians: not to worry about anything, but to pray about everything with thanksgiving to God, and allow his peace that transcends all understanding to guard our hearts and minds in Christ Jesus (Phil. 4:6–7).

Cecil Hawkins was now in Dallas where a few Sharanahua New Testaments had been sent by mail from South Korea. Knowing how much it would mean to us to have at least one copy, he had one sent by mail to us in Washington State. What a thrill it was to hold in our hands this beautiful Word of God in the heart language of the Sharanahuas! We had looked forward to the day when the Sharanahuas would hold this life-giving Word in their own hands.

Now, whenever we would speak in a church or with friends, we could show them a copy of the New Testament, which their prayers had helped to produce.

—59—

THE DEDICATION

South America Mission pilot Craig Gahagen flew low over Gasta Bala the early part of May 1997 and brought back the disturbing report that the airstrip was unusable, as the grass was too high with even a tree growing in the middle of the strip. Wheel planes would need to land in Gasta Bala the day of the New Testament dedication.

On May 7 pilot Jim Roberts flew Marie and me out to the Purus in a floatplane. I asked the Lord to give me the words to say to Gustavo and the other Sharanahuas that would motivate them to get the airstrip cut. The Lord was way ahead of me and had something far better in mind. He was already doing "immeasurably more than all we ask or imagine." As Jim let down for Gasta Bala and circled it, we could see that the airstrip was already cleared off. I could not suppress shouting a heartfelt "Hallelujah!"

Jim said, "Had we known, we could have come out in a wheel plane." But coming in a floatplane was also of the Lord. We wanted to visit the Sharanahua communities of Santa Margarita and San Marcos, neither of which had an airstrip, to invite the people to come to Gasta Bala on the 18th to celebrate God's Word now in book form in their own language.

The other good news that greeted us was that Gustavo had come back to Christ after a lapse, and for several months he had again been teaching the Sharanahuas the Word. Later that day, when he returned with some men from a hunting trip, it was obvious by his warm greeting that the Lord had indeed been working in his life.

Finally, the great day we had worked, waited, and prayed for, May 17, 1997—the dedication of the Sharanahua New Testament— dawned bright and beautiful for the flight out to the Purus. Back at Yarinacocha five planeloads of people were waiting with keen anticipation for this trip they had looked forward to for many years. These, too, had waited and prayed as partners with us and the Sharanahuas. Some were our co-workers in Peru, and some had come from the States.

Gasta Bala will probably never again see so many airplanes arrive in their community in one day, each bringing guests for the celebration. Besides two Helios on wheels and one on floats, SAMAIR sent their Cessna on wheels also. Having the pilots there was almost like having four apostles with us: James (Roberts), John (Schmidt), Peter (Lawrey), and Paul (Smith).

Tents were quickly set up to accommodate the guests. Those who did not sleep in tents were put up in the schoolhouse for the night. We were so glad that Ivagene Shive and Mary Ann Lord were already in Gasta Bala on a project and were able to make preparations: boiling water for drinking, having a latrine made, and giving weather reports to the pilots.

The Sharanahuas were excited to have so many come to share in their joy of having God's Word in their language. Among those who came were all four of our children and their spouses, with the exception of Steve's wife, Leila, who was expecting and needed to be near a physician. Also present were Lucy Eakin Lindholm, Willie and Kay Gesch, Janice Loewen, Rick and Priscilla Mellen,

Gary Rich, Larry and Carol Sagert, Karen Smith, Pastor Bob Zoba and his wife, Wendy, plus the four pilots.

Our son-in-law Jim Mottola had printed three big banners in Sharanahua to put on the walls of the church: John 14:6 at the front and John 3:16 and 1 John 4:11 on the side walls.

Cuscopindi, the master of ceremonies, began the service with welcoming words and then led in several Sharanahua hymns. Then Gustavo spoke, saying how glad they were that so many guests had come to share in their joy. Then Becky and Priscilla sang a song in Sharanahua based on Acts 3:6–8.

After that, Larry Sagert spoke about the wonderful power of Christ and his Word while I interpreted into Sharanahua. We sang another song or two in Sharanahua, followed by a few words from Pastor Zoba while I interpreted. He used an illustration that fit right in with the Sharanahua culture. He told how Christ bought us from the devil by giving his life for us.

Gustavo welcomes visitors to the dedication.

In conclusion, I shared what this moment meant to Marie and me and our family and friends. Then we showed them the only New Testament in Sharanahua that we had with us. The look of joy on their faces was wonderful to see. Several of the Sharanahuas who had worked on the translation—Ifopini (Gustavo), Cuscopindi (Jaime), Fasanahua (Carlos), and Shinoyofu (Jaime)—came forward to look at what God had strengthened us and them to accomplish. With the promise that more New Testaments would be coming to them soon, the dedication ended by singing one of their favorite choruses in Sharanahua: "If I'm thinking about Jesus, I cannot be thinking anything bad. I will not put him behind me."

After all four planes had left with the guests, we invited all the Sharanahuas to come to the school, where we served *arroz con pollo* (chicken with rice) and sweet rolls, which our Yarina friends provided for the celebration. We were wondering what we were going to do because we didn't think there was enough to feed everyone.

Scotty shows the one New Testament copy available and promises more soon.

Before we ate, Cuscopindi led us in a word of thanks. He prayed, "Lord, just as you fed the 5,000 men plus women and children, using only the five loaves and two fish from the boy's lunch, it was enough with plenty left over. Now help Marie to make this come out just right for all of us. Thank you!"

And it was so ... but with none left over.

—60—

THE CELEBRATION CONTINUES

The celebrating wasn't over yet. Our colleagues and friends at Yarinacocha wanted to join in the festivities and praise to the Lord for the Sharanahua New Testament by having a dedication there too.

To give a Peruvian flavor, on the Saturday morning before the Sunday dedication, our dear Peruvian friends Aurora and Juan made a *pachamanca*. Pachamanca is a Quechua word meaning "earth pot," a tradition dating back to the Incas. They dug a hole on the edge of the lake in front of our house and lined it with rocks that had been soaked in salt water to increase heat retention and keep them from cracking. Then adding firewood, they brought the stones to a high temperature for about 30 minutes. Onions and sweet potatoes were added to spiced meat and marinated, and then the ingredients were placed on the rocks and covered with more hot stones, large banana leaves, and earth, forming a small mound. After several hours of cooking, the food was dug up. The hot rocks and banana leaves were pulled back revealing a delicious meal, which was enjoyed immensely by our guests and us.

That afternoon Priscilla sprained her wrist playing volleyball and had to have it put in a cast. We had hoped that she would be able to play her violin at the dedication the following day, but unfortunately that wasn't possible.

As Marie expressed in her diary, "What a wonderful day was Sunday, May the 25th at Yarinacocha!" All of our mission family at Yarinacocha, plus some of the missionaries from the South American Mission were there in the auditorium. Again, all four of our children and their spouses were with us: David and Julie, Steven and Leila, Becky and Jim, and Priscilla and Philip, with four little 2-year-old grandsons, one from each couple! Many of our stateside friends were with us too: Marilyn and Scott Anderson from Denver, Colorado; Bryan and Lavonda Kopsa with their daughters Rachel and Bethany from Cheyenne, Wyoming; and Bob and Bernie Ellens from Grand Rapids, Michigan; and our speaker, Lareau Lindquist of Barnabas International. Also the four Sharanahua spiritual leaders/co-translators were there. The only thing missing was the Sharanahua New Testaments.

Our director in Peru Steve Rowan served as the master of ceremonies. Willie Gesch led the singing and sang a solo. The four Sharanahuas sang a song in their mother tongue. At the request of Willie, Becky and Priscilla sang the Sharanahua version of "Silver and Gold Have I None." Later they tried to sing "My Tribute" ("To God Be the Glory"), but when their emotions overcame them, they had to stop. Everyone in the audience joined in and finished the song.

I then gave a brief history of the work among the Sharanahuas. Then I asked all the pilots to stand, all the mechanics, all the teachers who had taught our kids, all the administrators, the doctors and nurses who had taken care of us, and the printers. When I asked for all those who had prayed for the Sharanahuas to stand, everyone in the auditorium was standing. It was because of all these people that we were able to finish the translation of the Sharanahua New Testament. We wished that all the churches and people in the States who had stood by us all those years with their prayers and gifts could have been there for this joyful occasion. It was also because of them that this moment was a reality.

Midway through my talk the screen door at the back of the auditorium burst open and in came our son David and his father-in-law, John Mishler, carrying the precious cargo of two big boxes of Sharanahua New Testaments, each box containing 32 copies. What a beautiful sight it was, as David and John made their way to the front and deposited the boxes on the platform. The audience erupted in applause. No one was going to listen to anything more from me after that, which would have been anticlimactic. Alicia Palma, a United Airlines stewardess who delighted in helping God's work, had heard of the problem of getting the New Testaments to Peru. She felt the urgency, picked up the two boxes in Miami, got on an 11 p.m. flight, and arrived in Lima at 4:30 in the morning. She was met by John Mishler, who flew with her from Lima to Pucallpa, arriving at just the right moment. They were met by David and transported to Yarinacocha. What wonderful timing!

Emotions ran high as Dave arrived with a box of New Testaments.

Next, as four of our guests from the States presented each of the four Sharanahua men with a copy of the precious New Testament in their own language, excitement showed on their faces.

After the presentation, our dear friend Lareau Lindquist, founder and president of Barnabas International, who had been a great encouragement to all of us at Yarinacocha, brought a short message, which was just what Marie and I had hoped to hear. The heart of his message was that we should give all the glory to the Lord for this triumphant day. We all shall someday cast our crowns at Jesus' feet where they belong. Everything that has been accomplished among the Sharanahuas has been done through the prayers of God's people. It is our Lord who gives the strength, encouragement, wisdom, grace, and power to stay with it no matter the circumstances. Jesus said, "Apart from me you can do nothing." So all the glory goes to him who is worthy and to whom it rightfully belongs.

After Lareau had spoken, Steve Rowan ended this time of rejoicing by having each person present hold in his or her hand a copy of the Sharanahua New Testament and pray that the Lord would use it in the hearts of the Sharanahuas. Then we had a time of prayer dedicating the New Testaments to the Lord, asking him to use them mightily by his Spirit among the Sharanahuas to bring an awakening among the unsaved, and renewal and spiritual growth among the believers.

From the first lesson in linguistics to my first stepping foot on Peruvian soil to seeing the first Sharanahua come to Christ to putting the first Scriptures into the hands of the Sharanahuas, it was all by grace alone. To God be all the glory!

U.S. visitors gave testaments to the pastors. From left: Bernie and Bob Ellens, Bryan Kopsa handing a testament to Cusco, Scotty, Carlos, Lareau Lindquist, and Marilyn Anderson next to her son Scott Anderson.

AFTERWORD

As we stood in line at the Jorge Chavez Lima Airport in January 2004, thinking this would be our last sojourn in Peru, the customs officer said, "How long have you been in our country?"

I answered, "In eighteen more days it will have been fifty years since I first came to your wonderful country."

"Then you can't leave. You have to die right here." In some ways I would have been happy to do just that.

As a young man I never dreamed that I would live the majority of my years in the jungle of Peru, translating the Bible for a tribal group, and spending most of that time with my wonderful wife, Marie. Without her I wouldn't have made it.

After we finished the Sharanahua New Testament, we translated the whole book of Genesis. We then added selected passages from the lives of Moses, Joshua, Samuel, Saul, David, and Daniel, plus thirty psalms. These were published and distributed among the Sharanahuas. We wish we could have translated all thirty-nine books of the Old Testament, but we hope and pray that Sharanahua spiritual leaders, along with the help of others, will one day complete the remaining books.

Since our return to the States in 2004 we have been asked several times how the Sharanahuas are doing. Though we thought we would never return, we were asked three times during 2005 to 2007 to take short-term mission groups to Peru to introduce them to the country and Bible translation work there.

I took advantage of these trips to travel to the Purus and meet with some of the Sharanahuas. On one occasion we met with four Sharanahua pastors in Pucallpa for a short Bible course and to encourage them in their walk with the Lord.

On one trip my colleague Frank Doejaaren accompanied me on an overnight to Gasta Bala. I asked Pastor Gustavo if they would be having a meeting that night. He replied that they did *every* night. I was pleased to see young people leading the meeting. Gustavo's son Portacio, who had studied for four terms at the Swiss Indian Mission Bible School, gave a message, then the Sharanahuas sang hymns in their language, and several of the young people gave testimonies. Gustavo spoke, and they asked me to speak too. It was a thrill to see them continuing to worship and hear the Word.

Technology has also come to the Sharanahuas, who can now email us in the States and even share up-to-date family photos. And more recently still, we receive phone calls, sharing news of new believers and baptisms. Some Sharanahuas have become missionaries themselves, reaching out to related-language communities with the gospel.

CHRONOLOGY

1927 Gene born

1945 Gene joins the US Navy

1946 Gene's promise to God to serve him

1948 The promise kept

1952 Linguistic training in Norman, Oklahoma

1953 Jungle Camp orientation

1954 Gene and Dave Farah arrive in Peru

1955 Short tribal assignments

1956 Gene meets Marie in Lima

1957 Marriage in Bolivia

1958 Marie meets the Sharanahuas; David born

1959 First furlough

1960 Steven born

1964 Becky born

1965 Fire burns down first tribal home; move to San Marcos

1966 Adult literacy campaign

1968 Gustavo, the first Sharanahua believer

1971 Search for Stone Axe People; Priscilla born; LANZA crash

1972 Training Sebastian, the first bilingual school teacher

1973 First bilingual school

1975 Furlough

1976 Government threat to expel SIL

1977   Whooping cough epidemic; "termite flight" and flu epidemic

1981   Trip to visit Sharanahua schools

1982   Flood destroys San Marcos

1983   Furlough; challenging message by Ray Ortlund

1984   Revival in Gasta Bala

1985   Yora contact

1987   David joins the team

1989   Furlough

1996   Completion of the New Testament; furlough

1997   New Testament dedications

Made in the USA
San Bernardino, CA
12 June 2019